The Southern Exodus to Mexico

BORDERLANDS AND TRANSCULTURAL STUDIES

Series Editors:

Pekka Hämäläinen
Paul Spickard

| Todd W. Wahlstrom

The Southern Exodus to Mexico

| Migration across the Borderlands
| after the American Civil War

University of Nebraska Press | Lincoln

A portion of chapter 1 originally appeared as "A Vision for Colonization: The Southern Migration Movement to Mexico after the U.S. Civil War," *Southern Historian* 30 (Spring 2009): 50–66.

Library of Congress Cataloging-in-Publication Data

Wahlstrom, Todd W.
The southern exodus to Mexico: migration across the borderlands after the American Civil War / Todd W Wahlstrom.
pages   cm.—(Borderlands and transcultural studies)
Includes bibliographical references and index.
ISBN 978-0-8032-4634-8 (hardback: alkaline paper)
ISBN 978-1-4962-2221-3 (paperback)
ISBN 978-0-8032-7422-8 (epub)
ISBN 978-0-8032-7423-5 (mobi)
ISBN 978-0-8032-7424-2 (pdf) 1. Americans—Mexico—History—19th century. 2. American Confederate voluntary exiles—Mexico—History—19th century. 3. United States—History—Civil War, 1861–1865—Refugees. 4. Southern States—Emigration and immigration—History—19th century. 5. Whites—Southern States—Attitudes—History—19th century. 6. Coahuila (Mexico: State)—History—19th century. I. Title.
F1266.W34 2015
972'.07—dc23
2014036545

Set in Sabon Next by Lindsey Auten.

For Meghan, Liam, and Owen

Contents

| Illustrations and Tables

Figures

Tables

Map

Acknowledgments

I would like to express my gratitude to Matthew Bokovoy, senior acquisitions editor at the University of Nebraska Press, for his help with reshaping and finalizing my manuscript for publication. I would also like to thank Heather Stauffer, Joeth Zucco, and Joy Margheim for all their help with completing this book project. I extend much appreciation to Adam Arenson and an anonymous reviewer for reviewing several drafts of my manuscript and for providing critical insights into how to develop my arguments and analysis. Likewise, series editors Pekka Hämäläinen and Paul Spickard have been instrumental in guiding the project to its completion and making the manuscript worthy of publication. John Majewski, my former advisor, and Sarah Cline, both at the University of California, Santa Barbara, have also been very supportive and vital contributors to this book.

I would like to thank the personnel at the archival institutions that I have visited while working on this project, especially Reader Services at the Huntington Library, Miguel Ángel Muñoz Borrego and Lucas Martínez Sánchez at the Archivo General del Estado de Coahuila, and the Virginia Historical Society. While working at these research institutions and others, I was able to examine fascinating historical materials and enjoy very productive periods of research and writing. I am likewise thankful for the fellowship and grant support I received while doing the bulk of my research, including a History Department Dissertation Fellowship from the University of California, Santa Barbara, a UC MEXUS (University of California Institute for Mexico and the United States) Dissertation Research Grant, a Mellon Match Fellowship from the Huntington Library, and a Mellon Research Fellowship from the Virginia Historical Society.

I was fortunate enough to present portions of my research at several conferences. The Richards Center Conference "The Civil War in Global Perspective" at Penn State University and the MESEA (Society for Multi-Ethnic Studies: Europe and Americas) Conference "Migration Matters" at Leiden University were especially valuable to developing the project. I also published an earlier version of chapter 1 as an article in *Southern Historian* and coauthored an article on Matthew Fontaine Maury for the *Virginia Magazine of History and Biography* that helped advance my analysis of southern migration to Mexico after the Civil War.

I extend my largest debt of gratitude to my wife, Meghan, for her unfaltering love and support over these years. My two sons, Liam and Owen (age five and two), have likewise provided support, or more accurately, inspiration for completing this book and brought immeasurable happiness to our lives. My mother, Barbara, brother, Erik, father, Paul, and grandmother, Laura, have also been great sources of support and encouragement. To my family, I extend my greatest appreciation.

Introduction

Isham G. Harris left for Mexico with a price on his head. As the former Confederate governor of Tennessee, Harris fled the country after the American Civil War. In mid-June 1865, "with my baggage, cooking utensils and provisions on a pack mule," he wrote, "I set out for San Antonio, where I expected to overtake a large number of Confederate, civil and military officers, en route to Mexico." He was too late. Having missed that group of Confederate migrants, he decided to head for Eagle Pass, Texas, which he reached "on the evening of the 30th, and immediately crossed over to the Mexican town of Piedras Negras." The next morning he set out for Monterrey, Mexico, the meeting ground for Confederate exiles crossing the border away from Reconstruction.[1]

Harris was among the vanguard of white southerners who migrated to Mexico after the Civil War, one of the elite Confederates who composed the leadership of the southern migration movement and helped establish the first Confederate colony in Mexico. These Confederate officers were vital to defining southern colonization in the post–Civil War era. Indeed, the planning largely sprang from another top-ranking Confederate—Matthew Fontaine Maury, a renowned scientist and Confederate naval officer who came to the helm of this initiative. For Maury, Mexico represented an enticing opportunity for white southerners in the post–Civil War world. His fellow white countrymen could escape from U.S. Republican rule and make a fresh economic start by taking advantage of Mexico's agricultural resources. These migrants were expected to contribute their farming skills and a labor force—especially their former slaves—to stimulate the Mexican economy through commercial agriculture. In return, they would secure a prosperous postemancipation life after their lifestyle predicated on slavery had vanished.

Important as these Confederate leaders were to southern colonization, they were ultimately not the backbone of the southern exodus to Mexico. Instead, they were soon eclipsed by a swell of enterprising white southerners of lesser socioeconomic standing. As Harris described, "Mexico presents the finest field that I have ever seen."[2] Thousands agreed with him—approximately five thousand white and black southerners migrated to Mexico from 1865 to the early 1870s. This population shift, while seemingly small, had the potential to substantially reconfigure the sparsely settled northern Mexican borderlands, a region reduced over the previous decades by Comanche and Apache raiding.[3] Common white southern migrants (in economic and social terms) came to define southern colonization along lines that both supported the social and political outlook of the leadership and moved it in new directions.

While undertones of racial supremacy helped impel common white southern migrants across the border, the bulk of them were attracted more by the geographic and economic promise of Mexico. That is, more-average white migrants may have harbored a white supremacist perspective that coincided with the attitudes of the leaders of colonization, but they were not as driven by the fear of persecution and "Black Republican" rule. In seeking out Mexico, most migrants prioritized the transborder economic possibilities of the postwar era, even while sharing in the racialized prism that was central to the American South, and the United States, during the nineteenth century.[4] They represent a key layer in redefining the dimensions of southern migration to Mexico after the Civil War, shifting away from an existing interpretation that views southern colonization only as an attempt to resurrect antebellum plantations on Mexican soil.

Southern colonization in Mexico began at the end of the Civil War but was actually embedded in a preexisting web of international power struggles. By the 1850s Napoleon III of France, the nephew of Napoleon Bonaparte, plotted to establish a monarchy in Mexico in hope of advancing other monarchies in Spanish America and thereby strengthen

France's political and economic power on the world stage while brushing back U.S. influence and expansion. Napoleon III searched in earnest for an appropriate monarch to lead the imperial Mexican nation. Austrian archduke Ferdinand Maximilian Joseph eventually accepted this position, landing in Mexico at the end of May 1864. The arrival of Emperor Maximilian von Hapsburg coincided with the French army successively gaining control over much of Mexico.[5]

Napoleon III came to see southern immigration as a key component of these imperial designs for Latin America, especially the idea of building the population base and establishing commercial outlets to the American South. By 1865 Emperor Maximilian had issued several decrees to make public lands ready for the anticipated influx of immigrants and had established a commission on immigration. These were the initial steps toward opening an extensive colonization enterprise.

In the summer of 1865 Emperor Maximilian teamed up with Matthew Fontaine Maury to formally launch a colonization initiative in Mexico with the goal of attracting white southerners from the failed Confederate States of America. Maximilian sponsored southern colonization as a means to establish control over the country and invigorate the Mexican economy, and he subsequently appointed Maury the imperial commissioner of colonization. Maury proved to be the key facilitator of an enterprise that promised to aid his fellow white southerners while contributing to the rise of the Mexican Empire.[6]

Past studies about the migration of Confederates to Mexico after the American Civil War have emphasized the movement's inherent flaws and concluded that their attempts to resurrect an Old South in Mexico were doomed from the start. As historian Andrew Rolle has claimed, "The exodus was striking for its futility, the depth of delusion of its participants, and the inevitability of its failure."[7] Such arguments, however, ignore the degree of planning that went into colonization and the scope of the vision behind it. The colonization plans coalesced around firm ideas about how to develop agriculture, industry, railroads, and markets within advantageous geographical surroundings. The initial plans also included a very specific proposal to use former slaves as the main labor force in order to make these

visions a reality. This "intriguing episode" had the potential to reshape the Mexican economy and put the American South on an entirely different course of Reconstruction, one not solely bent on Lost
Cause delusions.[8]

Southern Colonization in Mexico and the
Nineteenth-Century Western Hemisphere

From the antebellum era to the post–Civil War period, the American
South was connected to the Caribbean world largely through slavery
and emancipation. These hemispheric connections informed and abet-
ted southern colonization in Mexico. Maury, for one, gleaned some
of his ideas about labor control from Jamaica. His apprentice system
drew upon exslaveholder ideas about how to transition to a free labor system without allowing too much freedom. Similarly, the planter and slaveholding class of the American South wrestled with how
to maintain control over a newly freed workforce. The earlier precedent set by Jamaica offered an example of labor control, but it also
sent a warning about lost power and a collapsed economy. The early Reconstruction South took clues from this hemispheric context
to formulate the Black Codes, the rigorous state laws aimed at controlling freed people. While congressional Reconstruction banned
these specific laws, it did provide a framework for the segregationist
South that emerged in the late nineteenth century. The early colonization plans in Mexico tolled a similar note in their efforts to control
a black migrant workforce while remaking the social and economic
landscape in Mexico.[9]

Maury was one of the white southerners who bemoaned the effects that emancipation would supposedly have on the South and
the world. As he wrote in one article in 1866, "The industry of Jamaica, San Domingo, the Spanish Main, and of every other part of the
world, where African emancipation has been tried on a large scale, has
suffered, and the whites have come to grief." Maury borrowed from
the measures of labor control introduced in Jamaica but wished to
avoid its particular fate. "Emancipation in Jamaica was accomplished
in a rational way," he indicated, "not by violence; by compensation,

not by total loss." Yet in just one generation, "we see that island almost completely Africanised," he stated, "its industry destroyed, and its plantations are in ruins." In connection, he asked, "Why should we expect for our once happy and sunny South a better fate than that which has fallen upon that lovely island?" His answer to this riddle was to promote immigration to Mexico, accompanied by a labor force composed of lower percentages of "loyal" freed people and greater mechanisms of control. These plans contributed to the emerging responses of ex-slaveholders and other white southerners to emancipation in the trans-Caribbean world.[10]

Some high-ranking former Confederate officers and politicians went north to Canada to avoid imprisonment for treason or the fate of living under Yankee rule. Former Confederate secretary of war John C. Breckinridge went to Toronto, as did Jubal A. Early eventually, after going to Mexico and Cuba. Most went south, though, with Cuba serving primarily as a stopping place for migrants as they journeyed to and from Mexico and elsewhere in Latin America. The initial migration of Confederates was driven by a fear of persecution and a desire to resurrect slave-based plantation life in areas of the Western Hemisphere where it still existed. Brazil appealed to former Confederates directly in these ways and also spoke to the engines of economic expansion.[11]

American southerners had looked to Latin America to expand their fortunes since the 1840s. Many southern slaveholders shared a similar worldview with Cuban slaveholders and saw the Caribbean as a slave-driven commercial basin. In 1859 Louisiana governor R. C. Wickliffe focused on the commercial prospects in acquiring Cuba, with the port of Havana becoming "the great *entrepôt* of southern commerce." The Confederate government had also sought to establish commercial relations with Mexico, Cuba, and Brazil.[12] An expansionist and profit-oriented motivation sometimes became tangled with political grievances and helped fuel postwar migration to Brazil and Mexico.

Brazil was the second most promising location for white southern migrants after Mexico in the postemancipation world. Texan Frank McMullen formed one of the leading migrant groups that went there. Born in Georgia in 1835, McMullen moved with his family farther west in pursuit of cheap lands in Mississippi. This same idea brought him to Hill County, Texas, in 1853. He already had an inclination to move to acquire better economic footing. During the Civil War, McMullen had gone to Mexico while he struggled with tuberculosis and had remained there throughout the war as an unofficial Confederate intermediary. Confronted with a devastated southern economy after the war, he next turned toward Brazil as a place to secure his fortunes, most likely because slavery still existed there.[13]

The Confederacy and Brazil found common ground in slavery, and the possibilities of a political alliance lingered until the end of 1864. Emperor Dom Pedro II welcomed ex-Confederates to Brazil at the end of the Civil War. The *New York Herald* estimated in September 1865 that fifty thousand southerners might emigrate from the South, principally for Brazil.[14] This estimate was an exaggeration, but it reflected the serious southern interest in Brazil. McMullen would be among those southerners attracted to Brazil mainly because of the existence of slavery and the economic potential of plantation agriculture.

Both in Brazil and Mexico, the allure of remaining "unreconstructed" was thus strong, and this was especially appealing to the planter elite of the South. One of the key differences between Mexico and Brazil, though, was that southern migrants in Brazil continued to believe in slavery as the institution that would provide this more prosperous future. This fact boosted McMullan's confidence in the Brazilian government, which he considered "the best system of government known to man" since "it guarantee[d] PRACTICAL EQUALITY to ALL its citizens."[15] Mexico instead became a beacon for those southern migrants who still may have held political grievances but were motivated more by a path to prosperity that did not depend on slavery, at least not so overtly. At first the prioritizing of economic benefits may have only partially concealed a strong undertone of white supremacy, but the reality became increasingly clear—an alternative pathway of economic and social advancement would have to be pursued in Mexico, especially for common white southerners as the initial enterprise unfolded and folded in on itself.

Matthew F. Maury published letters in southern newspapers that focused on the economic potential of Mexico. One such letter was published in *DeBow's Review*, a publication that did not agree with Maury's emigration plan. However, *DeBow's* expressed respect for the "eminent Southern gentlemen who [were] at its head," especially Maury, and the editors explained that southern migrants could find "desirable locations" across Mexico "suitable for the cultivation of any staple they prefer, or the raising of any kind of stock." *DeBow's* also printed the report of a journalist from the *New York Tribune* who had visited the Córdoba region. This reporter provided such descriptions as, "The fields in this blessed country are mostly banana and pineapple plants," adding that other fruits were also "found in great abundance." Such reports also gave validity to southern colonization as it began to spread across Mexico by 1866.[16]

Maury wished to provide a clear picture of the agricultural paradise that awaited southern migrants. In another one of his letters to the South, he indicated that the "most desirable locations" were in Córdoba and Jalapa, a "sort of Steppe" in central Mexico that "abound[ed] in garden spots as beautiful as Eden itself." Córdoba and Jalapa, he explained, were fertile areas where "the farmer there and at many other places, may reap from the same field, two or three crops annually, with an increase of three or four hundred fold, upon the seed sown." With increased market outlets, this agricultural production would drive the Mexican economy. To this point Maury stated, "A Railway is to be completed, from each of these points, to Vera Cruz, which will bring them fairly within the domains of foreign commerce."[17] Maury was a promoter who spoke in similar terms as agricultural boosters of the American West and Southwest at this time, but he was also a physical geographer who had spent years studying different locations for their geographic economic potential.[18] Thus Maury exhibited a blend of boosterism and belief in Mexico as a promised land that beckoned southern migration. And it appeared that those back in the South took heed of his words.

Although Maury initially targeted his fellow Virginia gentlemen as the primary migrants, along with the ex-slaves he thought would accompany them, the net had widened by 1866. The largest number of white migrants that can be identified from 1865 to 1866 actually came from Texas, a state that joined the Union in 1845. Among the original thirteen colonies, Virginia and South Carolina, with their more established planter class, showed much less interest in the colonization plans. As chief spokesman of Virginia, Robert E. Lee responded to Maury's invitation to join him in Mexico by saying, "The thought of abandoning the Country and all that must be left in it, is abhorrent to my feelings." While Lee admired Mexico's "salubrity" of climate, "the fertility of its soil, [and] the magnificence of its scenery," he preferred "to struggle" for the South's restoration in the Union and "share its fate." Virginia newspapers likewise expressed little enthusiasm. The *Richmond Daily Dispatch* printed unfavorable reports about the movement, while the weekly publication the *Richmond Dispatch* more vocally urged Virginians "Don't Leave Your Country." Although "many of our countrymen . . . have emigrated," the *Dispatch* went on to say, "we would advise no one to follow their example."[19] Maury's home state seemed to frown upon the venture, even as it gained more momentum.

Maury was aware of the disinclination to emigrate from the older Atlantic states. As he stated, "The doctrine held, especially in Virginia, Carolina, and Georgia, discourages emigration" since the people of these states, "especially the young men," had been "told that interest and honour, duty and devotion, all required each man to stick by his state." Dedication to one's home state after a devastating war appealed to the younger generation of the Old Dominion. The planter class likewise had a much stronger desire to rebuild their home state because of the amount of wealth they had accrued, especially through the transfer of slaves to the Deep South. Hence the prospects of postwar renewal inside the United States seemed more certain for the established Old South.[20]

Yet even in Virginia immigration appeared to be a hot topic of conversation, if not outright action. The prominent Virginian Robert Lewis Dabney also came around to thinking emigration would be the best, or only, option under a Yankee government. He had initially been hesitant on the matter, but by January 1866 Dabney was plainly

interested in leaving the South and recognized a growing interest within the state. He saw "the steady and extensive leavening of the mind
of our people, with the desire for emigration." He was not convinced
that Mexico would be the optimal location since it was "too near the
Yankees" and the imperial government was not completely established.
Brazil, on the other hand, with its stable monarchy and slave plantation economy, seemed more promising to him. Dabney had a point.
Brazil turned out to be the second-biggest destination for southern
migration and played a significant role in expanding the scope of colonization under the direction of former top Confederate officials.[21]

White southern migrants also made their way to Honduras, Venezuela, and even to Egypt after the Civil War. In 1867 the ex-Confederate
major Washington Goldsmith of Georgia and Major Malcolm of Kentucky secured land grants in Honduras and within a few months over
two hundred migrants (mostly from Georgia) formed a short-lived colony. Conditions were rough, and most went on to British Honduras
(now Belize), where perhaps one thousand southerners lived by 1869.
As in Mexico, though, most of these migrants eventually returned
to the South, largely because of the changed political circumstances
in the United States. Colonization plans also sprouted in Venezuela
in 1867 before fizzling out by 1870. Around the time that most exiles
were returning to the United States, a small group of migrants left for
Egypt, including about twenty ex-Confederates. Among the departed were former major generals William W. Loring and Henry Sibley,
who arrived in Cairo in 1870.[22]

Southern emigration efforts thus stretched into Latin America as
well as across the Atlantic in the post–Civil War period. Taken together, the immigration and development efforts of southerners in Mexico, Brazil, and elsewhere pushed transnational social and economic
relations in new directions, although not toward greater equality and
freedom. While providing a means for individual and family-based
economic advancement, southern migration attempted to connect the
American South with channels of trade in the Western Hemisphere.
A major focus from the start was to develop circuits of economic development beyond and across borders.

The Stages of the Southern Exodus

My investigation of Maury and the other planners, or boosters, of southern colonization in Mexico is principally aimed at revealing the viability of the colonization movement in the wider realm of the Western Hemisphere and new dimensions for understanding these leaders. Throughout the book, but especially in chapters 1, 2, and 5, we see how the success of southern colonization seemed all the more possible because of the simultaneous migration of southerners to such Latin American destinations as Brazil. Emigration to countries within the Western Hemisphere created avenues for economic advancement, especially for white southerners, and generated routes of commercial exchange between the South and Latin America that promised to bolster white southern efforts to maintain their social and economic position in a postemancipation world. It was the combined paths of southern migration that gave more validity to what Maury envisioned for Mexico and the American South as several plans for colonization circulated back to the idea of modernizing both the host countries and the South.

Exposing the potential for economic renewal through hemispheric colonization provides one primary dimension for understanding southern migration to Mexico. A second dimension is how common white migrants focused more on the possibilities of economic revival than on political convictions. The existing literature on colonization in Mexico and Brazil has focused almost exclusively on "irreconcilable" Confederates such as Isham G. Harris who could not submit to defeat or "recalcitrant soldiers, who would rather flee abroad than surrender."[23] However, southern colonization in Mexico was a more complex movement than such perspectives reveal, not just a cause formed around stalwart generals and politicians.

In chapter 2 I focus on the more numerous white southern migrants who have garnered less attention in the historical literature and who pushed forward this aspect of colonization. These white southerners were largely small to middling ex-slaveholders who had previously relocated from such states as South Carolina and Georgia to Texas. They largely went across the border into Mexico after the Civil War to pursue new economic opportunities, rather than fleeing foremost from the threat of punishment and Republican Reconstruction. The pursuit of economic opportunities may have been tucked under the umbrage of racial supremacy, but these migrants strove forward most overtly as men on the make who provided the foundation for the colonization plans. As chapter 4 reveals, when the colonization plans were forced to change direction, economic priorities became even more pronounced and reframed the immigration venture.

Chapter 2 also examines the involvement of black southern migrants in the immigration initiative. Even though the vast majority of African Americans did not migrate to Mexico, some freed people, especially along the Texas-Coahuila border, did decide to go in an effort to find greater social and economic freedom. A number of former slaves unwillingly accompanied former owners to Mexico, with some leaving them behind once across the border. Other black migrants, who had been taken to Texas as slaves before and during the Civil War, migrated on their own to a country with a history of welcoming fugitive slaves and being more racially inclusive. Including black southerners in the analysis fills a key gap in the historiography and likewise reveals a more complex movement of people across the border.

Shifting the geographical emphasis also provides new dimensions to the southern colonization venture. Previous scholarship on Confederate migration to Mexico has given the most attention to central Mexico, where the largest colony, Carlota, was located, along with other, smaller colonies in the Córdoba district. By doing so, it has revealed the most important reason for the failure of colonization—the success of the Mexican Republican forces over the French-Conservative Imperialists in the summer of 1867 and Maximilian's subsequent execution.[24] U.S. military and diplomatic efforts to stop emigration and remove the French after the Civil War were also major impediments to the success of the venture. Likewise, high land prices and the racial prejudice of Confederates, which provoked conflicts with Mexicans, were key factors that contributed to the downfall of Carlota.[25] Thus we have come to understand the failure of Confederate colonization as the result of the loss of imperial support, U.S. diplomacy, lack of funds, failed crops, and the negative racial attitudes of southern migrants.[26] These conclusions are insightful and merit attention. And yet a key factor that helps explain why colonization failed is missing from the analysis.

The immigration plans, as developed by Maury and others in the summer and fall of 1865, called for the establishment of colonies outside of central Mexico in order to meet the anticipated level of white and black southern migration. By early 1866 the planners recognized that the time was ripe to make a push into northern areas. However, in ways that they did not fully understand, the borderlands of northern Mexico would not accommodate their plans. The planning for the initiative had been sound overall, but it did not fully grasp the dynamics of the border region, specifically between Texas and Coahuila (where an important land survey was conducted). Ultimately, the colonization efforts began to falter not from an overall lack of planning but from faulty assumptions about how to modernize Mexico, which depended on settlements in the borderlands. The failure to secure these settlements presaged the decline of the colonization venture.

During the 1860s the Texas-Coahuila borderlands were almost a world apart from the United States and Mexico. The area drew upon a history of separateness fostered by its distance (literally and figuratively) from state or central authority on both sides of the border. An intricate network of violence, theft, and trade prevailed across this stretch of the border in the American Southwest and northern Mexico, making it a virtually autonomous zone. Chapter 3 investigates the dynamics of the Texas-Coahuila borderlands, where such American Indian groups as the Comanches and Apaches dominated the area through their involvement in a raiding-trading network. Examining such Mexican political leaders as Governor Andrés S. Viesca likewise reveals the role played by the Mexican Republican military forces in the raiding-trading network and the Imperialist-Republican war. Collectively, both American Indians and local Mexicans along the border were responsible for two major developments: (1) they barred southern colonies from taking hold in the area, and (2) they prevented a centralized Mexican government, Imperialist or Republican, from overtaking the region.

Chapter 3 thus exposes not only the unraveling of southern colonization but the intersection, or collision, of regions, nations, and peoples. By examining the contours of a raiding-trading economy in the Texas-Coahuila borderlands, we gain insight into the complex array of interactions and motivations that formed in this geographic zone. For example, the Lipan Apaches were instrumental to establishing a "shadow trade economy" focused on stealing livestock for consumption and trade, which corresponded with their views on "harvesting," or capturing resources and property within what they saw as their dominion. The Comanches operated in a similar way to contribute to a debatable ground of control along a great swath of the border. The Kickapoos were likewise important to creating this environment, although the Kickapoos in Mexico engaged in more retaliatory behavior against a history of American expansion and, more specifically, in response to a Confederate attack against them in Texas late in the Civil War.[27] Southern colonization in Mexico was enmeshed in the U.S.-Mexico borderlands and its denouement was bound up with it.

In chapters 4 and 5 I disclose the ways in which southern colonization actually continued after the fall of the Mexican Empire in June 1867. During the Restored Republic, a new group of southern leaders emerged and carried out more modest colonization plans. Instead of completely abandoning Mexico, such white southerners as Jo Shelby and John Henry Brown took charge of pushing southern migration away from central Mexico to areas along the Gulf of Mexico. These plans focused even more on commercial agriculture and market-driven strategies to develop southern colonies and Mexico's economy. The southern publication the *Two Republics* emerged at this time as the main promotional vehicle and, out of necessity, expressed a more inclusive and politically neutral stance while emphasizing ways to develop Mexico's agricultural and industrial potential. Collectively, southern migration did not end but entered a new, less expansive phase that continued into the early 1870s.

In chapter 5 I stress how southern migration and colonization need to be juxtaposed against other economic development plans arising from within and outside of Mexico. Southern promoters focused on agricultural and commercial development plans, especially through railroads, to connect Mexico and the South that coincided with and departed from U.S. and Mexican modernization plans.[28] Southern colonization in Mexico likewise resonated with a southern conservative ideology that came to be embodied in the Lost Cause and New South movements as well as the scientific politics of the Científicos.

Southern colonization emphasized the merits of economic development in ways that resembled New South theorists' drive for industry and railroads—that is, by defending southern identity through connections to the Lost Cause. A major part of the cultural movement called the Lost Cause was the belief in preserving the plantation ideal without the scars of slavery in the postemancipation world, and New South promoters, as well as the planners of colonization initially, paid homage to this worldview. However, circumstances in Mexico rendered greater separation between these frames of thought, with white southerners in Mexico stressing economic growth beyond the ghosts of the Confederacy.[29] During the late 1870s and early 1880s political theorists associated with the presidencies of Porfirio Díaz advocated a conservative liberalism focused on order, material progress, and an administrative government that reverberated with southern colonization too. This thinking framed the political party dubbed the Científicos in the 1890s and their trust in economic progress through scientific and technical management of social regeneration. Political-economic theorizing from Mexico and the American South thus intersected with the business elements of southern colonization, providing lasting connections beyond the years of settlement.[30]

Southern colonization in Mexico influenced the course of U.S. and Mexican history in two major ways. First, southern colonization, especially in its first manifestations, contributed to a conservative political ideology that transcended borders. While ultimately distancing itself from Lost Cause rhetoric, southern colonization did not seek to reshape the social landscape on more equal terms. Second, and more importantly, southern migration facilitated the development of a hemispheric economy and a hemispheric South. In their search for an alternate destiny to U.S. Reconstruction, southern promoters and the migrants who followed contributed to the larger impulse to bridge economic borders—a major theme during the second half of the nineteenth century in the United States. Southern promoters actually sought transborder mutual benefits, more so than northern promoters did. Although short-lived, southern migration and colonization in Mexico thus played a pivotal role in remolding and reshaping the South, the United States, and the Western Hemisphere in the post–Civil War era. The movement contributed to the main economic impulses of the time period and made an effort to depart from a nationalist focus that so imbued U.S. visions of the postwar world.

The Southern Exodus to Mexico

Chapter One

Migration across the Borderlands after the American Civil War

Perhaps one of the most intriguing episodes of Alexander Watkins Terrell's life was his trek across the border to Mexico after the Civil War. Terrell was among a small sea of Confederate migrants taking leave of the South in the war's aftermath. After news of defeat reached the Southwest, groups of officers and soldiers departed Texas for Mexico, while Union troops moved to intercept them. Terrell's group eventually managed to escape, dogging a dangerous path that would get even more perilous as they entered Mexico.[1]

As a soldier of the Trans-Mississippi District, Terrell had been cut off from the eastern Confederacy after the fall of Vicksburg, Mississippi, on July 4, 1863. By the spring of 1864, Colonel Terrell moved to Mansfield, Louisiana, to support Confederate defenses under General Richard Taylor. At the height of battle on April 8, Terrell's Texas Cavalry (as the Thirty-Fourth Texas Regiment was called) charged across an open field into Union fire; Terrell then led the pursuit after the retreating Union forces under General Nathaniel P. Banks. During the fight Terrell's coat was shot through, but amazingly he was not injured. As this wartime incident reflects, Terrell witnessed much with the Confederate army in the West, his home region. Secession and the Civil War were monumental milestones for the region, nation, and him. Yet Mexico loomed ahead as perhaps an even more stirring episode in his life.[2]

Just across the U.S.-Mexico border, Terrell ran into a Mexican group led by Juan Cortina, a borderlander who had carried out an infamous raid on Brownsville, Texas, in 1859. "They were a rough looking set of scoundrels," Terrell recorded, "and their chief, Cortina, . . . had long been a terror on the Texas border." These southern migrants narrowly avoided a fight with these new foes before making their way to Monterrey, Nuevo Léon, arriving on June 28, 1865. The next day, Confederate general John B. Magruder, renowned for recapturing Galveston, Texas, late in the war, joined them with a small group of soldiers. More southern migrants came as well, including Henry Watkins Allen, a former governor of Louisiana, and General Kirby Smith, the commander of the Trans-Mississippi Department, to whom Terrell had reported. Sterling Price, a former governor of Missouri and southern hero of the Battle of Lexington in 1861, came a little later. In all, around fifty ex-Confederate officers held a Fourth of July banquet before heading to central Mexico. Besides seeing themselves as bearers of the true American nation, they were probably also celebrating their ability to escape from both the Yankees and Mexican Republicans hovering along the border.[3]

One of those Yankees was Union general Phil H. Sheridan, whose primary task was "to force the surrender of the Confederates under Kirby Smith." But there was also another pressing concern. As Sheridan stated, Grant "looked upon the invasion of Mexico by [Emperor] Maximilian as a part of the rebellion itself, because of the encouragement that invasion had received from the Confederacy, and that our success in putting down secession would never be complete till the French and Austrian invaders were compelled to quit the territory of our sister republic." To that end, Sheridan sought to stop the burgeoning exodus of Confederates heading for the border.[4]

Sheridan received news of Kirby Smith's surrender en route to his command in the American Southwest, although "the surrender was not carried out in good faith, particularly by the Texas troops," since many of them "had marched off to the interior of the State in several organized bodies, carrying with them in their camp equipage, arms, ammunition, and even some artillery, with the ultimate purpose of going to Mexico." Accordingly, Sheridan decided to "make a strong showing of force in Texas" and sent a column of cavalry to San Antonio and another to Houston, as well as called for reinforcements from across the Mississippi River. Sheridan soon discovered that these troops had fallen upon "the trail of my old antagonist, General [Jubal A.] Early," another top Confederate officer headed for Mexico. The Union troops chased the party and captured their horses, but the group got away. "A week or two later," Sheridan wrote, "I received a letter from Early describing the affair, and the capture of the horses, for which he claimed pay, on the ground that they were private property, because he had taken them into battle." This amusing demand was not all: "The letter also said that any further pursuit of Early would be useless, as he 'expected to be on the deep blue sea' by the time his communication reached me." While Early joined the Confederate rush out of the United States, Sheridan poised himself to be the gatekeeper of the West and stanch the flow of escaping Confederates. Sheridan eventually commanded over fifty thousand troops along the border and coast of Texas for this purpose, a testament to the formidable task he faced.[5]

As for Early, he had become a hardened Confederate officer who, like other high-ranking Confederates, chose exile over subjugation after the Civil War. After traveling through Texas and stopping off in the Bahamas, Early migrated to Mexico in the summer of 1865; he then went to Cuba and eventually to Canada.[6] Early wrote that Mexico was the place where he could "get out from the rule of infernal Yankees." His motivation for leaving matched that of most early southern migrants streaming across the border. "I go therefore a voluntary exile from the home and graves of my ancestors," he stated, "to seek my fortunes anew in the world."[7] During the summer of 1865, Confederates leaders such as Early and Terrell sought to escape from the developing cloud of Republican Reconstruction.

Matthew Fontaine Maury also sought to flee from punishment for his role in the war and the anticipated ruin following southern defeat. He had already become famous as a brilliant navigator and scientific writer; his contributions to the fields of oceanography, astronomy, and meteorology led to international acclaim. Moreover, Maury was an economic thinker who had written extensively about the potential for trade with China and the Far East, the importance of a transcontinental railroad for the United States, the commercial development of the Amazon Basin, and the creation of direct trade between Europe and the South.[8] Maury had thus already had distinguished himself from the rest of the Confederate leadership and would continue do so by attempting to orchestrate a transnational reconfiguration of Mexico and the South.

During the summer of 1865, Maury began to develop a colonization plan to bring white and black southerners to Mexico. He was not yet officially the imperial commissioner of colonization, but he had already conceived an immigration plan of significant proportions. While war raged in Mexico between the Imperialist forces under Emperor Maximilian and Benito Juárez's Republicans, Maury drafted a plan to help stabilize the imperial government and invigorate the Mexican economy. As a distinguished scientist and former Confederate navy captain, Maury appeared to be the right leader to carry out this venture, even under such unstable conditions. He became the centerpiece for the southern migration movement and pushed the contours of southern colonization in Mexico beyond the parameters of irreconcilable Confederates bent on re-creating an Old South.

Maury envisioned that the physical geography of Mexico would ensure the success of the colonization enterprise—he planned to capitalize on its bountiful landscape and unique location between the Pacific Ocean and the Gulf of Mexico. Maury also enlisted the support of numerous ex-Confederate migrants to aid this ambitious project. Many were prominent southerners, such as General Sterling Price, who founded the main colony of Carlota in central Mexico, or former governor Henry Watkins Allen, who published the *Mexican Times* newspaper, which focused on promoting immigration. With Maury at the helm of the venture, a well-formulated plan began to emerge by the fall of 1865 that promised to reshape the economic and social relations between the United States and Mexico.

Through an examination of Maury's plans for colonization, we can

determine that white southern migrants hoped to restore a large mea-
sure of control over their postemancipation lives in ways that corre-
spond with existing interpretations about this movement. However,
Maury also established a path for searching out Mexico's economic
promise that guided colonization beyond his tenure and bestowed it
with dimensions left unexplored by the existing scholarship on this
topic. To better understand how Maury's plans took shape and to open
up new windows into U.S. and Mexican history, we first turn to the
nineteenth-century South, the United States, and the Western Hemisphere to frame his ideas and to demonstrate the viability and breadth
of southern colonization in Mexico after the American Civil War.

El Dorado to Filibustering:
Southern Colonization in View of the Nineteenth Century

It seems true enough that both the initial colonization plans and the
early Confederate exodus to Mexico in the summer and fall of 1865
were largely driven by the desire to replicate a racially subordinate labor system as close to slavery as possible. Confederate figures such as
Maury, Price, Allen, and Terrell all seemed to be drawn to Mexico under this guise and an impulse that resonated with the developing Lost
Cause, which wished to cherish the defeated South while ridding itself
of the hated Yankee foe. True, too, Maury and other top Confederate
leaders partly justified their venture on the grounds that the mixed
and lowly racial composition of Mexico called for the establishment
of an imperial government—they also thought the country was too
unstable for a republican form of government.[9] Yet the colonization
movement that Maury guided soon developed into something larger.

The most compelling evidence that southern colonization was more
than just a Confederate fantasy is the migration of middling white
southerners who came to Mexico primarily for economic opportunities. As discussed more in the next chapter, the motivations for these
more common migrants, although still connected with racialized visions, spoke much more to the dream of upward mobility through relocation and commercial farming, rather than an insistence on racial
control and support of the Lost Cause. These migrants drew on the

antebellum tradition of moving west to find better lands and places to make money, as Alexander W. Terrell had done by moving to Texas.

Since the 1830s white southerners had migrated at an unprecedented rate from Atlantic states such as South Carolina and Georgia to inland ones such as Alabama and Mississippi. They left to take advantage of the open lands to the west. One witness to this out-migration described these southerners as "wanderers" in "pursuit of the Elysian fields, cheap lands, and golden prospects."[10] In this respect, southern migration before and after the Civil War took on the American overtones of a quest for upward mobility. Many of these white migrants, however, also brought slaves to support their economic ambitions and thereby gave a southern twist to the pattern. By the 1850s Texas joined Mississippi, Louisiana, and Arkansas as a top destination for these westward-moving slaveholders.[11]

The majority of these new Texas residents owned fewer than ten slaves, but the acquisition of land and slaves was still the primary objective for both large and small westward-bound slaveholders. Letters sent back home from relatives and friends who had already relocated emphasized the fertility of the new western lands and the ease of acquiring more slaves (either through reproduction or through the domestic slave trade). New migrants were enticed by a recurring message: "move and make your fortune, further west and further south." Indeed, the exaggerated claims of transplanted white southerners helped attract a large following; so did the example set by their parents' generation, who had left the seaboard behind for greener pastures.[12]

As with the post–Civil War southern colonization venture in Mexico, antebellum promoters tended to exaggerate the abundance of fertile land and promised riches in the Southwest during the antebellum period. Critics of southern out-migration condemned these distorted messages and drew explicit comparisons to dreams of El Dorado going back to the days of Spanish conquistadors. Some feared that the Southwest represented a future in which mobility would become the focal point of southern society—the directionless wanderings of a doomed culture. For better or worse, southwestward migration, lured by the idea of improved economic standing, did not abate after the Civil War, but gained momentum.[13]

In some respects, the westward movement of southerners took pages from the intensified migration to California during the midcentury Gold Rush. That California filled up with "a land of adventuring strangers" with "a fixation upon the quick acquisition of wealth" partially conveys the motivations behind southern migration before and after the war.[14] But both situations were also inspired by the simpler quest of finding work in the West. Going back to the 1830s, American traders and trappers had moved into such areas as northern Mexico and set a precedent for southern migration in their willingness to relocate to where economic prospects seemed brighter. The circumstances had changed since then, but opportunities still abounded. Perhaps migrants of the 1860s, as depicted in one study about the U.S.-Mexico borderlands, still saw themselves as "agents of a new fugitive landscape between nations." The borderland region can accurately be described as fugitive terrain not only because "it resisted efforts to fix or police territory" but because "it represented an ambiguous, shifting blank space on most mental maps of North America." That is, southern migrants dreamed of the open possibilities in a land that shifted between two nations, one of the "Wests" that still existed as a zone where work could be found and capitalist ventures could be launched.[15]

Two earlier migrants, Charles Debrille Poston from Kentucky and the German-born engineer Herman Ehrenberg, help illustrate the long-standing economic dream associated with westward migration. Both dreamed of El Dorado and pursued mining in the 1850s along the Arizona-Sonora borderlands. Attuned to the nineteenth-century version of golden opportunities, Poston secured financial backing for the Sonora Exploring and Mining Company in 1856. One of his backers was Robert J. Walker, the former secretary of the treasury under President James Polk and current head of the Texas Western Railroad. The capitalist emphasis of their endeavors was clear: "Where Poston saw silver, Walker saw railroad traffic." By the late 1850s other mining operations sprang up alongside U.S. military posts, establishing a trajectory of newfound visions of prosperity in the Southwest. Because of increased Apache raiding, cash shortages, and labor conflicts, these particular initiatives would not survive past the early 1860s. Yet the vision of upward mobility through mining, agriculture, and trade persisted during the Civil War.[16]

Although conceived as part of wartime strategy, a number of Confederate initiatives during the war aimed to spark southern economic expansion. For example, John Forsyth, the ex-U.S. minister to Mexico turned Confederate agent, sought to establish commercial relations with Mexico, including a transcontinental railroad between Texas and Mazatlán.[17] The Confederate agent working in northern Mexico, José A. Quintero, likewise attempted to develop a railroad line with the governor of Nuevo León, Santiago Vidaurri. This latter plan proposed to link the northern states of Mexico to the Confederacy and provide a railroad route to the Pacific. By early 1864 Confederate secretary of state Judah P. Benjamin ordered William Preston, serving as Confederate commissioner to Mexico, to secure a more accessible route to the Pacific Ocean than afforded by the Gadsden Purchase.[18] Fearful of antagonizing the United States, however, Emperor Maximilian did not support these ventures, and they went down with the Confederacy.

Once the Confederacy, and slavery as a system for upward mobility, collapsed in the spring of 1865, white southerners in Alabama, Mississippi, Louisiana, and Texas increasingly looked to the West to restore their economic fortunes. By the hundreds, they shifted southwest in support of the southern colonization venture in Mexico, following a pattern of southern out-migration and capitalist opportunities that helps establish the larger context for understanding Maury's colonization plans.

That the allure of economic opportunity took priority is also evident in how the boosters of colonization attempted to attract white southerners to Mexico. Henry Watkins Allen, who crossed the Mexican border at Eagle Pass/Piedras Negras in late June 1865, headed up the *Mexican Times* newspaper to promote the economic promise of Mexico. Ostensibly the newspaper was to be "devoted to the best

interests of the Mexican Empire," with its "special object" "to advo-
cate immigration and progress in their fullest meaning and extent."
Indeed, Allen's publication would prove to be a dedicated, if short-
lived, champion of modernization in Mexico. "For many years Mexico, convulsed with her own internal dissensions," Allen stated, "has
remained inactive in regard to immigration, railroads and internal
improvements."[19] He thought southern immigration presented a cure
for these ills, as it offered a grand vision of economic welfare for these
very immigrants. As chief of colonization, Maury likewise accentuat-
ed the economic prospects of Mexico, rather than the benefits of leaving a Yankeefied United States or cherishing a defeated South. Mexico
was well known for "its mineral wealth," but "as a source of riches,"
Maury stated, minerals were "by no means equal to its soil."[20] Maury
focused on the vast landscape of economic vitality with a foundation
in commercial agriculture to attract white southern migrants. It was
this type of message that underwrote the Mexican colonization venture from the very beginning.

This type of message is not too surprising, given the long rush of
migrants prompted westward by promises of economic reward during
the nineteenth century. The American West, Southwest, and Mexico
all held dreams of riches, or at least upward mobility. These dreams
and ambitions foreshadowed the southern thrust across the border,
but southern migration after the Civil War also departed from the
earlier migration patterns by attempting to secure an economic space
between national projects.

Confederates heading southwest also reflected a sense of being
"exiles" cast out from their native land. It was a sense, imagined or
real, of being driven from their homes, as such migrant groups as the
Irish framed their emigrant experiences. Beyond the pursuit of economic gain shared by many westward-moving migrants, white southern migrants, especially in the early Confederate phase, shared with
Irish migrants the idea of trying to relocate "home" to wherever one's
kinsmen were. For both migrant groups, home became "less a geographical concept than a social one." Perhaps the idea of "a movable
nation," from a work on Irish migration to the West, better gets at

the comparison, given the brief existence of the Confederacy but the palpability of a southern nation.[21]

Confederate migrants sought refuge across or in the southwestern borderlands, as did Chinese and Mormon migrants from the late nineteenth into the early twentieth century. Chinese immigrants who came to Arizona in the 1870s and 1880s established separate communities and later turned to Sonora after the United States passed the Chinese Exclusion Act of 1882. Chinese migrants were most associated with railroad and mining work, but many found work as cooks, farmers, merchants, and restaurant owners. The Mormons left for Mexico in an attempt to maintain the practice of polygamy. In the 1880s Mormon migrants established six colonies in Chihuahua, and in the next decade two in Sonora. They mostly centered on agriculture and supplied mining camps. They too carved out separatist enclaves away from the pathways of U.S. and Mexican national objectives.[22]

In more basic terms, like Irish migrants going West, white southerners in Mexico sought to escape economic insecurities—although the Irish were fleeing an oppressive industrial East, not the perceived economic and political combustion of the post–Civil War period. Irish emigrants have been portrayed as "instruments of America's western advance," making up almost 25 percent of the U.S. western army in 1870, for example, and playing a large role in the development of the transcontinental railroad as well as mining and agriculture. White southerners diverged from this course in that they sought to carve out an economic space between nations. In the end, however, most southern migrants joined the Irish in simply "building lives," or really rebuilding them, first in Mexico and then back across the border by the late 1870s.[23]

For black southerners, the West called as well, especially after the Civil War when they were no longer forced migrants. During the nineteenth century the overall black population shifted southwestward, but the pace quickened during the 1870s. "Although most migrants stayed within the South," as one historian has noted, "the prospect of leaving the region entirely for truly free soil fired the imaginations of Blacks who realized that their oppression was inextricably bound up with Southern or perhaps American life." Black southerners shared in the dream or vision of western landscapes opening up better economic tomorrows, while the prospect of crossing borders fueled ideas about obtaining true freedom.[24]

By framing the colonization initiative around economic imperatives, the planners thus tapped into a preexisting mental logic that prevailed throughout most of the nineteenth century. The planners also set this migration movement on a path to find both refuge and economic prosperity outside the boundaries of the United States and separate from the Mexican nation. In that sense, they also drew from a reservoir of southern antebellum expansionist plots.

Southern connections with filibustering projects were well established by 1865, including forays into Cuba, northern Mexico, and Central America. During the early 1850s Narciso López's second invasion of Cuba in support of an independence movement, for instance, attracted the support of the governor of Mississippi, John Anthony Quitman. The expedition was defeated, and López was executed in late summer 1851, but Quitman backed ongoing filibustering efforts before another invasion plan fizzled out. At the same time, the Tejano leader José María Jesús Carbajal drew on southern support when he captured the Mexican village of Carmargo, Tamaulipas, in September 1851. He not only drew supplies and launched the invasion from Texas but also enlisted the help of Texas Ranger John S. "Rip" Ford. The army of four hundred failed to take Matamoros, but Carbajal's filibusterers managed to invade twice more from Texas, in 1852 and 1853, although with less impressive results.[25]

The most notorious fillister campaign, William Walker's into Nicaragua in 1856, likewise had southern connections. Walker's campaign appealed to slaveholders not only because he established slavery in his short-lived republic but also because Walker was the former part owner and coeditor of the *New Orleans Daily Crescent*. By July 1856 Walker managed to become president of Nicaragua, until a Central American coalition army squelched his filibuster initiative in the spring of 1857. Back in New Orleans, he plotted again; after three more attempts he had not gained a nation, and he lost his life in 1860. Somewhat less

recognized is Walker's earlier invasion of Baja California, Mexico, in
October 1853. He proclaimed the Republic of Lower California, a state
based on free trade, pushed into neighboring Sonora, and then re-
named this expanded territory the Republic of Sonora in early 1854.
After Walker's expedition failed, former Vicksburg, Mississippi, attor-
ney Henry Alexander Crabb attempted to seize Sonora as well, but
only one person out of his party of seventy survived.[26]

Those who focused on both the expansion of slavery and southern
commercial development included George Bickley and his organization the Knights of the Golden Circle. A Virginian by birth, Bickley
had formed the Knights in Kentucky in 1855; the group's main purpose
was the creation of a new slave empire, extending out from the South
into Mexico, Central America, and part of South America. He especially focused on Mexico, emphasizing how it would provide "advantages of climate, soil, productions and geographic position of a very
marked character." His rhetoric about Mexico's geographic bounty is
reminiscent of Maury's. While Bickley planned and recruited for an
invasion of Mexico, he never carried out his colonization project.[27]

Although these filibusterers were unlike Maury in that they were
uninvited participants—Maury at least had the sanction of the imperial government—these campaigns sparked the southern imagination about places in the Western Hemisphere that would be suitable
for the postbellum southern colonization venture. By proximity, Mexico became ground zero for Maury's plans that focused on harness-
ing the riches of Mexico without outright slavery.

William M. Gwin has the most immediate connection to the postwar colonization venture in Mexico, bringing together the strands of
thought that preceded southern migration. Born in Tennessee, Gwin
had owned plantations in Mississippi before becoming a California
senator. Since the Mexican-American War, Gwin had favored expansion southward. At the time of the Gadsden Purchase in 1853, he urged
the United States to push the boundary to thirty miles south of Mazatlán on the Pacific Ocean. After being arrested as a suspected Confederate leader in 1861, Gwin hatched a colonization plan for Mexico.
He set his sights on the mineral and agricultural wealth of Sonora,

and, for a time, he received the unofficial backing of Napoleon III. Gwin warned the French emperor about the possibility of discharged Union soldiers overrunning northern Mexico and instead advanced the idea of settling ex-Confederates and other southerners. By 1865 he had drafted a broader plan to populate and develop an area that swept across Chihuahua, Sinaloa, Durango, and Sonora.[28]

Gwin's project was secretly backed by Napoleon III, but it never received the support of Emperor Maximilian (in contrast to Maury's). Without full imperial backing, Gwin was forced to abandon his efforts in the summer of 1865, but his plans were geared toward the same kind of modernizing strategy that underlay Maury's ideas. Gwin aimed to develop a mining and agricultural colony that would open up a robust trade with China, Japan, and other countries of the Pacific. As one historian has concluded, "The chief purpose of Gwin in his plan for colonization of North Mexico was to exploit the silver mines and to lay the foundation of a commercial empire."[29] This plan for a Mexican empire spoke to commercial agriculture as an engine of progress as much as its successor did.

Alexander W. Terrell crossed paths with Gwin while the latter was retreating back toward the U.S. border in the summer of 1865. Gwin, whom Terrell described as "a venerable looking man, with a long snow-white beard," hailed Terrell's stagecoach as it traveled outside of Hidalgo, Mexico, and "cautioned" Terrell "not to trust the French."[30] But Terrell continued onward. As one colonization scheme evaporated, a more extensive one was taking hold. Confederates converged on Mexico City, to be followed soon afterward by larger waves of exiled southerners seeking new prospects in a war-torn hemisphere.

A Plan for Southern Colonization:
Matthew Fontaine Maury in Mexico, 1865–66

Before the Civil War ended, Archduke Maximilian of Austria (soon to be the emperor of Mexico) had already been corresponding with Commodore Matthew F. Maury about naval and scientific matters. By the time Emperor Maximilian landed in Veracruz at the end of May 1864, he too thought southern colonization was an attractive idea for building up Mexico.[31] Maury arrived in Mexico City in June 1865; he had been in England securing ships and munitions for the Confederacy before he set sail for the West Indies in early May. Once he arrived at St. Thomas in the Virgin Islands, he learned that the Confederacy had collapsed. So he traveled to Cuba and, fearing punishment for his role in the war, decided not to return to the United States. Instead he took advantage of his friendship with Emperor Maximilian and offered his help with the new Mexican Empire.[32]

The desire to avoid punishment, however, was not Maury's only motivation for migrating to Mexico. Rather, he recognized Mexico as a place to launch his ideas on economic development, an area of study that he had pursued for quite some time. By the time he arrived in Mexico, Maury had become a world-renowned scientist and economic thinker. In 1825 Maury had joined the U.S. Navy and begun focusing on science, mathematics, and navigation. In 1839, at the age thirty-three, Maury had written a series of articles on naval reform. He subsequently became famous with his "Wind and Current Charts and Sailing Directions." Before the Civil War, Maury published the fifth and revised edition of *The Physical Geography of the Sea*, a book that established him as one of the founders of oceanography. By this time he was also head of the U.S. National Observatory.[33]

Beyond these scientific endeavors, Maury had also been involved in multiple economic development projects during the antebellum period. From building railroads and canals in the American Southwest to exploring the Amazon valley in Brazil, he demonstrated a faith in linking science and commerce. The key to the world's advancement, he argued, was to tap into the natural resources of a particular area. For example, the best way to develop the Amazon valley was to send forth "the emigrant, the Steamboat, the axe, and the plough" as "agencies of commerce" to spread civilization.[34] Maury invoked similar ideas in his colonization plan for Mexico.

Even before he became the official leader of southern colonization, Maury began drafting an immigration plan, or "project," which he sent to his son Richard in late June 1865. He also requested that Richard forward it to Robert E. Lee, who was also in Virginia. The essence of his plan was to offer "such favorable inducements" to his "fellow countrymen" that they would choose to emigrate and establish a "New Virginia" in Mexico. These incentives included exemption from taxation and conscription for five years and "a grant of 640 acres of land to the head of every family," with an additional 160 acres for each additional family member. Maury had expressed the idea for a New Virginia the previous month in Cuba. Now he set down to the task of making it a reality.[35]

Although Robert E. Lee did not respond favorably to his ideas, Maury was undeterred. He saw in Mexico a chance to create a commercial agricultural haven for white southerners and saw himself as the primary architect of the plan. Maury recognized a tremendous opportunity in supporting Emperor Maximilian's burgeoning empire. As he wrote to Reverend Francis W. Tremlett in England in early August 1865, "From such a wreck [in the South] Mexico may gather and transfer to her own borders the very intelligence, skill, and labour which made the South what she was in her palmy days—except her bondage."[36] Maury thought first of the planter class in Virginia and elsewhere in the South as the key ingredient for success in Mexico. He also thought former slaves should accompany former masters to provide the backbone of the labor system. This two-pronged approach was at the heart of his initial plan.

While Maury did not attempt to revive slavery, he did want loyal ex-slaves to accompany their former masters to Mexico as "agricultural and other labourers." The dual migration of white and black southerners, Maury imagined, would produce three results: rebuild the lives of white southerners, stimulate the Mexican economy, and advance "a humane system of African emancipation." These objectives connected with his antebellum ideas. Maury came from a slave-owning family, but he had owned only one slave himself and had argued for gradual emancipation in the United States. Like other gradual emancipationists, he sought to "drain off" the slave population from Virginia. In the 1850s, for instance, he wrote of his desire to send American slaves off to "the valley of the Amazon" in Brazil. This "safety-valve" approach was meant to *relieve* the *curse* of slavery in the South.[37]

As he published letters in the United States to attract white and black migrants, he expressed his belief that Mexico was the optimum location to resurrect a southern postwar life without slavery. Although he had previous made "the physical geography of Brazil a special study," he now argued that it was not the best destination. The primary reason was that Brazil was "a slave country, and for the Southern people to go there, would simply be 'leaping from the fire back into the frying pan' again." Mexico, on the other hand, would be a great leap forward, for white southerners could bring their "willing" former slaves to Mexico to work as apprentices, an idea that spoke to unfree labor schemes even if Maury did not want to phrase it that way.[38]

By June 1865 Maury had presented the idea of a dual migration movement to Emperor Maximilian, who "strong[ly] and heartily" supported the idea of white southerners bringing "their negroes not as slaves, but as *apprentices* bound by indentures."[39] From the summer to the fall of 1865, Maury worked out the details of this apprentice system, which placed former masters in charge of former slaves to develop commercial agriculture in Mexico.

Although nominally free, black southern migrants would thus be drawn back into a labor system that resembled slavery. "The head or patrón of each family introducing coloured apprentices," Maury stated, "shall be bound to care for them in a patriarchal and paternal manner during their apprenticeship," including providing food, clothing, and lodging. Maury even granted white southern migrants "the necessary authority" to establish "the proper and requisite police on his plantation and to compel these apprentices who may be disposed to idleness and vice to conform to the laws and to render service." Moreover, once the apprenticeship had been fulfilled, after ten to twenty-one years, "the liberated apprentices" would still be required "to render to his patron such an amount of labour and at such a rate of wages as being not inconsistent with the usages of the country."[40]

As outlined by Maury, ex-slaves who came to Mexico would find few advantages. For instance, Maury stipulated that ex-slave laborers were to be made "the tenant of a comfortable dwelling" with a small parcel of land of their own ("not less than 10 acres"). They would also receive an education, particularly about how to conduct themselves after emancipation. Under his apprentice system, "emancipated negros" were "bound to serve until they can learn the language of the country, its customs, and be able to take care of themselves."[41] Maury was much more concerned with the advantages of emigration for white southerners and thought that second- or third-class citizenship for freed people was sufficient.

Emperor Maximilian modified some of the benefits that Maury proposed for white southern migrants. For example, he reduced the amount of uncultivated land offered to a white migrant family from 640 to 320 acres; he also limited the exemption from property taxes from five years to only one year. Still, white migrants could rely on such advantages as bringing "labourers with them" who were then bound to serve for five to ten years (instead of ten to twenty). Black southern migrants were thus slotted to provide the primary workforce in Mexico, while white migrants played the role of quasi-masters.[42]

Maury's ideas for colonization, especially his apprenticeship system, resonated well with the former southern master class in the postemancipation world. He certainly was not alone in thinking about racial and labor control alongside economic modernization, with the intention of reviving southern planters. While other elite southerners swept their gaze across the Caribbean, Maury focused on Mexico but drew lessons, as others had before him, about the proper path to emancipation and how to deal with the "problem of freedom." First and foremost, Jamaica's apprenticeship model provided the framework for understanding what to do and what not to do.[43]

The West Indian sugar industry had declined precipitately since British abolishment of slavery in 1833. On the larger islands of Jamaica, Trinidad, and Demerara, the sugar economies plummeted by 9 percent in 1838 (at the end of the apprenticeship period) and by 35 percent in 1846. Thus, while an apprentice system offered ideas for racial control, it likewise had to be modified to ensure economic productivity. Moreover, the islands spoke to the dangers connected with emancipation. Fellow Virginian Robert Monroe Harrison, U.S. consul in Jamaica in the 1830s, not only commented on economic decline but also warned about the prospects of open rebellion and the slaughter of whites. Even though no rebellions actually occurred in Jamaica, Harrison was convinced that the South faced a race war, fated to be "deluged in blood." This turned out to be true, but from the Civil War, not slave rebellion. But Maury could learn from these pre–Civil War warnings as well as from the coinciding influx of indentured laborers from British India to the West Indies. By 1850 over thirty thousand indentured Africans and about the same number of Indians had emigrated to work on the sugar plantations. Maury undoubtedly thought that without proper controls and the requisite plans for economic revival, including controlled immigration, emancipation would be the ruin of the planter class, in Mexico or the South.[44]

The labor system that Maury conceived had much in common with arrangements for emancipation in the British West Indies during the 1830s, especially the apprenticeship systems in Barbados and Jamaica. British Jamaica, for example, had employed an apprenticeship model in 1834 that required "free" laborers to work forty and one-half hours per week in exchange for food, clothing, and shelter. As with Maury's plan, these measures were supposed to "properly prepare" freed people for postemancipation life, but they were primarily aimed at securing a dependable labor force.[45]

During the early stage of U.S. Reconstruction, the planter class in the South also drew upon similar measures to resolve their "labor problem." The state laws collectively known as the Black Codes attempted to keep former slaves tied to plantations by limiting economic alternatives and regulating personal freedoms. Mississippi and South Carolina passed the first and most severe codes at the end of 1865. The apprentice law in Mississippi, for example, required that all blacks and mulattoes under the age of eighteen who were orphans or whose parents could not support them be bound to a white person (usually their former owner). A male apprentice could be held until age twenty-one, a female could be retained until age eighteen, and corporal punishment was permissible. Maury's labor system in Mexico called for similar actions for white economic advancement and racial control.[46]

In September 1865, when Maury officially became imperial commissioner of colonization, he unfurled his immigration plan to bring about the South's recovery and Mexico's expansion. He saw his plan as "the quickest, most certain and best means of affording relief to their [white southerners'] sufferings, of giving quiet to this country, stability to the throne, and peace to America." Maury wrote a memorandum to accompany Emperor Maximilian's official immigration decree in which he offered further inducements to white southern migrants, such as "a free passage by sea for their families and effects." For those without means, he offered not only a free voyage but also "a traveling allowance." He also planned to place immigration agents at "convenient points abroad" to help migrants make the journey.[47]

As monitor of the border, Union general Phil Sheridan watched these plans develop with keen interest and contempt. As he stated in the fall of 1865, "Within the knowledge of my troops, there had gone on formerly the transfer of organized bodies of ex-Confederates to Mexico, in aid of the Imperialists, and at this period it was known that there was in preparation an immigration scheme having in view the colonizing, at Cordova and one or two other places, of all the discontented elements of the defunct Confederacy." He named "Generals Price, Magruder, Maury, and other high personages" as the main "promoters of the enterprise, which Maximilian took to readily." As Maury and Sheridan recognized, Emperor Maximilian saw in southern colonization "the possibilities of a staunch support to his throne, and therefore not only sanctioned the project, but encouraged it with large grants of land," titles of nobility, and a system of peonage, "expecting that the silver hook thus baited would be largely swallowed by the Southern people." Under Maury's direction, that silver hook was cast across the South to boost the sagging spirits of the planter class and more common white southerners searching for better economic opportunities.[48]

To help urge the southern exodus to Mexico, Maury expressed his full confidence in the imperial Mexican nation. He told potential migrants that it was the unique geographic location of Mexico between the Gulf of Mexico and the Pacific Ocean that bestowed the country

with rich agricultural resources." Maury conjured up a vast landscape
of economic vitality with a foundation in agriculture just waiting to be
properly developed by white southern migrants who oversaw a black
southern workforce. "The staples of agriculture in Mexico," Maury
explained, were "as diverse as its climates." With the help of southern
migrants, Mexico was poised for greatness.[49]

It was precisely the dual migration of former masters and slaves
that Maury thought was crucial to improving Mexico. Mexico might
have been "a country of perpetual harvests," but in many areas "agriculture was in a rude state." Maury claimed (with exaggeration) that
some Mexican farmers were still "ploughing with a stick, and sawing
with an axe." He expected white southern migrants to innovate this
process while black southern migrants made the fields more productive. As he stated, "A few of our clever farmers, bringing with them
their agricultural apprentices, would give new life and energy to the
country." Under the influence of more "improved implements of husbandry" and a reliable workforce, he expected "new centres of agricultural life, energy, and improvement" to sweep across the land.[50]

Maury's plan ultimately dismissed the abilities of Mexicans themselves to place their country on a path to modernization. As he explained, "The present population of Mexico is said to be eight millions,
more than seven of which belong to what with you is called the laboring classes." However, only a small contribution to the "commerce
of the world" had been realized, he argued. In comparison, "the laboring classes of the South, though but little more than half as numerous as these, enabled that country to throw into the channels of
commerce an amount of raw produce annually that was worth more
than $300,000,000," or more than eight times the amount Mexico pro-
duced. His conclusion: "You may well imagine the effect, therefore,
upon the prosperity of this country, and the stability of the Empire,
which would follow the introduction of a few hundred thousands of
these very laborers, guided, as they should be, by the skill and experience of their former masters."[51] He did not spend time analyzing the
ethno-racial diversity of the country, with its Hispanic, indigenous,
mestizo, and multiethnic populations, but contented himself with the

idea that only white southern migrants, with their improved farming techniques and their properly monitored black labor force, could effectively build up the nation.

Thus his plan was shortsighted in some important respects (especially its racial outlook) but not haphazard. In fact, Maury found common ground with leading Mexican thinkers who had likewise argued that white immigration would bring economic advancement to Mexico. During Mexico's post-Independence period, for example, liberal politician José María Luis Mora sponsored European immigration to help stabilize and build up the nation. Mora believed wholeheartedly in the superiority of some races over others and saw Mexican Indians as inherently unproductive. In the 1830s and 1840s Mora and other liberals looked to the white race to develop a strong Mexican nationalism. Throughout the second half of the nineteenth century in Mexico, the idea of improving social conditions through the "whitening" of the nation's racial composition was an integral part of most modernization plans.[52] Similar to Maury, leading Mexican politicians believed that only the educated elite would be able to contribute to the country's economic development.

Maury's ideas also found commonality with colonization efforts in Brazil, especially his focus on commercial agriculture. For example, South Carolinian James McFadden Gaston collaborated with the trading firm Nathan e Irmão (Nathan and Brother) in Brazil to relocate southern migrants to raise staple crops. Charles Nathan of this company had forged long-standing commercial ties between New Orleans and Rio de Janeiro through the coffee trade. In mid-1867 Nathan secured a contract with the Brazilian minister of agriculture and commerce to relocate over five thousand southerners. These combined efforts, much like the plans in Mexico, focused on settling migrants on farmlands to produce crops for local and transnational trade. By July 1867, around the same time that Mexican migration peaked, it was reported that large yields of corn and cotton were being produced in Brazil.[53]

Nathan also sought out industry, especially textile manufacturing, to accompany commercial agricultural exchange. By the 1870s

the southern migrant Dr. Russell McCord from Alabama had likewise established a strong business relationship with the Carneiro da
Silvases in Brazil, a prominent sugar-growing family with significant
international connections who sought to modernize the sugar industry. As one study has indicated, migration to Brazil and the associated
plans for economic development had been facilitated by transnational business and kinship connections forged over the eighteenth and
nineteenth century in a capitalist Atlantic-world setting.[54] These efforts paralleled Maury's vision for Mexico and the South.

Maury's plan likewise drew on the support of other southern migrants in Mexico. Former Louisiana governor Henry Watkins Allen
was among the most prominent, with his English-language newspaper
the *Mexican Times*. Like Maury, Allen thought it was the geographic
location of Mexico that afforded a new economic start for southern
migrants, and he fully backed Maury's plans.[55] In due time, survey
agents would confirm Maury's and Allen's assessment of Mexico. William Marshall Anderson, for example, provided some of the ground-
level support for establishing southern colonies and expressed similar
views. "A more varied, animating, satisfactory agricultural scene," he
wrote about the valley of Puebla in central Mexico, "would be hard
to find, or difficult to imagine." This fertile valley was one of the locations that held the most promise for southern migrants. "Trees in
bloom, trees in fruit—Wheat fields green, barley ripe—corn up &
sugar-cane planting," he commented. To capitalize on this agricultural abundance, Anderson agreed with Maury and Allen that railroad
development was needed to create new markets. "The completion of
her Rail-Road system," he wrote, "would make [Mexico] the most desirable farmer's home on earth." Elsewhere in Mexico seemed just as
promising to Anderson too. Once he undertook his survey mission
in the northern state of Coahuila, Anderson made note of the innu-
merable advantages of soil and climate just waiting to being fully developed. In February 1866, for example, Anderson noted how the
landscape was "admirably adapted for pasturage, and if supplied with
water, [was] as good farming land as an honest man ever took from
the hand of nature." As he peered out from this vista, he recorded, "In

[my] imagination I see cotton, sugar, tobacco—cattle, horses, sheep and Angora goats of the very best class" cropping up along the countryside. To Maury, Allen, and Anderson, Mexico was an agricultural paradise just waiting for southern migrants to build up its economy.[56]

The first thrust of southern colonization went straight into central Mexico. On September 19, 1865, Sterling Price, Jo Shelby, Trusten Polk, and Isham G. Harris, all prominent ex-Confederates, left Mexico City to embark on the colonization mission. They arrived in Córdoba three days later; members of the group were particularly hopeful about the prospects of revitalizing Mexico and their own lives by establishing colonies in central Mexico. They and some thirty other Confederates took to surveying the land, giving the choicest spot to colony leader Price—a 640-acre plot—while allotting twenty-four acres for the town square. The Carlota colony, named after the empress of Mexico, soon became the focal point of southern immigration.[57]

By early December 1865 Price felt confident enough in the colony's future to invite his wife, Martha, and family to join him. After a harrowing shipwreck, his family did arrive in May 1866. By July Martha Price wrote about the prospect of creating a "pleasant society" and the potential that awaited southern immigrants: "If no unforeseen accident occurs the Americans will do well, and most of them be comfortably settled in a few years." Sterling Price shared these views and likewise wrote letters to friends and family members still in Missouri. He also expressed confidence in the abilities of the French army and the Mexican people to stop the Juaristas. While he envisioned an agricultural aristocracy rising up from among transplanted southerners to join landowning Mexicans, Price looked upon the Mexican workforce through a lens similar to that with which he had viewed his slaves in Missouri. He thought that both Mexican and former slave workers needed supervision and care in exchange for working the fields.[58]

Maury explained that "a number of Haciendas" at Carlota had formerly been confiscated by the Juárez government and then taken over by Maximilian for colonization. "These lands [were] sold to immigrants at $1 per acre in five equal annual instalments." Among the notable migrants at this location were the ex-Confederate generals

Price and Jo Shelby (both from Missouri), former Tennessee governor Isham G. Harris of Tennessee, and Judge John Perkins of Louisiana. Maury further reported that they were "all highly pleased with their prospects" and that by the time the railroad was completed to Veracruz and they had "improved their farms," most expected their lands to be worth "$10, $20 and even $50 the acre." The rising land values were connected to the staple crops that were produced in this area. For instance, one "gentleman from Louisiana" who had been in the Córdoba region for seven to eight years had established an eighty-acre coffee plantation with a crop valued at $16,000 for the previous year.[59]

By the fall of 1865 the colonization plans were in full swing, as evinced by the Carlota colony. Migrants were told to come by the hundreds and remake the land to bring forth its full bounty. Railroads were just waiting to be constructed across the countryside to form links with vibrant new markets. With the help of such agents as Anderson, the press of Allen, and colony leaders such as Price, Maury was ready to draw white and black southerners down from the American South to the rich haven of Mexico. He had begun to orchestrate a transnational revival of white southern fortunes in a postemancipation world.

Chapter Two

White and Black Southerners Migrate to Mexico after the American Civil War

William Marshall Anderson first stopped off in Havana, Cuba, before landing in Mexico. In April 1865 he arrived in Veracruz looking for work as a land surveyor. As both a supporter of the Union and a Confederate sympathizer, he had not fought in the Civil War, but he soon aligned himself with the southern colonization plans.[1] As migrants such as Anderson reveal, southern migration to Mexico was not solely a Confederate enterprise. Although the focus of previous historians has been on high-ranking Confederate officers, a wide range of white southerners took part in the Mexican colonization plans.[2] It would be worthwhile to shift our attention to these less known and more numerous white migrants, many of whom had been small to middling slaveholders before the Civil War and had previously migrated westward from the Southeast to the Southwest. While most probably harbored grievances against Republican Reconstruction, these migrants went to Mexico primarily to pursue new economic opportunities. They were men on the make who provided the foundation for the colonization plans but have been overshadowed by the Confederate leadership. By bringing these migrants to the forefront, we uncover a more complex movement—one that reflected the American drive for upward mobility while pushing economic development across the border.

It is important to also recognize the movement of black southern migrants to Mexico after the Civil War. Although most African Americans decided to stay in the United States after the war, a select number of black southerners, particularly along the Texas-Coahuila border, decided to search for a better postemancipation life in Mexico. Some freed people unwillingly accompanied former owners to Mexico, with some managing to leave them behind once across the border. Other black migrants, who had been taken west to states such as Texas as slaves before and during the Civil War, left on their own accord in search of greater social and economic freedom than that offered in the American South.

By examining this dual movement of southerners, although it is greatly skewed to white migrants, we can gain a better understanding of the social history of southern migration to Mexico.[3] Existing scholarship on this topic has not captured the full range of migrants in this episode of U.S. and Mexican history, nor its importance to the histories of both nations. Below we gain insight into how white and black southern migrants gave life to the colonization plans and pushed the U.S. Reconstruction period into a transnational framework, thereby enhancing our understanding of nineteenth-century U.S., Mexican, and borderlands history.

The Crossroads of Texas:
White Southerners Migrate across the Border to Mexico

William Marshall Anderson provides a sense of the broader range of white migrants who went to Mexico after the Civil War. Anderson had been born in the border state of Kentucky but spent most of his adult life in Ohio, which helped forge both his strong support for the Union and his deep sympathy for the South. It might also help explain why he fought for neither the Union nor the Confederacy.[4] Like other white migrants at the end of the war, he saw Mexico as a place of opportunity, rather than foremost as a political refuge. In their prioritization of economic motivations, Anderson and the bulk of other white migrants reconfigure the meaning and significance of the southern colonization movement to Mexico.

After landing at Veracruz in April 1865, Anderson traveled to central Mexico. Spending a terrible night in Córdoba with "no shelter or place of rest but a miserable grass covered shanty" and leaving "before day light" the following morning, Anderson would have to wait to get a real sense of the area on which white southerners were converging. As the *New York Tribune* later reported, the valley of Córdoba was "situated in the mountains, sixty-five miles from Vera Cruz" and "for salubrity of climate, beauty of scenery and fertility [was] unsurpassed anywhere in the world." A similar report was printed in another U.S. newspaper about the main colony of Carlota, where "a dozen large farms of land, adapted to the production of cotton, cocoa, coffee and tobacco," had taken root. The valley and city of Córdoba, and especially Carlota, were the primary destinations for white southern migrants after the Civil War.[5]

A large portion of the white southerners who migrated to Mexico reflected the trend of southwestward movement before and after the Civil War. Once the Confederacy collapsed in the spring of 1865, and with it slavery as a system for upward mobility, white southerners in Alabama, Mississippi, Louisiana, and Texas sought other avenues to restore their economic fortunes. Some went by ship to Mexico from ports like Galveston, Texas, while others crossed the border by land into the Mexican states of Coahuila and Nuevo León.

A review of the emigrant lists in the *Mexican Times* newspaper indicates that around one thousand white southern migrants arrived in Mexico from June 1865 to June 1866 (thirteen out of forty-three issues contained lists).[6] If we take into account the number of southern colonies in Mexico, though, we arrive at a higher figure. Based on a count of eight to ten colonies (see the map, "Southern Colonies and the Texas-Coahuila Borderlands," in chapter 3), somewhere between sixteen hundred and three thousand total migrants may have come to Mexico from the summer of 1865 to the end of 1866. This estimate is based on the assumption that two hundred to three hundred migrants, at most, settled at each of these locations. Mediating between these two estimates, it seems likely that over two thousand white migrants came within the first two years of colonization (summer 1865 to summer 1867). The evidence shows that migration started to slow in mid-1866 and the numbers dropped dramatically in 1867 (after Emperor Maximilian's execution). Thus we can deduce that the total migrant count was larger than provided solely from counts based on the *Mexican Times* but less than previous estimates. In all, around five thousand southern migrants came to Mexico from 1865 to the early 1870s.[7]

Among those white southerners who arrived during the peak time period was Dr. William D. Lyles, who chose to migrate from Macon, Mississippi, to Mexico during the early months of 1866. Born and raised in South Carolina, he was one of those westward-bound slaveholders who had attained a higher socioeconomic standing before the Civil War through the use of slave labor. In the 1860 U.S. Census, Lyles was listed as a planter as well as a doctor; he had $4,000 worth of real estate (above average for a slaveholder) and $8,000 of personal property, representing the seven slaves that he owned.[8] However, his slaveholdings were quite modest by planter standards, usually defined as an owner of twenty or more slaves. By 1850 the median value of a slaveholder's land was just below $3,000, while median slaveholding was about five slaves per owner, or more typically five to eight slaves.[9] Hence Lyles appears to have been a slightly above-average slaveholder who continued his search for better economic opportunities after the war had ended and slavery and the southern economy lay in ruins.

Lyles made his journey with a group of twenty-eight fellow Mississippians, including C. M. Thomas. Thomas came from the same county as Lyles and was also a farmer. He also had been born in the neighboring state of North Carolina. However, Thomas was younger than Lyles (age thirty-five in 1866; Lyles was forty-eight) and had owned more slaves (eleven total, valued at over $14,000) and land (valued at $5,000).[10] With such wealth holdings, Thomas fits the definition of a planter more than Lyles does, but he was really only slightly better off than an average slaveholder (on a regional level).

Both Lyles and Thomas provide us with a picture of the small to middling slaveholders who had only recently acquired better economic footing before the war. The rising international demand for cotton during the 1850s helped push men like Thomas and Lyles into the middling slaveholder ranks, since slave prices also rose and increased the value of their human property. The cotton boom in the 1850s and the increased demand for slave labor that accompanied westward movement caused the average slave price to rise from $700 in 1840 to over $1,000 in 1860.[11] In 1860 Thomas owned five male slaves who were in the prime of their lives (ages fourteen, fifteen, eighteen, twenty-one, and twenty-eight), a key factor in determining a slave's value (other factors contributing to a slave's worth included health, gender, and skills).[12] Both Thomas and Lyles were part of the shift westward of slave owners, slaves, and cotton from the seaboard South to the states of Alabama, Mississippi, Louisiana, and Texas. These two migrating white southerners had benefited from the use of slave labor before the war, and after it they sought to sustain or improve their social and economic status by migrating to Mexico.

Like Lyles and Thomas, many white southern migrants had served in the war but were not among the top tier of command. Lyles might have rubbed shoulders with some of the top brass while serving as a surgeon in the Confederate general and staff officers corps. But other migrants were common soldiers, such as J. S. McMorris, the wealthiest member of the Mississippi group, who had been only a private in the Fifth Mississippi Infantry Regiment. Since the South needed all the manpower it could muster, the wealthy sometimes served on the lower rungs of the Confederate ladder. Oftentimes military rank did reflect one's socioeconomic status, though. J. A. McDonald, from the same migrant group, did not have any real estate wealth in 1860 and had been a private in the Civil War.[13] H. C. Gillespie likewise was a laborer, with a wife and one son, and he had no real estate or personal property listed for his household before the war. His military service is absent from the records, but assuming he did enlist (or was drafted), as more than three-fourths of white southerners age eighteen to forty-five did, it can be safely concluded that he did not rise very high in the ranks.[14] Both McDonald and Gillespie trekked over the Mexican border (or sailed to Veracruz) at the end of February or early March 1866, beckoned by the possibilities of economic advancement.[15]

Table 1. White southern migrants from Mississippi who arrived in Mexico in February or March 1866

Name	Age, 1865	County	Birth state	Family/household, 1860	Occupation	No. of Slaves, 1860	Confederate military rank
William D. Lyles	48	Noxubee	South Carolina	Wife, 5 sons, 3 daughters	Planter, doctor	7	Surgeon
C. M. Thomas	35	Noxubee	North Carolina	Father, overseer	Farmer	11	1st Lieutenant, Captain
C. A. Durham	48	Kemper	North Carolina	Wife, 5 children	Farmer	11	1st Lieutenant, Captain
J. S. McMorris	49	Winston	South Carolina	Wife, 5 sons, 2 daughters	Farmer (planter)	40	Private
J. A. McDonald	36	Lawrence	Mississippi	Wife, 1 other	Not listed	None	Private
H. C. Gillespie	45	DeSoto	South Carolina	Wife, 1 son	Laborer	None	Private (most likely)

Sources: Mexican Times; U.S. Census Bureau, 1860 Federal Census; and U.S. Census Bureau, 1860 Slave Schedules. For detailed citations, see chapter 2, notes 9–16.

From other states, like Missouri and Alabama, more average white southerners (in economic terms) migrated as well, especially in the first months of 1866. John Thrailkill from Callaway County, Missouri, for example, migrated to San Luis Potosí, south of Coahuila, in January 1866. He was a single, thirty-year-old farm laborer with a small amount of personal property and had served as a private in the Confederate army before going to Mexico.[16] Edward Ferguson from Mobile, Alabama, brought his whole family with him to Córdoba (central Mexico) in February or March 1866. He was a carpenter who had been born in Ireland (as was his wife, Eliza) and had been a private throughout the war.[17] With the strong religious connection between Spain, Ireland, and Mexico, Ferguson and his family found hospitable ground in Catholic Mexico.

These white southerners help reveal diversity in the social classes of migrants. Unlike elite Confederate officers, who were more afraid of the punishment they might receive for the leading part they had played in the war, these more average white southerners were not so much trying to re-create a new Dixieland in Mexico but were pursuing a strategy of upward mobility founded on the notion of relocating to wherever the future seemed brightest.[18] A larger migrant group from Texas helps illustrate this point.

In February 1866 an even more diverse group of white southerners (seventy total) that included planters, farmers, carpenters, blacksmiths, and lawyers decided to migrate to Mexico from Clinton, Texas, in DeWitt County (southeast of San Antonio).[19] Some migrated with their whole families, while most sent forth the men of the household to scout out the area around Córdoba. Arriving in early to mid-March 1866, this migratory group also helps illuminate the range of white southerners who went to Mexico after the Civil War. The colonization venture might have started off as an exodus of recalcitrant Confederates, but it was turning into a wider movement. By the early months of 1866, small to middling (former) slaveholding farmers made up the bulk of travelers, interspersed with richer and poorer emigrants.

Table 2. The Clinton Group (DeWitt County, Texas),
arrived in Córdoba, Mexico, March 1866

Name	Age, 1865	Birth state	Family/household, 1860
William S. Booth	56	Georgia	Wife, 4 sons, 2 daughters
Ben Cage	46	Tennessee	Wife, 6 children
Gilbert Gaye	44	Georgia	Wife, 4 children, 1 other
Felix Greer	49	Georgia	Wife, 5 daughters
William L. Pierson	39	Alabama	Wife, 2 sons, 1 daughter
Benjamin A. Milligan	50	South Carolina	Wife, father, mother
Oliver H. Stapp	47	Kentucky	Wife, 3 sons, 2 daughters, 2 others
M. V. King	30	Georgia	Wife, 1 son
William A. Blair	44	Missouri	Wife, 3 daughters, 3 others
John R. Wright	29	Mississippi	Wife, 1 other
James Brown	70	Tennessee	Wife, 3 children
Nancy Brigham	59	Florida or Georgia	Husband (died 1863), 1 son, 3 daughters

Sources: Mexican Times; U.S. Census Bureau, 1860 Federal Census; and U.S. Census Bureau,

William S. Booth, for instance, had been a fairly prosperous farmer and slave owner before the Civil War. In 1860 Booth owned $3,000 worth of real estate and fourteen slaves valued at $12,400. Thus Booth fits the profile of a slaveholder who was slightly above average in terms of wealth and who had hoped to attain planter status by investing in slave labor. In 1866, at age fifty-six, instead of being able to draw upon this slave labor force, Booth instead struck out for Mexico with his four sons.[20]

At the same time, other migrants in the group came from the lower end of the economic scale. Gilbert Gaye and Felix Greer offer two examples. In 1860 Gaye was a farmer with a modest $300 in movable property, representing two slaves. He traveled to Mexico without his wife, Martha, and four children. Felix Greer was a forty-nine-year-old farmer with no personal property, and hence no slaves, and he

Occupation	No. of Slaves, 1860	Confederate military rank
Farmer	14	Private, 2nd Lieutenant (possibly)
Farmer (planter)	26	Private
Farmer	2	Unknown
Farmer	None	Sergeant or private (most likely)
Farmer	12	Private (possibly)
Carpenter	None	Sergeant, then private (possibly)
Carpenter	None	Unknown
Blacksmith	None	Private, then artificer
County court clerk	2	Private (possibly)
Wagon maker	None	Private, then corporal; or third and then first lieutenant
Tavern keeper	3	Did not serve (most likely)
None listed; husband was farmer	4	Did not serve

1860 Slave Schedules. For detailed citations, see chapter 2, notes 19–24.

also struck out on his own. Elenor, his wife, and their five daughters would have to wait to join him. In the case of Gaye, Greer, and Booth, we can see the continued migration southwestward that began in older Lower South states like Georgia, where all three were born. After moving to Texas and enduring the Civil War, all three saw greater potential in moving farther southwest to Mexico.[21]

The decision to migrate also appealed to white southerners in other occupations. Both Benjamin A. Milligan and Oliver H. Stapp were among those white southerners who continued westward, but not as farmers or planters. Both were carpenters, married, in their late forties, and held only a small amount of personal property.[22] The group also contained a blacksmith originally from Georgia, a wagon maker from Mississippi, and a tavern keeper from Tennessee. These migrants allow us to see that the migration movement was composed of a broad range of white southerners, including less wealthy nonslaveholders who worked in a variety of professions.[23]

Not all of those leading the way across the border were men either. Nancy Brigham left with the Clinton group for Mexico with only her son Benjamin. At age fifty-nine, Brigham was heading the family; her husband died in 1863. Her twenty-two-year-old son helped her navigate the new surroundings of central Mexico, and she may very well have stayed in Mexico past 1870, since there is no record of her in the U.S. Census for that year. Her involvement reflects the appeal of Mexico as grounds for economic revival, a way to resuscitate her family's future.[24]

As the *Mexican Times* stated in March 1866, "the people of Texas are in the emigrating fever" and they were "determined to seek new homes" across the border. Back in November, the newspaper reported that "over 600 immigrants [had] arrived in this country" and called it "a very good beginning." White southern migration to Mexico appeared to be building momentum. U.S. general Phil Sheridan, the former (and ongoing) nemesis of Jubal Early, estimated that "perhaps 3,000 or 4,000 men," had already migrated across "the Rio Grande into Mexico" in May and June 1865. His count was undoubtedly too high, but it gives a sense of the significant departure of white southerners during the summer and fall of 1865.[25]

Texas was the primary launching point for Brazilian emigration as well. One study indicates that of the 154 families that arrived in Brazil between 1865 and 1875, 103 came from Texas.[26] Frank McMullan led one of the Texas groups that migrated to Brazil; as with the Texan migrants who went to Mexico, most were small to middling farmers. The McMullan farmers sought out territory that still allowed slavery and the chance to continue their aspirational climb into the small planter ranks. The McMullan group in the São Paulo region of Brazil also contained a number of professional men, such as two judges, an engineer, a teacher, and a saddlemaker.[27] This mixture of backgrounds helped make the Brazilian expedition something slightly more than an ex-Confederate redoubt, but southern migrants to Brazil harbored overt slave-based-plantation intentions. By May 1866 McMullan confidently wrote, "Here are lands equal to any in the world and within three or four days' run from the great Capital of the nation [Rio de Janeiro], a climate unsurpassed, neither hot nor cold, and where frost is never known, water as cold as the mountain spring, and so equally distributed as to allow every man to run his plantation machinery from it." As in Mexico, McMullan described a land of plenty, brimming with opportunity for agriculture. All that was needed were hearty southern migrants to harness nature's abundance.[28]

Maury and other colonization planners saw the same promise in Mexico and moved to promote the allure of this nation. As the *New Orleans Daily True Delta* recorded in February 1866, "The letters of Governor [Isham G.] Harris, [Henry W.] Allen, and Captain Maury, written from Mexico, are having their influence." The newspaper prophesied that if migrants confirmed "the glowing accounts given by our distinguished exiles" then it would result in "a general exodus from this country." Indeed, it started to look that way by early 1866.[29]

Southern newspapers also reprinted letters sent by Americans who traveled to Mexico, touting the same promise of migration. One letter from August 1865 emphasized not only the open immigration policy of Emperor Maximilian but also how the emperor had "given contracts to Americans for telegraph lines" as well as "offering great inducements to capitalists to work the rich and exhaustless mines with which Mexico abounds." Under the heading "Steamships, Railroads, and Telegraphs under the New Regime," this story named "a Mr. Clute, of Texas," who had received "some interior telegraph privileges of great value." Railroad and telegraph lines were being plotted to "connect Vera Cruz and Matamoros, Guanajuata and Matamoros, and San Luis and Durango" under the guidance of southern initiative. Clearly others were becoming convinced that "the true key to the regeneration of Mexico consists in the infusion of new blood, new energy, ambition, courage and enterprise."[30] These larger economic impulses came to define the enterprise more concretely as the migration movement grew in the early months of 1866.

Letters seeking information about migration came flying across the border as quickly as those sent back across it by the leaders of colonization. By January 1866 Sterling Price indicated that Isham Harris and he were receiving "more than fifty letters by the last steamer from persons asking for themselves and others information regarding this country." In response, Price issued a glowing report of the "unsurpassed" fertility of the soil ("producing two crops in a year") and how sugar and coffee were grown "in great abundance and of excellent quality." As leader of the Carlota colony, he had previously set aside 20 acres from his 640 for the town.[31]

Even in the face of General Phil Sheridan's tightening blockade of New Orleans and the border, southern migration continued. In February 1866 Sheridan had successfully stopped a group of forty or fifty migrants from leaving New Orleans. But by early April 1866 it was reported that the steamship *Savannah* was on its way from New Orleans to Veracruz with "emigrants bound [for] Cordova," described as a "new and flourishing settlement." As this notice urged, "Do not neglect this chance for the land of future promise."[32]

Such activity followed the path already set by southerners close to the border. "The enterprising Mr. Frank M. Campbell and a number of gentlemen associated with him," for example, had "made a purchase of 20,000 acres of land from the Government, to settle in the district of Cordova" back in August 1865. Such "settlers" were "allowed to introduce, free of duty, all implements, machinery, stock and fixtures necessary for carrying on their agricultural pursuits."[33] By February and March 1866 the movement was less about stalwart Confederates looking to evade punishment of the new political order and more about individuals and families searching for new opportunities. The *Mexican Times* noted the changing nature of the migrants by January 1866, describing the families that came together, along with the "stock and farming utensils" that some carried with them. It appeared that white southerners were answering Maury's call. As this newspaper reported in February 1866, "Preparations are being made in the United States for emigration to Mexico on a very large scale." At this point, who should come? "All those who have no employment and but little means," as well as "those who are discontented and cannot be made satisfied with the new order of things."[34]

As the migration movement evolved, the future in Mexico seemed to burst forth with opportunity for white southerners of all backgrounds. The emperor was reported to be "bending his energies to throwing open the country, wherever practicable, by railroads penetrating the most valuable mineral and agricultural sections of the empire." Toward this end, "skillful engineers are planning highways to connect with these [railroads], so that industrial populations will have every facility for sending produce to market." In addition, "steamship companies" had been established "on both sides of the continent, to form the nucleus of a commerce for which few countries in the world offer a more substantial basis." Hence, telegraph lines connecting Mexico with the South were only one part of "the great system of internal improvement." Colonization rolled forth hand in hand with this modernization strategy, drawing heavily upon common white southern migrants.[35]

A Different Sort of Crossroads:
Black Southern Dreams of Mexico

A small number of black southerners migrated to Mexico during the peak of southern colonization. Similar to white southern migration to Mexico, black migration drew upon earlier movements across the Southwest, but the decision to move westward before and during the Civil War was usually not in the hands of black southerners. As the Union army advanced deeper into Confederate territory during the Civil War, many white southerners tried to protect their human property by moving their slaves to a location away from the opposing army. For example, the slave Allen Manning was taken from Clarke County, Mississippi, to Coryell County, Texas, and recalled moving in a caravan and being hired out to planters along the way, until it seemed they were far enough away from the Yankees. Such caravans of slaves, wagons, and livestock were common sights in the South during the war, especially heading west from Louisiana and Mississippi. As Manning later said, "It look like everybody in the world was going to Texas." This was an astute observation—an estimated 150,000 slaves lined the roads going to Texas from mid-1862 to the final days of the war.[36]

Fred Brown recalled how he had been taken from a plantation in Baton Rouge Parish, Louisiana, to Kaufman County, Texas, toward the end of the war. "Jus' 'fore freedom come," he had been whisked away to what his owner thought would be safer ground. The same logic prevailed in Alabama. Former slave Cato Carter commented, "Near the close of the war I seed some folks leavin' for Texas." Apparently, slave owners from Wilcox County believed "they'd have to live in Texas to keep slaves." So, Carter said, "plenty started driftin' their slaves to the west." Mattie Gilmore had previously been pulled away from Mobile, Alabama, while Yankee troops tightened their grip around the area. As she remembered, they traveled at night and were "scart to make a fire." Masters hastily pushed their slave property onward across the Mississippi River, "dead men layin' everywhere, black and white." As Carter said, some slave owners were so intent on keeping their human property that they even "took slaves to Texas after the Fed'rals done 'creed the breakin' up."[37]

Although more hurried and panic-driven, these forced relocations to Texas during the 1860s built upon a history of forced migration to the Southwest from the previous decade. Slaves brought to Texas in the 1850s included Monroe Brackins from Monroe County, Mississippi. In 1855 Brackins came with his owner, George Reedes, to Medina County, Texas, when he was only two years old. His father, mother, and two sisters were also pressed into Texas. Gus Bradshaw was a "good sized kid" when he was forced to migrate from Keecheye, Alabama, to Port Caddo, Texas.[38] During the war, then, white southern slaveholders were following a well-worn path in an effort to protect their property.

At the end of the war, some former slave owners decided to move farther west and south across the border into Mexico, bringing ex-slaves with them. At least two former slaves migrated with former Tennessee governor Isham G. Harris. They traveled over the border from Texas to Coahuila at the end of June 1865, arrived in Monterrey, Nuevo León, on July 9, went to Mexico City, and then made their way to Carlota in central Mexico.[39] Likewise, a freedman named Charlie crossed the border with ex-Confederate general Thomas C. Hindman from Arkansas in June 1865. Hindman was previously the commander of the Trans-Mississippi Department and was dismayed by the defection of his other former slaves once in Mexico. As he wrote from Monterrey in early July 1865, "All our Negroes decided to leave us upon arrival here, and did so, except Charlie, whom I employed until I could get Mexican servants." Charlie was intent on leaving too, however. As Hindman wrote, "He [Charlie] will leave tomorrow. Negroes are worse than worthless in this country." At least some former slaves were taking advantage of the cross-border migration to forge a new life on their own. A freedman named Albert, on the other hand, reportedly remained with the ex-Confederate Walter S. Stevens in Veracruz.[40]

The issue of remaining with a former master or leaving him behind highlights both the process of forced migration and the conflicted feelings that some former slaves felt during and after the Civil War. Certainly, most former slaves crossed the border under duress and with a lack of choice about the matter, and they strove to leave their former masters behind at the nearest opportunity. Others, especially those freed people who had worked closely with an ex-master, did not resolve the conflict between "fidelity to [that] master and the yearning for freedom" so easily.[41]

Body servants in particular were often torn between remaining loyal to those whom they had labored and cared for and pursuing their own precarious freedom. As Martin Jackson, who had been with his owner during the war, explained, "Just what my feelings [were] about the War, I have never been able to figure out myself." He "knew the Yanks were going to win," but he had hoped they would do it "without wiping out [his master's] company."[42] The former servant Ran displayed a sense of loyalty to his ex-owner Isham G. Harris by remaining with him throughout their time in Mexico.[43] A former slave named George who had been a body servant most likely struggled with this dilemma too when he went to Mexico. He was the guide for an ex-Confederate migrant group as they crossed through Texas. The group eventually made their way to Mexico City in the summer of 1865 and then left for the main settlement area in Córdova, where George probably went too. Or he might have gone off on his own.[44] The records do not reveal his path, but he most likely faced conflicted emotions, formed through years of service, while he entered a strange new country.

More former slaves instead reconceived their former masters as a means to greater freedom once in Mexico, a nation that had officially stipulated since 1824 that slaves were free upon entering its territory.[45] This was the case with the servants of Eliza McHatton, a plantation mistress from Louisiana who initially fled to Texas during the Civil War. Advancing Union armies prompted McHatton and her husband to relocate to Piedras Negras on the Mexican side of the border. She helped run a customshouse there until the early months of 1864, when they decided to return to San Antonio, Texas. Yet when they set out, McHatton discovered that her slave Delia had "disappeared," or rather struck off on her own, leaving McHatton and her family behind. It was later determined that Delia was living in the town of Mier, just across the Rio Grande.[46] When McHatton was living in Matamoros at the end of the war, two more slaves escaped. A wagon driver and cook named Humphrey took advantage of his relocation to Mexico and disappeared shortly after trying to liberate another slave-turned-servant named Martha. In early 1865 Martha was arrested by Mexican officials and taken from McHatton's home because Humphrey had informed them that she was about to be taken to Cuba without her consent. Martha, however, stated that she wished to remain with McHatton's family, and the case was dismissed. Humphrey, on the other hand, took a road away from his former owners.[47]

The surveyor William Marshall Anderson came across a former slave who appeared to have remained loyal to his former owner but upon closer inspection could be seen to have taken advantage of his forced relocation to Mexico to build a new life of his own. While Anderson was in the Córdoba district in early August 1865, in charge of clearing some land that had been acquired by another white southern migrant, he made note of one ex-slave named Domingo. Anderson was helping a friend lay the foundations for "a real 'Old Va. Home in Mexico,'" and so too was Domingo, supposedly. Yet one day when Anderson visited the work site with the proprietor's wife, their presence startled Domingo enough to make him "show the white of his eyes and catch his *bref* in fuss [first] rate style." Anderson explained why in a derogatory way: "The old fool! He began to think that Cacahuatal [the hacienda Cacaotal], Mr. Norris [the owner], all the wukmen, and even the engineer and the oxen belonged to him!"[48] Apparently Domingo was carrying out his work as he saw fit, and his work schedule went according to his own plans and not his former owner's. He probably did not truly think that the hacienda would become his own, but he was more than likely using his ex-master as a means to establish himself as a free man in Mexico, possibly carving out his own plot of land on this new settlement.

Ex-slaves who carved out niches of autonomy in Mexico during the 1860s connect with earlier precedents of pushing the boundaries of freedom. By the mid-1850s an estimated four thousand fugitive slaves resided in the upper regions of Mexico.[49] Mexican authorities actually encouraged the migration of black southerners into northern Mexico to provide a buffer against American filibusters and Indian raids. This was the idea behind allowing the Mascogos, or Seminole Maroons, to settle with a portion of the Seminole Indians in Coahuila in 1850. The Mascogos were an ethnic group formed from runaway slaves and free blacks who had an alliance with the Seminoles. Inviting such colonies helped spur higher rates of slave defections, as did Mexico's official political stance against slavery. In the early 1840s Mexican president Santa Anna clearly expressed his country's antislavery sentiments when he praised the refusal to increase the wealth of the nation "with the sweat, blood and tears of the African race." Mexico's liberal Constitution of 1857 likewise reiterated the offer of protection to fugitive slaves and outlawed any sort of extradition treaty. As one former slave recalled, "After the war starts lots of slaves runned off to git to de Yankees," but the slaves in the Double Bayou area of Texas (near Beaumont), "head[ed] for de Rio Grande river."[50] The more welcoming terrain in Mexico therefore attracted antebellum, wartime, and postwar black southern migrants.

Like white migrants, black southerners sought better economic opportunities, but they were often driven by basic survival. This factor helps explain why some former slaves stayed on with former masters in Mexico and the South. At the beginning of Reconstruction, freed people had to grapple over land and contracts with former owners or new employers in order to eke out a living. While the Freedmen's Bureau sought to ensure that slavery was in fact dead and to protect freed people from abuses, it also looked to turn former slaves into free laborers. During the summer of 1865, as former slaveholders often took matters into their own hands to stop freed people from taking temporary trips or relocating more permanently, they also urged the Union army and the Freedmen's Bureau to help them retain ex-slave labor. For example, one planter speaking for the plantations of Hilton Head and Port Royal, South Carolina, petitioned for "some system of 'permits' or passports by which the freed negro will be prevented from running all over the country" and "hold him to his engagements in labor." Military officials and the Freedmen's Bureau tended to comply with such requests. While stipulating that contracts were to be formed voluntarily, they acted to keep black southerners in their current locations. This was the case in Camden, Arkansas, where the bureau "advised" all freed people "to remain where they now are, for the remainder of this year" and told them they would "not be allowed to congregate in towns, about Military Camps, or spend their time in idleness and vagrancy."[51]

Taking a cue from President Andrew Johnson's lenient Reconstruction terms, including wholesale pardons to ex-Confederates and cancellation of the bureau's plans for land redistribution, southern state legislatures began adopting the Black Codes. Starting with Mississippi and South Carolina at the end of 1865, these state laws aimed first and foremost to compel black southerners to sign labor contracts and grant plantation owners slave-like control. At the end of the 1865 crop season, many ex-slaves were also deprived of proper compensation for their work. Confronting increased restrictions, many African Americans looked to other plantations or southern cities for a better livelihood, but they were quickly disappointed. These destinations were usually not any better, and most black migrants returned to their home states.[52]

Nonetheless, black southerners took advantage of their newfound liberty and elected to move about, if only locally, and take new stands on their own. Some, as in the case of James Boyd (originally named Scott Bird), made it across the border into Mexico. Boyd had been born in Oklahoma Indian Territory; his father was a Native American named Blue Bull Bird, while his mother came from Mississippi (possibly a runaway slave). Boyd was stolen away and enslaved by one Sanford Woolridge of Texas. Brought to the Waco area to work on a sixteen-hundred-acre plantation, Boyd recalled laboring "all week and sometime Sunday" along with a "big dance 'bout twice a year, on Christmas and sometime in de summer." When emancipation came to this pocket of the South, he remembered the ex-slaves "throw de hats in de air and holler." Once the initial euphoria wore off, though, Boyd, like many others, had to confront the reality of the situation. As his former owner asked him, "How you gwine eat and git clothes and sech?" These pressing economic concerns initially kept Boyd on the plantation, but about a year later he managed to get a job on a cattle ranch in South Texas. "I druv cattle into Kansas," Boyd said, and he became a "top hand" at this line of work.[53]

Around mid- to late 1866, Boyd started driving "some cattle to Mexico" for his employer, who had become ill and instructed Boyd "to sell de cattle and send him de money and git de job down dere." So he went down to Mexico and carried out this business; he also married "a gal name Martina in 1869, down in Matamoras." James Boyd had come a long way, figuratively and literally, from the days of slavery. He had earned solid work for himself and found a Mexican bride, with whom he had four children. Boyd managed to cross both national and ethnic boundaries after his transition to freedom. Some years later, after his wife died, he came back to Huntsville, Texas.[54]

Skilled or semiskilled work such as Boyd's cattle driving granted some freed people more means to migrate out of the South. After the Civil War, Felix Haywood also went to Mexico because of his work skills. Haywood was born and worked as a slave in Bexar County, Texas (where San Antonio is located). By working as a sheepherder and cowpuncher (or cowboy) before and during the war, he honed the abilities that would allow him to migrate to Mexico. As he recalled,

"I went there after the war for a while and then I looked 'round and decided to get back." Haywood came back to San Antonio and eventually took a job at the waterworks, "handling pipes."[55] Haywood completed his circular migration in less time than Boyd, but his sojourn still demonstrates the desire to move beyond the local area after emancipation.

The ability to get out from under field labor helped propel these two freedmen out of the South. Other forms of nonagricultural wage labor such as steamboat, railroad, and lumber work also provided avenues to relocate and improve one's economic circumstances. Most black southerners who moved made local migrations within states and counties. The majority of southern blacks remained in rural areas and migrated at most to a neighboring plantation. Cities such as Norfolk, Virginia, and Mobile, Alabama, also began to attract large numbers of black migrants. For black southerners, the exception was to migrate to destinations such as Mexico or Liberia, where several thousand blacks (many from South Carolina) went from 1866 to 1871 with the aid of the American Colonization Society.[56]

Between 1865 and 1868 about twenty-two hundred African Americans had already migrated to Liberia, mainly from Virginia, the Carolinas, Georgia, and Tennessee (as in the antebellum period). While the numbers going to Liberia dwindled from 1868 to 1873, black southern interest in leaving the South made new strides in the latter part of the 1870s. This renewed interest coincided with increased white southern political control, violence, and racial oppression.[57] During the 1870s black southerners more often moved to Kansas in the Exoduster movement. When a Kansas fever of sorts occurred in 1879 at least six thousand blacks migrated to Kansas from Mississippi, Louisiana, and Texas, whereas almost ten thousand had gone in the previous ten years. This latter movement, though, was much more motivated by the desire to escape the repressive Redemption politics that closed over the South. As one black Texan said about this exodus, it was built on "the necessity of fleeing from the wrath and long pent-up hatred of their old masters." Dreams of economic security certainly worked their way into the imagination of migrating black southerners, but the impulse to escape from "political terrorism," violence, and dis-crimination certainly underwrote African American motivations to leave the South during and after Reconstruction.[58]

For most black southerners it was just too difficult to go to Mexico. The abject poverty that confronted ex-slaves pressed upon them the immediate need to work, wherever it was possible and safest. As El-vira Boles, the freedwoman who came to Texas during the war with only one dress, indicated, "Dat's de way all de culled people was after freedom, never had nothin' but what had on de back." After the war ended, "marster turn us loose in de world, without a penny." So the primary goal was to work to keep oneself alive. For some that meant traveling to another county, state, and sometimes country. As Boles said, "Oh, dey was awful times. We jus' worked from place to place af-ter freedom." The freedman Wash Anderson (short for George Wash-ington Anderson) echoed these sentiments. "After freedom come," Anderson explained, "I went 'roun' doin' dif'rent kind of work. I uster work on steamboats, and on de railroad and at sawmillin.'"[59] Like oth-er freed people, Anderson took most work that came his way, and that was the priority—finding a way to survive, which sometimes, but not often, meant going to Mexico.

African Americans appear sporadically in Coahuila town records from the later nineteenth century, offering further evidence of black migrants who made it across the border. In Piedras Negras, for in-stance, a black resident named Charles Luis was named as an escaped fugitive from a Mexican jail in early 1875. A few years later, another possible black migrant worker who lived on a ranch in Monclova was accused of taking a donkey from his employer. Such incidents surface only when a crime or dispute was at hand and provide only a glimpse of what was certainly a larger presence of African Americans in Coa-huila. The most well-known black migrants, the Mascogos, appear in the records somewhat more frequently. In 1884, for example, three black representatives of this group, Rafael Aldape González, Hilario Sánchez, and D. Cesario, renegotiated a land contract in Múzquiz, demonstrat-ing this group's longevity in the border area. Such records allow us to see only a small portion of the black southerners who went to Mexico.[60]

By the late nineteenth century, dreams of expanded freedom still floated along the border. One of the greatest examples is the colony of William Ellis, an African American who envisioned that the U.S.-Mexico borderlands would offer pathways of economic mobility and social liberation not available in the United States. The Ellis colony, formed in 1894 in the Laguna region of Durango, represented a possibility that had been so elusive to southern blacks. As one study states, "African Americans might [have] finally achieve[d] the independence and self-sufficiency so long celebrated in American agricultural ideology—yet so long denied them north of the border." Ellis recruited black field laborers from Alabama to work on a Mexican hacienda in exchange for land and funding; he brought back over six hundred migrant workers. The colony was short-lived, however, as the Mexican government did little to protect these agricultural workers from exploitation, while a swath of yellow fever broker over the land. Nonetheless, about seventy of these colonists picked up their hopes and went to the mining town of Mapimí to continue their pursuit of expanded freedom.[61]

Mexico offered the possibility of greater social and economic freedom for black migrants before and during the Civil War. For some, migration across the border after the war had ended also became a reality, at least temporarily. As Felix Haywood explained, "There wasn't no reason to *run* up North. All we had to do was to *walk*, but walk *South*, and we'd be free as soon as we crossed the Rio Grande."[62] Although black southerners did not migrate to Mexico at nearly the same level as white migrants, they add a vital dimension to the immigration movement. They allow us to see that the path across the border was filled with other people beyond Confederate generals and politicians.

Combined with that of lesser-known white southerners, the migration of black southerners provides greater insight into the broader range of migrants involved in this transnational episode in U.S. and Mexican history. Both migrant groups help reframe this history more along the lines of economic pursuit and upward mobility. They also instill a sense of the multiple meanings of freedom and how the term could be redefined by crossing the border.

As we will see in the next chapter, the U.S.-Mexico borderlands, where most of these migrants entered Mexico, played a vital role in shaping the contours of southern colonization and the associated meanings of freedom. Turning back to the pivotal year of 1866, we will see how Indians and local Mexicans along the border responded to this movement of people. We will also see how the colonization plans reached their peak and began to unravel in this geographic crossroads.

Chapter Three

Southern Colonization and the Texas-Coahuila Borderlands

On May 30, 1865, Mexican military commander Anacleto R. Falcón spotted about one thousand Confederate soldiers crossing the border from Texas into Coahuila. As he watched these war-hardened soldiers go across at "Paso de la Aguila" (Eagle Pass) along the Rio Grande, Falcón was witnessing the first rush of southern migrants fleeing to Mexico after news of General Robert E. Lee's surrender at Appomattox reached the American Southwest. Falcón grew concerned, suspecting that these armed riders would cause problems in northern Mexico and wreak havoc on communities along the border. He even thought they might join up with the Imperialist forces, seen by Mexican Republicans such as Falcón as traitors to the nation. He thus sent a message to the town of Guerrero to warn its inhabitants of the potential danger headed their way.[1]

For these self-exiled ex-Confederates—and for the broader movement of southerners to follow—northern Mexico would not be a welcoming place. Some southern migrants seemed aware of the dangers as they crossed into the borderlands. John Henry Brown was among the first waves of ex-Confederate migrants who crossed over the Texas-Coahuila border in the summer of 1865; he commented on the instability of northern Mexico, with "a border population" that had become isolated "from the more potent centre of the nation." As Brown explained, "rival, predatory chiefs" controlled the area and contended with one another for power. According to Brown, it was the corrupt ways of these local strongmen along with "their inability to resist the inroads of wild Indians, or to suppress organized bands of robbers" that made the region inhospitable to southern colonization. These contending lines of local power, he thought, provided "sufficient reasons to prevent prudent American farmers, mechanics and artisans from desiring to settle in that part of Mexico at the present time."[2] And yet this is just what Maury and the other colonization planners proposed to do.

While Brown crossed the Rio Grande in June 1865, "from that sink of iniquity, Eagle Pass, on the American side, to its twin sister, Piedras Negras, on the Mexican side," he further attested to one of the chief obstacles confronting the colonization plans along the Texas-Coahuila borderlands. As he wrote, "a fine stallion, work horse and mules" had been stolen from him, along with "four other animals" belonging to his migrant group. As he continued his journey, Brown concluded that "thieves abounded and honest men constituted the exception to the visible mass" along the border. Ex-Confederate general Thomas C. Hindman formed similar conclusions as he crossed over the border in the summer of 1865: "Stealing is the one thing to be dreaded."[3] Brown's and Hindman's remarks provide insight into this border region, indicating that acts of theft were quite commonplace, even embedded, in this landscape.

By the 1860s a network of violence, theft, and trade had become entrenched across this stretch of the border in the American Southwest and northern Mexico. The primary protagonists were Indian groups and Mexican Republicans. Through their involvement in this raiding-trading network, the Comanches, Apaches, Kickapoos, and Mexican Republican armies loyal to Benito Juárez erected a localized power structure that subverted external attempts to control the Texas-Coahuila borderlands. Collectively, both Indians and local Mexicans would strike back at the advancement of southern colonies into Coahuila, as both groups likewise effectively prevented either a federal Mexican Imperialist or Republican government from laying claim to the state.

The colonization plans, as developed by Matthew F. Maury in the summer and fall of 1865, called for the establishment of southern colonies outside of central Mexico to meet the anticipated level of white and black southern migration. By early 1866 both Maury and Henry Watkins Allen (the publisher of the *Mexican Times*) deemed that the time was ripe to advance into northern Mexico. Allen had been an early Confederate arrival who knew of the dangers that confronted these plans—his group had been on the alert for "roving marauders" as it crossed the border from Eagle Pass to Piedras Negras in late June 1865. Nonetheless, as Allen reported in the *Mexican Times* in March 1866, "Emigrants in large numbers have already arrived; a great many more are coming, to say nothing of scores of agents here who are seeking locations for entire colonies." "The great demand," Allen continued, was "for land." In response, Maury commenced his "operations," which culminated in sending William Marshall Anderson on a survey mission in Coahuila. Maury, Allen, and Anderson expected that they would "very soon" open up "as fine a body of land as any in this vast Empire."[4]

Anderson was a surprise recruit to southern colonization in Mexico. As seen in the previous chapter, he had divided loyalties to the American North and South and fought for neither side during the Civil War. However, he was drawn to the colonization venture largely because of its economic potential, and his background as a surveyor fit well with his mission. Mexicans and Indians in the borderlands, however, would vigorously contest his part in the colonization plans and prevent the immigration plans from fully unfolding.

The plans for the immigration movement had thus far proceeded in a logical manner, but the organizers did not fully grasp the dynamics of the Texas-Coahuila borderlands. While such Confederates as General Edmund Kirby Smith wrote about "the fear of attack by both Indians and the 'Liberal Robbers,'" these warnings fell by the wayside in the quest for southern colonization dreams.[5] Ultimately, the planners of colonization underestimated the obstacles that awaited them in northern Mexico and thought too narrowly in terms of their own ambitions and not enough about the Mexican people and nation.

This shortsightedness ultimately led to the downfall of southern colonization in its initial form. Here in the U.S.-Mexico borderlands we see the seeds of destruction and the roots of recasting colonization.

Coahuila: A Land for Southern Colonization?

By early 1866 white southerners had started to march into the northern stretches of Mexico. In response, Maury first sent former Confederate brigadier general William P. Hardeman to the state of Durango, immediately south of Chihuahua and southwest of Coahuila, to map out potential colonies. Hardeman's survey resulted in the Palacio colony in the northeastern section of the state (bordering on southern Coahuila). Major General George W. Clark from Arkansas was placed in charge of settling white southerners there.[6] Despite his misgivings about northern Mexico, John Henry Brown also conducted a survey for Maury on the suitability of the Yucatán Peninsula for colonization and compiled a report on the viability of the Tuxpan and Pánuco River valleys, about three hundred miles to the north of the city of Veracruz. Brown was so pleased with his findings that his family and four others moved to this location in July 1866. Two years later, Brown reported that forty families along with forty-seven single men and thirteen single women lived at this Tuxpan colony. Both the Palacio and Tuxpan colonies spearheaded the efforts to expand out from central Mexico.[7]

Maury and Allen solicited and published land offers from northern states to press the move northward forward. As one "Mexican gentleman" near the city of Durango expressed, "I feel the greatest desire to co-operate to the colonization of our country." He thus offered to furnish two colonists and their families with a farm, stating, "I will give them *gratis*, for five years," an allotment of "fertile land," along with "a yoke of oxen, two cows with their calves, two mares, one horse, two ewes." At the end of five years, if profits were in hand, he expected to collect pay for the animals and tools and to arrange for a new contract. His primary remuneration before that time was for colonists to "assist [him] in defending [his] property, in case of attack by wild Indians or robbers." This last item would prove to be a

formidable task. Still, the land offers continued. Rodrigo Durán offered a similar arrangement on his neighboring farm "nine leagues
east of Durango." His relative Jesús Durán likewise sought to enlist
colonists on his farm farther to the west.[8]

Maury received a more significant land offer from the state of Tamaulipas, located on the Texas border along the Gulf of Mexico. In early
February 1866 a resident named J. O. Forns offered up "640 acres to a
man with family, 320 to an unmarried man" for a total of "25 square
leagues of land (108.459 acres)" on his hacienda called Limon situated on the Pánuco River.[9] Maury responded with excitement, writing,
"the offer of Mr. Forns is most princely" and adding that the lands
would be "admirably adapted to the cultivation of coffee, cotton, sugar, rice, tobacco, and the whole list of intertropical fruits." It was also
"a good stock country, with an abundance of timber." Maury advised
only that emigrants be aware of the timing of their journey, careful to
avoid the rainy season and the attendant fevers and "to send out their
pioneers [male migrants] first, to make ready for their families to follow."[10] These last instructions were already being followed by most
of the migrants coming over the border in early 1866.

Forns offered to "give, also gratis, enough land for a town, as well,
as for a road 16 yards wide traversing the entire colony from North to
South."[11] Such actions were aimed at building the infrastructure of
the colonies and aligned perfectly with Maury's modernizing vision.
As Maury proclaimed in a letter meant for U.S. newspapers, "The Empire is continually gaining ground. Enterprise is abroad; many works
of internal improvement are already under way, and about to be connected." He believed the momentum for colonization was at hand and
stressed that financial investment was coming to the surface. "Capital
is leaving its hiding places," he wrote, "and the columns of the newspaper press are daily, and for months have been, filled with the names
of liberals, who looking upon the Empire as a success, and their cause
as a failure, have laid down their arms, and are giving in their adhe-
sion."[12] By early 1866 Maury thought the time had come for the full
realization of his plans.

By the time Maury turned his attention to Coahuila, he had already

laid the groundwork to expand beyond central Mexico and incorpo-
rate the northern regions. Nine colonies were already established or
currently being developed across Mexico: the Palacio colony in Durango; the Tuxpan colonies in Veracruz; the Forns colony in Tamaulipas; the Ridley colony near the Pacific coast city of Mazatlán; and
five more that Maury took great pride in describing. "[John F.] Bryant
from Arkansas has established a colony in Chihuahua," Maury indicated. F. T. Mitchell of Missouri had established another "on the Rio
Verde in the Department of San Luis Potosí," and "[David S.] Terry
of Texas erected another in Jalisco [called San Lorenzo]." There were
also several smaller colonies around Córdoba and Orizaba that, taken
collectively, can be counted as the eighth colony (e.g., one at Omealca). "Then," as Maury proudly said, "there is the fine colony of Carlota near Córdoba."[13]

Maury contended that the lands around Carlota in central Mexico were ripe for development and that agricultural production would
provide the economic foundation for Mexico's future. However, Maury also sent out a warning: "All the lands of this colony are already, or
soon will be taken up." Perhaps this claim was another promotional
device to lure immigrants to Mexico. Yet land was being purchased at
an accelerated rate, especially since a white migrant family could obtain 320 acres and was exempt from property taxes for a year. Moreover, land speculation had become an integral part of the Carlota
colony, with early migrants gobbling up the valuable tracts in hope
of selling them for a much higher price later. Hence Maury was con-
firming what he already knew. The demand for land brought on by
increased migration called for a push into the borderlands.[14]

This is where William Marshal Anderson came into the picture;
his mission was to conduct a survey of northern Mexico. In fact, while
Maury wrote his letter for publication in the United States in early
February 1866, Anderson was already charting out new stretches of
paradise and making headway toward implementing the colonization plans. Maury reassured incoming migrants that "the speedy filling up of this [Carlota] colony should not be disheartening, under
the ideas that there are no more good lands and choice spots." To the

contrary, agents were currently "at various convenient points to assist immigrants on their arrival in the country," and, although "it ha[d] not been as yet practicable to establish agencies on the Rio Grande," soon that would be accomplished. Most likely after the completion of Anderson's survey, he planned to station an agent at Presidio del Norte. This immigration agency would be added to those already established at Córdoba under John Perkins, at Veracruz under Y. P. Oropesa, at Monterrey with J. T. Lux, at Mazatlán with Alonso Ridley, and others at Tampico and Matamoros.[15]

With these plans underway, it is not too surprising to find that some southerners were already making a home in northern Mexico. The movement northward had started with such Confederates as F. T. Mitchell and his family, who settled in San Luis Potosí near the town of Río Verde in the fall of 1865. Mitchell had gone into "cotton planting on an extensive scale, having rented two large haciendas for the term of ten years." In addition to Maury's efforts, the American and Mexican Emigrant Company had also begun to recruit migrants for the district of San Luis Potosí. It called attention to 150 leagues "of the very best land in Mexico," located in "what is called the Huasteca [Wasteca] country, back of Tampico." This was near the area in which John Henry Brown had started a colony, known for its remarkable lands that produced "sugar, coffee, cacao, rice, indigo, and all the tropical fruits." Such efforts began to push the colonization movement northward, out from central Mexico.[16]

From the colonization planners' perspective, this course of action made sense. The land farther north was comparatively rich for both agriculture and livestock grazing. Maury reassured migrants that such crops as cotton and corn would "do well in almost all parts of the Empire" but that "the cotton especially of Tamaulipas . . . Durango . . . and the States north, are said to be of a better staple—save sea island— than any produced in the United States." These areas were a veritable "vegetable kingdom" and farmers would be wise to settle there.[17] Furthermore, the countryside of northern Mexico was not the only place in which to prosper.

As the capital of Nuevo León with a population of fourteen thousand,

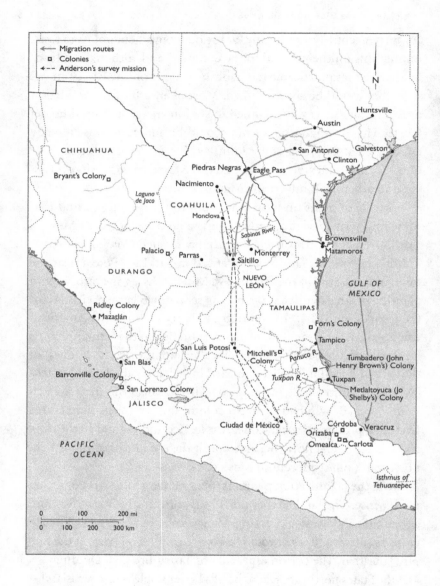

Southern Colonies in Mexico and the Texas-Coahuila Borderlands. Created
by William L. Nelson.

the city of Monterrey was a prosperous location for businessmen and farmer alike.[18] S. G. Sneed of Travis County, Texas, had migrated to this city in the fall of 1865. A successful lawyer and former slaveholder, Sneed had moved with his family to Texas before the Civil War and then on to Mexico.[19] The engineer John C. Moore followed a similar course to Monterrey. He started in Tennessee, married his wife, Martha, there, and had four children along the way to Missouri. Because he had almost no property holdings, however, his march to Mexico was more pressing than the Sneed's. More prominent Confederates such as former judge T. J. Divine had also arrived in this northern Mexican city, as had young upstart farmers. A young nonslaveholding farmer by the name of Thomas Daniels, for example, had moved from Missouri to the city of Monterrey in the fall of 1865.[20]

In nearby Coahuila the same process was underway. The southern migrant Dr. D. McKnight had practiced medicine in the capital city of Saltillo before joining up with fellow Texan and ex-Confederate general Hamilton P. Bee to lease a hacienda in nearby Parras. Besides intending to "carry on extensive farming operations," they had entered into "a grape association" to produce wine and brandy. They would later extend their operations to include "the paper manufacturing business."[21] With such encouraging signs, the planners of colonization thought they had every reason to believe that Coahuila would soon become a shining home for a diverse array of southern migrants.

General Jo Shelby and the Borderlands

At the same time, if Maury and the other planners had heeded the warnings sounded by some Confederate migrants, they would have more readily recognized the difficulties that awaited the push northward. Even in the early stages of the immigration venture, there were signs that northern Mexico would not be so receptive to southern colonization. Accounts of the initial waves of Confederates pouring over the border indicate that most northern Mexicans were not very keen on their arrival. In fact, members of the local Mexican Republican armies would contest their migration through Coahuila and make it known that the state was terra non grata.

Before and after the estimated one thousand Confederates spotted by Mexican Republican Anacleto R. Falcón crossed the border at the end of May 1865, smaller groups of migrants drew the wary eye of Mexicans living along the border.[22] During the Civil War, northern Mexican officials had feared attacks by Confederates in Texas, which helped lay the groundwork for cross-border animosities. In April 1864, for example, Gregorio Galinda, the principal commander of the Rio Grande district, instructed the town of Guerrero to prepare for such an attack.[23] Since the annexation of Texas and the Mexican-American War, there had been plenty of reason for Mexicans to distrust Federals and Confederates alike, including a history of Anglo-Americans unscrupulously gobbling up lands owned by Mexican-turned-American citizens.[24]

Meanwhile, fleeing Confederates such as General Jubal Early steered clear of the borderlands because of the reported deaths of migrant soldiers at the hands of Mexican Republicans. As we saw in chapter 1, Early had fled from Virginia in late May 1865, making his way through South Carolina, Georgia, Alabama, and Louisiana before arriving in Texas at the end of July. From there he chose to go to Galveston rather than continue across the border because, as he wrote, "The Rio Grande was of such a character as to show that it would be very difficult to pass the river in safety by reason of the guerillas, who were murdering all Confederates." He thus sailed out to the West Indies before making his way to Mexico.[25] In this case, the perceived actions of local Mexicans deterred even this high-ranking Confederate officer from joining the main thrust of the colonization movement.

Other Confederates instead chose to travel straight through the borderlands and paid the price for doing so. Among them was General Jo Shelby (Joseph Orville, but called Jo) of Missouri's Iron Cavalry Brigade, who crossed the border with John Henry Brown or shortly afterward. On June 15, 1865, General Shelby had brought together a group of three hundred southern men in San Antonio, Texas, for the trek across the border. Such prominent Confederates as General Danville Leadbetter of Alabama joined him, as well as other lesser-known white southerners. Two days later they moved out toward the

Rio Grande. Before crossing over the border at Eagle Pass, Shelby and his group apparently held a ceremony, sinking a Confederate flag in the river to mark the Fourth of July. This was their last symbolic act on U.S. soil as they continued across a borderland that would be full of surprises and difficulties, even for such war-hardened Confederate soldiers.[26]

Shelby's group entered Piedras Negras on the Mexican side of the border and set a course for Monterrey. Before leaving the town, Shelby sold their remaining cannons and most of his rifles to Andrés Viesca, the Juarista governor of Coahuila.[27] Although Shelby's group did not favor the Republican cause and would later side with the Imperialist forces, they were prompted to sell their arms because of both the insistence of Mexican authorities and Shelby's need for funds. The exchange allowed the group to pass through Viesca's terrain.[28] This was not the last time that Viesca would make his presence felt; he would prove to be a formidable force obstructing colonization. Shelby's group avoided a conflict with Viesca, but they did have a shoot-out with local Mexicans in Piedras Negras over accusations that Shelby's men had stolen some horses.[29]

Shelby's Confederates soon faced another, more serious fight as they went farther south into northern Mexico, through a stretch of the borderlands between Piedras Negras and Monterrey. This area was described as "a kind of debatable ground—the robbers had raided it, the Liberals had plundered it, and the French had desolated it."[30] Once the group crossed the Sabinas River, about eighty miles south of Piedras Negras, a combined force of Apaches and local Liberal Mexicans ambushed them. John Edwards, one of the Confederate officers in the group, wrote that they knew "a powerful war party of Lipan Indians" lay "crouched in ambush upon the further side of the Salinas [Sabinas], four hundred strong." He also claimed that "there were three hundred native Mexicans" in league with the Lipans. Yet these southern migrants pressed onward anyway. Before crossing the river they traveled through a small village that had been already plundered: "Men hung suspended from door-facings literally flayed alive. Huge strips of skin dangled from them as tattered garments might hang."

The joint Mexican-Apache force confronting these white southern migrants was presumably quite fearsome.[31]

The actual ambush was a fight for dear life. Edwards recalled "that terrible charge across the Sa[b]inas, water to the saddle-girths, and seven hundred muskets pouring forth an unseen and infernal fire." "As they struck the water," he wrote, "some Indian skirmishers in front of the ambush opened fire." Soon "the stray shots deepened into a volley." At the same time, "a yell arose from the woods, long, wild, piercing," and the Lipan Apache–Mexican force sprang into full attack. "The terrible volley had reached the column in the river, and a dozen saddles were emptied," Edwards wrote. "Some horses fell in the stream never to rise again, for the bullets plowed up the column and made stark work on every side." Then, just as suddenly, the southern migrant group's counterattack prevailed—"the attack was a hurricane" and the battle became "a massacre." "The Mexicans first broke," he said, "and after them the Indians." In the end, "no quarter was shown."[32]

An estimated two hundred of the combined Mexican-Apache raiding force were killed (probably an exaggeration), with Shelby losing twenty-seven killed and thirty-seven wounded.[33] Regardless of the true losses, what is apparent is that even these Civil War soldiers struggled to make it through northern Mexico. They forged ahead with their journey through this violent land while the blistering sun "left their heads pounding" and the almost daily march from "water hole to water hole" made their maneuvers through hostile terrain even more challenging.[34]

Finally, outside the city of Monterrey, 250 miles from Eagle Pass, Texas, Shelby and his group decided to rid themselves of any neutrality and openly declared their support for Emperor Maximilian and his French backers. It was a well-timed decision since they were entering a city controlled by the Imperialists. On August 3, 1865, Shelby met the French general Pierre Jeanningros, who presided over five thousand French and Mexican troops. After a near confrontation with Jeanningros, Shelby affirmed that his group would offer their services to Maximilian. Next they moved through Saltillo and then to Parras, where Shelby had a run-in with another French commander, who was unaware of their newly stated allegiance. The two leaders narrowly avoided a duel, and the war-torn, beleaguered group finally completed the journey to Mexico City, where they found the southern colonization plans already underway.[35]

These Confederates were among the initial southern migrants who crossed through the borderlands after the Civil War. They encountered several obstacles along the way, especially the fight with the Mexican-Apache forces, that foreshadowed the difficulties that awaited the colonization venture. While Maury plotted to move northward, the combination of Indians, local Mexican Republicans, and French and Mexican Imperialist troops, all in motion and competing with one another across this part of northern Mexico, created a volatile atmosphere that would prove to be hostile to southern immigration.

Comanches, Apaches, Kickapoos, and the Texas-Coahuila Borderlands

During his survey mission in Coahuila, William Marshall Anderson directly encountered a main participant in the raiding network along the border. In mid-January 1866 Anderson was "a little north of Las Adjuntas," a hacienda north of Monclova (the former state capital), and had "entered upon the lands of Don Carlos Sanchez Navarro." The Sánchez Navarro family had numerous tracks of lands running across Coahuila, and at this point in his journey Anderson passed over "a fine grazing country" that "with irrigation" might someday "teem with cereal wealth." This lush landscape, however, had already attracted Native Americans to it.[36]

As he neared the Sánchez Navarro hacienda at Hermanas (still north of Monclova), Anderson noted that a German cotton dealer (of the firm H. Meyers & Co.) from San Antonio, Texas, had recently been slain, along with a Mexican companion. The responsible party, he wrote, was "the Camanches." Hacienda las Hermanas was a favorite target of American Indians as well as the Mexican Republican armies in the borderlands. Anderson would later record that the cattle had "nearly all disappeared" at this ranch because the "Liberal patriots" had plundered it for livestock. Several Indian groups likewise recognized the site as a wellspring of goods for trade and consumption.[37]

While Anderson was at the junction of the Alamo and Sabinas Rivers, he learned more about the plundering of livestock in the borderlands. One of the estate administrators for the Navarro lands informed him that ten years earlier "30,000 head of cattle could be seen from this point." However, Anderson noted, "now there is scarcely one to be seen." Anderson also described some Indian camps he encountered that were "marked with the skins, entrails and bones of the wild cattle they have killed." Undoubtedly the cattle included those from Mexican and Texan ranches within the area. In fact, he thought the "vacas" would soon be as "few in these plains as deer." Indian raids had taken their toll on this section of the borderlands.[38]

For centuries raiding had served as an organizing principle along the Rio Grande borderlands of the American Southwest and northern Mexico. By the beginning of the nineteenth century, livestock and slave raiding had developed as a system of exchange that exemplified both the changing power relations of the region and the intrusion of capitalist forces. From the 1850s through the 1870s, commerce in livestock and human captives reached an apex. From 1860 to 1867, for example, more than three hundred thousand Texas cattle were stolen and resold to ranches in New Mexico as part of the illicit trade of Comanches, Kiowas, and Anglo and Hispanic New Mexican ranchers.[39] While the degree to which all people living along the border bought into this raiding and trading economy is debatable, it is clear that it was a longstanding characteristic of a broad swath of this borderland region.

A microcosm of this trade network existed along the border between Texas and Coahuila in the 1860s. Native American groups such as the Comanches and Apaches had dominated the Texas-Coahuila borderlands for generations and were leading players in this particular swath of raiding and trading. By the early nineteenth century, the Comanches were still the leading political-economic power in Texas and the leader in marketed goods in New Mexico. At the same time, Apaches continued to drive across the border on raiding expeditions, especially the Lipans in Texas and Coahuila, disrupting Mexican and

American efforts to consolidate the region. The Kiowas also played a key role in border raiding, particularly as an ally of the Comanches in the 1860s and 1870s.[40]

Comanche raiding and trading were well established in Texas and Coahuila by the 1860s, while the tribe pushed their raiding activities farther and farther into Mexico. According to a leading work on the Comanches, this Indian group reached the peak of their power in the 1830s and 1840s and had intensified "the range and scope of their plundering operations until vast expanses of Mexico's Far North had been turned into an extractive raiding domain." By the 1860s, due to ecological instability and U.S. military expansion, Comanche power had declined, but they were still a key force within a violent trading network operating in the zone between Texas and Coahuila.[41]

From the mid-nineteenth century to the Civil War period, Comanche raiding was a defining element of the borderlands environment in which southern colonizers sought to establish settlements. From 1849 to 1853, for example, Coahuila witnessed over 250 raids, mainly by Comanches—Mescalero and Lipan Apaches sometimes joined them or carried out their own raids—resulting in about seventy captives, nearly two hundred deaths, and hundreds of stolen livestock. A Mexican government commission on Indian raiding later claimed it was the prospect of trade with Americans that was the primary motivating factor for these raiding expeditions. No doubt trade with Texans, as well as other Indian groups, helped stimulate these violent raids.[42]

During the American Civil War, the Union army in the West had to contend with raiding Comanches. In November 1864 a large military expedition pursued the Comanches through the Territory of New Mexico along the boundary line with Texas. At one of the main battles, Lieutenant George Pettis of Company K of the First California Infantry gave a sense of the Comanches' continued strength. He recorded that his troops confronted "about two hundred Comanche and Kiowas," and that "the main body of the enemy" numbered about "twelve or fourteen hundred." He also specified that "a Comanche village of over five hundred lodges" lay in sight less than a mile away, which with "two fighting Indians to each lodge, which is the rule on the frontiers, would give us fourteen hundred warriors in the field before us." Even if inflated, this estimate indicates a formidable Comanche presence.[43] As at Hacienda las Hermanas in Coahuila, the Comanches held considerable sway over this part of the borderlands.

The Apaches were the second indigenous group centrally involved in raiding and trading between Texas and Coahuila. Like the Comanches, their raiding activities dated back to the Spanish colonial period. In order to quell Apache raids and stabilize their control of the North, Spanish authorities had sought political and trade alliances with the more dominant Comanches. By the 1780s the Apaches were the primary group targeted by the Spanish in joint military campaigns with the Comanches. These campaigns succeeded in suppressing Apache expansion for some time, but the struggle for Mexican independence, which resulted in the collapse of the presidio defense system against Apache raids, contributed to a renewed Apache presence across the borderlands.[44]

The 1830s were a time of intensified Apache raiding in northern Mexico (which included Texas until 1836). With a weak central government, defensive measures were largely left to local communities. In Texas, where already weakened missions withered away after Mexican independence, poorly funded and inadequately manned presidios coughed out their last breath and ceased to be an effective institution against Indian raids (if they ever had been). Local Mexican militia forces thus came to play a larger role. Although these troops had some success against some Indian groups, they failed to stem the raiding activities of the more dominant Comanches and Apaches.[45]

During the Civil War, George Hand, a sergeant in Company G, First Infantry Regiment of the California Volunteers, witnessed the Apache strength over the Texas–New Mexico–Mexico nexus. Hand's company and others pursued several hundred Apaches, reportedly led by Chiefs Mangas Coloradas and Cochise, who had attacked a lead unit of the California Column in July 1862 as they entered Apache Pass (in present-day Arizona, between the Chiricahua and Dos Cabezas Mountains). Stationed farther west in January 1863, Hand recorded a fight with the Apaches at Fort West, a new fort located along the New Mexico–Texas border, during which Mangas Coloradas was captured and later killed. Yet even with such reverses, the Apaches pushed onward with their established raiding customs. Hand, for one, reported on the continuance of the Apache raiding and trading circuit. At the end of March 1863, he recorded that the Apaches had stolen "about 60 horses" from Fort West. By August 1864, while at Fort McRae, New Mexico (about one hundred miles north of present-day El Paso, Texas), Hand pursued a group of Apaches who had "stolen 6,000 head of sheep & 50 mules." This estimate might have been an exaggeration, but we get a sense of the Apache-driven raiding activities that undoubtedly claimed much livestock.[46]

The persistence of Apache raiding and trading thus coincided with the continued, although diminished, power of the Comanches. Like the Comanches, the Apaches continued to be a force of their own largely because of their effectiveness in carrying out raids. Apache raiding had become an entrenched part of the Rio Grande landscape by the time of southern migration.[47] Theft was a necessary part of life, driven by reduced lands and depleted game hunting, and livestock raids took on a renewed importance as the Apaches became encumbered by U.S. expansion into the West. The Lipan Apaches, in particular, focused on stealing livestock for consumption and trade between Texas and Coahuila, a practice that corresponded with their views on capturing resources that lay within their domain.[48]

During the 1860s, Lipan Apaches and western Comanches were the leading Indian groups who relied upon raiding in Texas and Coahuila to both obtain goods and persons for trade and reassert their control over the region.[49] Theft, violence, raiding, and trading were intertwined means to generate wealth and create leverage. As one Lipan Apache (and later adopted Comanche) called Chevato expressed, "If a person came along, or a group of people came along, and decided that they wanted your land, they could take it from you. If they decided they wanted your cattle they could take them from you. And if they decided they wanted your children, they could take them from you." From Chevato's perspective, "that was the rule set forth in the frontier days." Surely others agreed. Native Americans, Anglo-Americans, and indigenous and Hispanic Mexicans all seemed to recognize, to some degree, that "if you could not protect yourself, then it was your fault" if goods or people were stolen away.[50]

Mexican authorities came to believe that it was trade with Anglo-Americans that fueled the Indian raids; Texans believed otherwise and argued that raiding stemmed from the other side of the border. Comparing evidence from Texas and Coahuila makes it clear, however, that raiding was conducted in both directions during the 1860s. That blame for raids was passed back and forth across the border indicates that several ethnic groups were involved in a raiding and trading network that transcended national boundaries. This transborder network not only led to tensions and conflict between the United States and Mexico but also created a hostile environment for southern colonization. William M. Anderson began to see this reality firsthand in 1866 as he scanned the horizon on behalf of the leaders of the migration movement.

In their recurrent petitions to the state government, Texan borderland residents also attested to the persistence of raiding and the extent of the trading system, which created serious problems for anyone seeking to live in this region. By the time southerners migrated across Texas in 1865, such residents as T. H. Stribling and P. Smythe had taken their appeals to a higher level, writing directly to President Andrew Johnson. They stated that "Comanche, Tonkawa and Lipan" Indians were raiding the "Western frontier of Texas." Likewise, "near the Rio Grande on the Mexican side of the River the tribe of Kickapoo" had been depredating the area, causing "a great deal of damage to this side of the River." Although such claims about Indian raiding may have been overstated, they still provide insight into the raiding, violence, and theft that permeated the Texas-Coahuila borderlands.[51]

From 1860 to 1865 Texas residents near the border wrote numerous letters to the governor's office begging for help against Indian raids. By November 1866 Governor J. W. Throckmorton wrote to the commissioner of Indian affairs in Washington DC and called attention to "a portion of the Comanche" who were holding a number of women and children captive. In fact, "for the last twelve months," he wrote,

"the depredations upon [the Texas] border [had] been of the most ap-
palling character." Governor Throckmorton wrote again the following month to the commissioner about a group of Kickapoo Indians
who had "left their home in Mo. or Kansas" during the war "and made
their way to Mexico, locating not a great ways from Eagle Pass on the
Rio Grande." Since that time, he complained, "they have constantly
depredated upon the South Western border of Texas."[52] As this letter
suggests, the Kickapoos were also involved in the network of raiding
livestock and captives for trade with other Indian groups or Mexicans or back to Texans.

The Kickapoos in Coahuila in the mid-1860s were a remnant of two
or more larger groups that had previously migrated to northern Mexico. The first group(s) came in the 1850s along with the Seminoles and
Seminole Maroons, or Mascogos, the ethnic group composed of runaway slaves and slaves of the Seminoles discussed in the previous chapter. The Seminoles returned to the United States in the early 1860s, but
a portion of the Kickapoos remained with some of the Mascogos in
Coahuila. During the Civil War, the Kickapoo chief Tobacco sought
to bring others from the United States into Mexico; in the fall of 1864
between two hundred and seven hundred Kickapoos left southern
Kansas and Missouri for Coahuila. This second group was undoubtedly the Kickapoo migrants referenced in the above Texas letter.[53]

As more sedentary Indians, the Kickapoos had not participated in
raiding as actively as the Comanches and Apaches. Members of the
group of Kickapoos in Coahuila in 1865 who raided into Texas over
the course of the next decade did so for the value of stolen goods but
also out of retaliation for the Battle of Dove Creek in January 1865. In
Texas, as they migrated southward, the Kickapoos had been attacked
by Confederate soldiers. This incident, along with a history of forced
migration out of the Michigan-Illinois region dating back to the eighteenth century and more directly to American expansion into Oklahoma and Texas during the nineteenth century, fueled their interest
in cross-border raids.[54]

The theft and trade that Kickapoos, Comanches, and Apaches
conducted thus crossed over a porous boundary between Texas and

Coahuila. J. B. Devenport of Bandera, Texas, (northeast of Eagle Pass and southwest of San Antonio) described another instance of this cross-border raiding that occurred in December 1866. Devenport wrote of "a neighboring child—a boy of about 13 years of age" who had been taken captive earlier in the year. He had discovered that the boy was "in the hands of Kickapoo or Lipan" who were encamped around Santa Rosa, Mexico, about eighty miles from Eagle Pass. South of Bandera in Medina County another boy was reportedly taken captive by the Lipan Apaches at the beginning of 1865 and was likewise being held across the border in Mexico.[55]

Statements of property losses likewise reflect the extent of the raiding-trading network in the Texas-Coahuila borderlands. Reports of stolen livestock, for example, from El Paso County, Texas, from August 1865 to March 1866 claimed that Apaches had stolen $8,805 worth of property and that raids had resulted in the death of fourteen men. These claims cannot be taken at face value since the numbers may have been inflated, but they do suggest the frequency of raids in southern Texas.[56]

That this theft and death were taking their toll on more than single municipal or county economies is evident in such petitions as the one from M. J. Denman of Lampasas County to Governor Throckmorton. Writing on July 15, 1866, Denman, along with fifty-nine other self-described "frontier people," signed his name to a petition claiming that the whole area lacked protection and that the Indian raids had increased "in number, boldness and violence." According to these borderland residents, "the frontier at this time [was] falling back." A second petition to the governor in July with 218 signatures from five counties along the "Western Frontier" corroborated such claims. By 1867 reports regularly came to the governor's office, reflecting a wide range of raiding activity in Texas.[57]

Raiding Comanches, Apaches, and Kickapoos likewise troubled the state and federal Mexican governments that struggled to maintain control over such northern states as Coahuila. As a Mexican commission reported about Coahuila during this time, "There were occasions when the same town was simultaneously approached from three or four different directions." The result was that "farmers were obliged to grasp with one hand the plow and with the other the rifle, and they were not unfrequently laid in the furrow." Such descriptions conjure the image of a Mexican farmer dutifully plowing his field along the border while simultaneously raising his gun to protect himself against raiding Indians.[58]

By 1867 the state newspaper *El Coahuilense* was reporting that Indian raiding had taken a perilous turn in Coahuila. "When serious evils with terrible and disastrous consequences exist in a society," it stated in reference to recent raids, and "when they paralyze with their harmful influence the most vital and important branches of progress," then it was time to take "some radical action" in order to prevent such evils, or at least "reduce their fatal effects." *El Coahuilense* spoke to the towns and states that formed the northern part of Mexico and asked rhetorically, "Who could ignore and not understand that they were facing a war with the savages?"[59] These words reflected a strained state of affairs in Coahuila and testify to the continuing Indian strength in the borderlands during the period of southern colonization.

By the mid to late 1860s, villages and towns in Coahuila such as Patos, Nadadores, Monclova, Allende, and Ramos Arizpe (all near Saltillo) regularly submitted long lists of men, arms, and horses that could be used against Indian attacks on the state capital of Saltillo. At the same time, Coahuila, along with Nuevo León, Chihuahua, and Durango, was due to receive 20,000 pesos from the central government for defense measures against the Indians of the region.[60] Although Coahuila's defenses appeared to be on the rise, the situation actually called for more help than general defense funding and the raising of local resident troops. In Saltillo, for example, a request was issued for an additional 1,000 pesos to pay for a force of Kickapoos to track down raiding parties. "The serious troubles that the Indians were causing in most of the towns in this state," it was reported, necessitated the raising of "una fuerza de Quikapóos" to repel the other Indian invaders.[61]

Both Mexicans and Indians living on the border between Coahuila and Texas fought for life and livelihood during the mid- to late 1860s. It was a multiethnic environment linked through a network of violent exchange. For many Apaches, Comanches, and Kickapoos in the borderlands, the raiding system was a means of survival, control, and trade. While some Mexicans living along the border likewise participated in this network, other local residents enlisted in the defensive efforts. A circular path of theft, violence, and trade worked its way around all of these borderlanders, with some participating, others fighting against it, and still others doing both.

The shifting and turbulent world around the border made the prospects for southern colonies quite dim. As with Shelby's group, southern migrants were apt to encounter solid and violent resistance to their plans for settlement. One such instance between "tres Americanos" (most likely from Texas) and "unos indios Quikapús" underscores this reality. It occurred at the end of March 1867 at the junction of the Sabinas and Alamo Rivers, the same site where Anderson had made his journal entry about livestock raiding. A group of Kickapoos from the village headed by Capitannillos Mamamaché (near Múzquiz) had a run-in with these migrants. The Kickapoos quickly killed them and took their belongings, which included rifles, pistols, and horses.[62]

Even closer to the Texas border, along the Sabinas River, Anderson again came across lands that were very "capable of making a generous return for agricultural labor" but now lay fallow. This represented the problem that the planners of colonization would never fully understand—there was great agricultural promise in the borderlands, but the barriers to settlement were too high. Two of the primary reasons why these lands would never become filled with eager southern migrants and instead would remain "almost useless," were the "civil war and the about, equally civil Indian, [who] ha[d] reduced the stock of cattle, horses and mules to the smallest number."[63] The actions of the local Mexican Republican armies under Benito Juárez, as discussed more below, certainly played the leading role in preventing the colonization initiative from unfolding as planned. The raiding and trading of Native Americans was likewise a major deterrent to the realization of the southern immigration venture.

Raiding, Banditry, and Local Control in Northern Mexico

Local power struggles were a central impediment to the colonization venture. One case in particular helps further illustrate the problem—that of Santiago Vidaurri. Vidaurri had risen to power in the 1850s when he overthrew the governor of Nuevo León and annexed Coahuila. By the end of the decade, Vidaurri had eliminated almost all of his opposition and was firmly in control of both states. His power soared because of his support for Mexican Liberals in the War of the Reform (1858–61) against the Conservatives before the landing of French and Austrian troops in 1862. During the French Intervention (1862–67), however, Vidaurri changed his allegiance and deserted the Liberal or Republican camp, apparently recognizing a greater opportunity to continue his control of northern Mexico through an alliance with the Imperialists rather than the faltering Republic of Mexico.[64]

At the beginning of the American Civil War, the Confederate State Department sent agent José Agustín Quintero to northern Mexico to establish friendly relations with Governor Vidaurri. Quintero arrived in Monterrey in June 1861 with orders from Secretary of State Robert Toombs to secure Vidaurri's help in stopping Mexican or Union troops from invading Texas through Nuevo León and Coahuila. As mentioned in chapter 1, Quintero also presented the idea of building a railroad across northern Mexico that would connect the Confederacy to the Pacific Ocean. A railroad line appealed to Vidaurri because it would connect his region to the Confederacy and create additional political leverage for him.[65]

Vidaurri used the cotton trade to gather wealth to fund his army and retain control of the northern states of Nuevo León and Coahuila. Other caudillos (regional strongmen) of the north pursued a similar course of action. In the neighboring state of Chihuahua, Governor Luis Terrazas had secured his political power through building an extensive economic empire. By acquiring massive tracts of land (usually expropriated church properties) and capitalizing on the cattle and mining industries, Terrazas reigned as governor from 1860 to 1873. Much like Vidaurri's clutch on power, Terrazas's economic dominance underwrote his political position and control of the state.[66]

Recognizing Vidaurri's power, Benito Juárez appointed Vidaurri *comandante* of Tamaulipas in July 1863 to help the struggling Mexican Republican war effort. It soon became apparent, however, that Vidaurri was not interested in aiding Juárez and the Republican cause. In January 1864 Juárez came to Saltillo, Coahuila, fleeing the French offensive. Instead of providing aid, Vidaurri pressed for independent control of Nuevo León y Coahuila, not willing to support either the invading Imperialists or the retreating Liberals. Juárez eventually forced Vidaurri to flee into Texas, where Vidaurri cultivated new relationships with the Confederacy before returning to Coahuila. In January 1865 he became a member of Emperor Maximilian's Council of State and thus came to openly support the Imperialists, but undoubtedly with the aim of restoring his control over northeastern Mexico.[67]

Vidaurri's activities in northern Mexico point to two significant conclusions related to the southern colonization enterprise and local power relations in northern Mexico. First, Vidaurri's power had translated into a brisk trade with the Confederacy, and this trade opened up friendly relations between the Imperialists and the Confederacy, paving a path for southern immigration. The turbulent and changing power struggle in the north could very well have switched back to favor Vidaurri, which would have established a key ally for southern colonization. Second, and more importantly, Vidaurri's struggle to control northern Mexico reveals that other contending powers were at work in the borderlands, powers that either Maury underestimated or that lurked beyond his view.

First and foremost were the Mexican Republicans, the various local troops under Juárez's command that would come to play the largest direct role in resisting the Imperialist forces and thwarting the colonization plans. In mid-1866, the Mexican Republicans, loosely under the command of Juárez, were still attempting to push the Imperialist forces out of Coahuila and increase their control over the state. Raiding ranches for livestock became one of the vital strategies they adopted to achieve this objective. In one instance, back in January 1864, a land manager for the Sánchez Navarro family in Agua de la Mula reported that Liberal troops had been taking cattle and breaking into granaries. By March of the same year, troops were taking more than cows and grain: "The forces from the Division of Guanajuato had struck one of Navarro's ranches, by order of Colonel Valdivia, and incurred a debt of over two thousand seven hundred and fifty pesos."[68] This colonel was one of many local leaders who sought to reassert Republican control over northern Mexico by drawing on local supplies to support the army. In January 1866, for example, Lieutenant Colonel Nicolás Ansures seized one hundred cattle from one of the Sánchez Navarro family estates outside of Monclova.[69] A few months later the ransacking of properties became widespread, and local leaders such as Valdivia and Ansures became an even more crucial layer of power within the borderlands.

By the spring of 1866, local Mexican Republican forces intensified their raids and made them a part of their war strategy. The Republican governor and military commander of Coahuila, Andrés S. Viesca (whom Jo Shelby had confronted), took this strategy to another level. Initially Viesca reported limited seizures, such as taking six cows from the hacienda of Mesquite (a Sánchez Navarro estate) to provide meat for the troops. Soon, however, Viesca issued orders to confiscate lands belonging to the Sánchez Navarro family. The Sánchez Navarros were cast as traitors to the country for siding with the Imperialists; raids upon their lands were quite permissible from Viesca's perspective.[70]

Viesca was a force of his own within the borderlands and was instrumental to pressing the raiding and confiscation strategy forward. An 1863 law had outlined this Republican strategy, but Viesca executed it within a region contested by French-Imperialist forces, Republican troops, Native American groups, and southern colonizers. By July 1866 he had set in motion land seizures in the districts of Parras and Saltillo; by September hundreds of cattle were stripped from Sánchez Navarro family lands around the capital of Coahuila for the Army of the North. In the same month, Viesca also issued formal regulations on how confiscated lands should be divided and sold to local citizens.[71] Juárez officially approved of the confiscation of the Navarro properties on September 13, 1866, the day after Viesca had issued his own regulation. This reverse decision making reflects how local leaders often made a move first and received approval from higher-ranking officials afterward, an indication of the degree of local power imbedded in the borderlands.[72]

By the end of 1866, the local Mexican Republican forces drew a cordon around the Sánchez Navarro lands, laid siege to them, and almost eliminated the possibility of using them for southern colonization. Although directed at supplying the troops, these confiscatory actions were certainly part of an overriding network of raiding. War made these seizures legitimate in Mexican Republican eyes, but it was still theft to those who were robbed. The Sánchez Navarro family could see these activities only as outright theft, which fit right into the ways and means of the borderlands.[73]

Even after Juárez and his allies took control of the Mexican government in the summer of 1867, theft and raiding in the borderlands was by no means ended. One of the major problems confronting Juárez was the banditry and theft that swept across the country but was especially endemic to northern Mexico.[74] Throughout the time period of southern migration—from 1865 to the early 1870s—banditry in Mexico, like raiding, was a significant force of destabilization that drew upon a long-standing history.[75] The raids on the Sánchez Navarro estates and elsewhere along the border served military ends, but they also spoke to an underlying resentment against particular families and the use of theft as a means for political-economic leverage.

Bandit-soldiers often saw migrating white southerners as more invaders, in league with the Imperialist government and open to attack. Back in September 1865, for example, Mexican bandits directly derailed the migration plans of one Confederate general and his party. As the *Mexican Times* reported, General Mosby M. Parsons was killed by "the robbers and assassins who have for three or four months infested the road to Monterrey," the capital of Nuevo León. Unfortunately for Parsons, who had been "traveling at the time peaceably in his carriage, with the intention of settling in Mexico," he ran into one of the groups of bandits who roamed the countryside in northern Mexico.

He and three former staff officers were seized, "then stripped and taken to one side in the chaparral, where they were barbarously murdered."[76] These bandits had been drafted into the Mexican Republican cause, but they still worked for their own benefit. Raids on haciendas and robberies of travelers often served their own purposes first and the struggling republic second. This is apparent in the fact that theft continued on a large scale even after Juárez was restored to power.[77]

In northern Mexico, theft and raiding seemed to take on a free-for-all nature, with numerous participants and less available means of prevention. Comanches and Apaches led the way in terms of livestock raiding up until the early 1870s, but Mexican Republicans under leaders such as Viesca came to play a significant role during and immediately after the French Intervention. By the early 1870s, the scale had actually tipped toward local Mexicans taking the lead in raiding along the border. One notable case in point was Juan Cortina and his band of raiders, the same ones who had confronted Alexander Watkins Terrell and his Confederate group in the summer of 1865. Local Mexican Republican leaders such as Cortina played a crucial military role in stopping the French-Imperialist Army and the southern colonization initiative. He did so largely by carrying out raids, which continued even after the war ended.

Cortina's success was embedded in the borderlands environment, with its fluctuating lines of power and reliance on raiding and banditry. Throughout the French Intervention, he sought to remain politically and militarily autonomous, and he relied upon raiding to carry out his plans. By the summer of 1865, Cortina launched raids against Imperialist supply lines from both sides of the border (with Union encouragement). For example, Cortina was greatly outnumbered, but he managed to cut off communications to and from Matamoros, and by August 1865 he controlled most of the roads leading into the interior. Cortina continued his raids on the Imperialist Army at Matamoros but also began raiding supply trains for his own use or for trade, especially robbing wagon trains and stagecoaches on the roads between Monterrey and Bagdad. In September 1865 it was reported that Cortina's men were also stealing cattle from Texas and driving the

livestock into Mexico. By the early 1870s he was orchestrating major
cattle raids into Texas, with some estimating that five thousand head
of cattle were being driven into Mexico each month.[78]

Cortina's raiders persisted throughout the struggling Republican
war efforts, chipping away at Imperialists' hopes and the possibilities
of southern colonization. With the onset of the Restored Republic in
1867, Cortina's raiding continued and actually eclipsed that of Comanches and Apaches. Yet this theft and trade was not one-way traffic. In
the late 1860s several stories appeared in the *Two Republics* describing
how Mexicans and Anglo-Americans were taking the lead in raiding
activities from various locations along the border. In one instance,
Mexican bandits outside Brownsville reportedly crossed into Texas on
a daily basis to steal cattle; in another, a headline proclaimed "American Bandits Again" were around the town of Baján, Coahuila. In still
another account, "organized bands of robbers, having their head quar-
ters on the Mexican side of the river, composed chiefly of Mexicans,
but embracing also more or less American outlaws, ha[d] been crossing over to the Texas side where immense herds of cattle and horses
are raised, and stealing these animals in great numbers." It was concluded that these combined Mexican and American raiders had "sys-
tematically driven them [the herds] over and sold them in Mexico"
for quite some time.[79]

By the early 1870s, Mexicans and Americans along the border played
more of a leading role in the raiding and trading network, perpetu-
ating the borderland reliance upon theft, trade, and violence. By this
time raiding activities had made the Texas-Coahuila borderlands ill-
suited for southern colonization, and the limited immigration that
did continue was directed to areas along the Gulf of Mexico.

William Marshall Anderson and
the Foreclosure of Colonization

On December 12, 1865, William Marshall Anderson departed from Mexico City to start his survey of northern Mexico. He traveled through
the cities of Querétaro and San Luis Potosí. He reached Saltillo, the
capital of Coahuila, right before Christmas, seeming calm and relaxed

as he visited "the old Cathedral" in the town square. In early January Anderson moved on to the Sánchez Navarro hacienda at Patos (west of Saltillo) and waited for the Mexican surveyor and engineer Jacobo Küchler to accompany him on his journey northward. Küchler was a local resident from the village of Alamo, Coahuila, who had been entrusted with preparing a map of the state to better evince its mineral and agricultural wealth. A representative of Navarro's estate also deemed it "proper to employ a certain Snr. Don Juliano Laing, alias Hugh Lang, as [their] companion and protector." Apparently, Señor Laing had considerable knowledge of northern Coahuila and possessed a passport from his brother-in-law Andrés S. Viesca, the Republican governor, to ease their passage through hostile terrain.[80]

With Küchler and Laing, and several guides and pack men, Anderson left the "well graded and well kept streets" of Patos for Monclova, which he described as a "shabby looking concern." Along the way, at San Felipe, he learned that Indians had robbed a small ranch "of all their horses and cattle," along with those of "the goats and the sheep that were fit for anything."[81] It was another indication of the obstacles to come in the borderlands. But for now, Anderson felt confident in his mission and headed in a northwestern direction.

On the morning of January 18, 1866, his party again entered the lands of Carlos Sánchez Navarro, just north of the hacienda called Las Adjuntas (north of Monclova). Anderson specified that it was "a fine grazing country" that with proper irrigation "might teem with cereal wealth." About a week later, Küchler started his "instrumental and scientific observations" around the hacienda at Nacimiento, noting "two perfectly level planes" along the Sabinas River that would be of great use to agricultural development.[82]

At this stage of their journey, Anderson and his survey party discovered what the planners had anticipated—"beauty in neglect." Thus far the group had found lands in a state of abeyance, but with great promise. As Anderson wrote, the area "as a general rule [was] very much neglected." But he believed "these lands [were] capable of making a generous return for agricultural labor." In places where irrigation had been properly provided, "the crops have proved abundant, and of superior quality." Accordingly, Anderson explained how a dam could be built at minimum expense to improve the supply of water. Anderson confided with "an old resident" of a nearby village who "also confidently expressed that, with an outlay of $1,000, a dam [could] be put in which would endure for ever." This idea seemed so promising that Anderson thought, "My present judgment is, that [the] valley, or rather broad plains, north and south of the Sabinas [River], will one day be the finest cotton producing regions of the world, for their extent."[83]

The borderlands of Coahuila had potential indeed. "At this point," Anderson later wrote, "we were of the opinion that a succession of mills and manufacturing establishments might be erected, sufficient to supply the wants of a large population." Around Palado, where the grandfather of Carlos Sánchez Navarro once lived, Anderson penned that he saw "the richest and most fertile looking lands" yet, reminiscent of "the best and most productive cotton lands of Texas, Louisiana and Mississippi."[84] These visions ran straight back to what Maury had in mind when he sent Anderson north.

Yet Anderson's visions of prosperity would soon confront the reality of the borderlands. Anderson's troubles began as they circled back to the south, intending to return to Patos. Throughout February 1866, as they crossed back southward through Hacienda las Hermanas (south of Nacimiento), Anderson continued to take note of the spectacular views and the promise of the lands before him. But on the third of March, while his party camped just south of Baján (south of Monclova), they caught word that "the Liberal or Illiberal troopers, under Don Pedro the Winker," also known as Captain Pedro de Valdez, were headed their way. Captain Winker was a local military leader from Monclova, loosely attached to the command of Juan Cortina. On the following day, when Anderson's party was camped at a place called Venado, Winker's troops confronted Anderson and informed him that "it had been resolved to take the arms and horses of Mr. Kuchler and myself." They were summarily detained and placed "under espionage of the nightguard, until morning dawn."[85]

This is when their companion don Juliano Laing, or Hugh Laing, came to their aid. Laing was "an old native of the United States" (from New Jersey) who had been in Mexico "for thirty seven years." He was the man with the passport from Governor Viesca that authorized the group to move through Coahuila. Laing appeared to be a shifty fellow whom Anderson did not fully trust, a man with "a mistress in every little town or hacienda between Saltillo and Piedras Negras." Nonetheless, Laing met with Captain Winker and returned with permission to keep their arms and horses, but Anderson's group were ordered to turn back north, toward Monclova.[86]

A few days before, Winker's men had also robbed "a private citizen, near that spot" of "eleven horses" and other personal items, leaving the person stripped down to nothing. Just like Viesca's men, these Mexican Republicans were carrying out raids and banditry for the war effort, but they were also enriching themselves by keeping or trading confiscated items. Anderson's group made their way back toward Monclova in early March, hoping to get beyond the reach of "the Captain and his sixty thieves." He saw these soldiers primarily as bandits, later testifying, "I have not heard and do not believe these soldiers have done anything else for some time, but robb passengers on the plains."[87] Such observations reveal that these local Mexican Republicans were fighting for their own cause as well as a political one. Such conduct fit right into the prevailing ethos of the borderlands.

Anderson and his group bunkered down for a month at Hacienda las Hermanas, just north of Monclova. From there he wrote a letter to his wife and told her of the recent incident with Winker and his bandit-soldiers. He also reflected upon the encroaching reality of the situation before him. He still noted that this hacienda produced such crops as wheat, barley, and corn and that it would surely produce cotton, but his outlook had shifted toward more pressing concerns. "The scourge of war has been felt here," he stated, especially in terms of livestock raiding. "There are now, but three horses belonging to this hacienda—the cattle also, have nearly all disappeared, and even pigs and chickens are rarely to be seen." Anderson pinpointed the culprits—the " Liberal patriots." It was "this nuisance of 'military necessity,' in other words, this excuse for stealing" that had become "a very great inconvenience to all the inhabitants" of this stretch of the borderlands.[88] Indeed, under the guise of military necessity, Mexican Republican forces plundered the Sánchez Navarro family estates.

One of the prominent coordinators of these raiding activities (as previously discussed) was the Republican governor and military commander of Coahuila, Andrés S. Viesca. Viesca would play a hand in unraveling Anderson's expedition. Curiously, however, Anderson received a passport from this very governor in Monclova in early April in order to make the return trip to Patos (from where he initially departed, outside of Saltillo). On April 19, 1866, Anderson, with only his guide Fruto Guzmán, passed the same point from which he had been turned back the previous month. This time he showed his passport to one of the army's colonels and was allowed to proceed on his journey, albeit trailed by a soldier. After passing a few more checkpoints, Anderson and Guzmán were ordered to camp at a lake village called Sauceda (north of Saltillo) for the night.[89]

When Anderson awoke on the following morning, he found that his "little mare [was] gone." With the intention of meeting back up with his guide, who had gone in search of his horse, Anderson traveled onward to Jaral, reaching it "about 2 o'clock p.m.—foot sore, hungry, & weary." At sunset, with no sign of his guide or horse, three "rogues" visited him and began to insist that he "should sell something, rather everything, even to the ring on [his] finger." These local Mexicans had spotted valuable items among Anderson's possessions, particularly his saddle, *chaparreras*, blanket, and bowie knife.[90] Anderson had fallen into Republican hands and a zone of theft and trade.

Anderson was held prisoner at a hacienda and kept under guard. Fearing for his possessions and his life, he decided to "make my escape that night," he later wrote, "and cross the mountain ridge that separated me from Patos." "On foot & alone," he set out as the light from a full moon fell across the sleeping bodies of the guards, who were "snoring soundly in drunken sleep" on the veranda. Fortunately, it was only a few steps from his room to one of the walls, enclosed in shadows, and he "made his way noiselessly, keeping close to the wall until he came to the side containing the entrance." Anderson took the road that led to "the mountains beyond which the French troops were stationed," but he was not in the clear yet.[91]

In less than an hour "a dozen men" on horseback accompanied by two bloodhounds were in pursuit of Anderson. He ran from the road into "a thicket of cactus" to hide from them but was soon discovered, and "the dog stood still giving forth low growls" for what seemed an interminable amount of time. Luck would have it that the hound stopped his growling, wagged his tail, "turned around and trotted off." Soon afterward, Anderson heard the horses and men return down the road, "and as they rode past he could distinctly hear them cursing him in the choicest Spanish."[92] The drunken parade of officers filed back out of sight, with foreign obscenities taking the place of the dog's growl, and then silence fell upon him.

Anderson was then able to make his escape, arriving at a hacienda near the town of Patos in the afternoon of the following day; fortunately he had stumbled upon friendly Mexican laborers in a tobacco field who aided him. After a journey of some forty miles over a mountain range, "barefooted and alone," Anderson had managed to save himself from the precariousness of the borderlands. He left for Mexico City about a week later, stopping off first "at Muchachos, with nothing but [his] old, worn-out and torn overcoat for couch and covering." In early June Anderson left Mexico, abandoning the colonization plans.[93]

The confrontation with "the rogues" and Anderson's escape foreshadowed the downfall of southern colonization in Mexico. This local Mexican force prevented Anderson from completing this key survey mission. Moreover, a detailed map and other important papers belonging to Küchler and Anderson had fallen into the hands of Governor Viesca. Küchler himself had gone missing, and Anderson feared that that he had been killed.[94] Anderson was lucky to have escaped with his life, even if most of his belongings were gone.

The local bandit-soldiers who had seized his possessions were a central part of the violent theft-trade network that existed in the borderlands during the 1860s. While the Native Americans who controlled the raiding-trading network disrupted colonization efforts along the border, local Mexican Republican forces had specifically stopped this survey mission. Both of these groups were key borderland actors, and these borderlanders struck a forceful blow at the colonization plans and started their unraveling. Without settlements in Coahuila, the initiative that sought to bring the American South and Mexico together in an economic alliance began to crumble. Commissioner Maury had made plans to push out into the borderlands in order to have enough land for the anticipated level of immigration into Mexico. Yet he and others did not sufficiently consider the difficulties that awaited them. They planned and prepared, but they lacked a sufficient understanding of the borderlands.

The confusing swirl of the Texas-Coahuila borderlands, where sovereignty, nationality, and dominance hung in the air, sank down over the colonizers' dreams. Borderland peoples came forth unwilling to accommodate the movement of southern migrants into this geographic crossroads. Southern colonization strove onward, but the original foundation had been cracked. What continued, as we will see in the next chapter, was a smaller, less grandiose movement balanced precipitously between two nations.

FIG. I. Matthew Fontaine Maury. Frontispiece engraving in Diana Fontaine Maury Corbin, *A Life of Matthew Fontaine Maury, U.S.N. and C.S.N., Author of "Physical Geography of the Seas and Its Meteorology"* (London: Sampson Low, Marston, Searle, & Rivington, 1888).

FIG. 2. Henry Watkins Allen. Andrew D. Lytle
Collection, Mss. 893,1254, Louisiana and Lower
Mississippi Valley Collections, Louisiana State
University Libraries, Baton Rouge.

FIG. 3. William Marshall
Anderson, 1866. This item is
reproduced by permission of the
Huntington Library, San Marino
CA.

Chevato Apache

FIG. 4. Chevato. From William Chebahtah and Nancy McGown Minor, *Chevato: The Story of the Apache Warrior Who Captured Herman Lehmann* (Lincoln: University of Nebraska Press, 2007).

FIG. 5. *Indios Kikapos,* by Francois Aubert. The
Getty Research Institute, Los Angeles (96.R.122).
This group of Kickapoos traveled to meet with
Emperor Maximilian, probably in 1866 to become
imperial Mexican troops, but the empire fell
after they returned to the border region. They
later joined another group of Kickapoos at
Múzquiz. See Nancy McGown Minor, *The Light
Gray People: An Ethno-History of the Lipan Apaches
of Texas and Northern Mexico* (Lanham MD:
University Press of America, 2009), 22.

FIG. 6. Joseph Shelby at the
court of Emperor Maximilian.
Photo Collection, the State
Historical Society of Missouri,
Columbia.

FIG. 7. Andrés Viesca. Nettie Lee Benson
Latin American Collection, University
of Texas Libraries, the University of
Texas at Austin.

FIG. 8. Benito Juárez. Nettie Lee Benson
Latin American Collection, University
of Texas Libraries, the University of
Texas at Austin.

Chapter Four

Southern Colonization and the
Fall of the Mexican Empire, 1866–67

When Matthew Fontaine Maury departed for England in March 1866, he vowed to return. He had written to his wife, Ann, and their children, who were already in England, "We are going to have happy times, a fine country and a bright future here [in Mexico]." On that note, Maury's eldest son, Richard, had acquired "land in my Carlotta Colony" (640 acres in fact) and "sent to China for labourers—12 or 15—to work it."[1] Maury had evidently opened up to other labor solutions for the southern colonies, and he entrusted his son and subcommissioner with the immigration plans while he was away. Leaving colonization in the hands of Richard L. Maury was a substantial down payment of trust in the success of the venture. Richard was "earnest in the cause," Maury wrote, and had "now in hand, a guidebook for immigrants" that would "soon be ready for the press." This guidebook represented another layer of the planning for southern colonization, as did a recent survey of "a fine body of public lands in Mitlatoyuca, one of the sub-districts of [the Tuxpan] region." Once Matthew Maury arrived in London, he published an article that reinforced his faith in the southern enterprise, concluding, "I now regard Mexican colonization on the fair way to success." It surely seemed that way at the time.[2]

At the end of March 1866, Maury reunited with most of his family in London, including his wife, Ann Herndon Maury, his daughters,

Diana Fontaine, Mary Herndon, Eliza Hull, and Lucy Minor, and his son Matthew Fontaine Jr., called "Brave" by the family. This must have been an exhilarating time for him, but at the end of April, Maury received disheartening news—the colonization office in Mexico would be closed. Emperor Maximilian's budgetary problems had prompted this decision, and it meant that Maury would no longer lead the colonization efforts. Maury wrote back to Mexico, "I am grieved to learn that your Majesty should be compassed with difficulties so serious as must be those which made it necessary to abandon such a cherished policy as I know that of colonization to have been."[3] Given the degree of planning that Maury had invested in the colonization initiative, this must have been difficult news to bear.

With Maury gone from the scene, where did that leave southern colonization in Mexico? The initial venture did indeed fail without him. Although not solely responsible, undoubtedly Maury deserves part of the blame for the failure of southern colonization. As several Mexican newspapers pointed out, Maury had concentrated on aiding southern immigrants while neglecting how his plans would help Mexicans. As El Cronista stated, "We believe that above all it is important to aid our poor, educate our orphans, and prevent our children from falling into crime; in a word, to better the lot of all destitute Mexicans, a thing to which Mr. Maury pays little attention."[4] Beyond building up its agricultural resources and infrastructure, Maury paid little attention to the social and economic state of Mexico, which had undergone two lengthy civil wars. Had he offered a more inclusive program of development and focused on how southern colonization would aid ordinary Mexicans, Maury would have drawn more support and possibly prevented the foreclosure of his plans. That is, if he had balanced his support for imperial Mexico with plans more attuned to the well-being of Mexicans and southerners in Mexico, his colonization plans might have survived the fall of the empire. As we see below, not all of the elements of colonization disappeared with the onset of the Restored Republic (1867–76), and those that continued took on a more politically neutral stance.

Maury had also not given enough thought to the obstacles that awaited colonization in northern Mexico. This shortsightedness, along with a racial exclusivity that included only elite Mexicans in the colonization plans, imbued Maury's ideas with some serious flaws. Notwithstanding these gaps in judgment, southern colonization was by no means doomed from the start or deficient in overall planning. In all, we can see how a substantial amount of planning had occurred in a short amount of time, which enabled a new phase of southern colonization to move forward.[5]

Colonization in Mexico did in fact continue, but on a smaller scale after the collapse of imperial support. This next phase was characterized by an emphasis on building railroads; seeking out labor solutions other than former slaves, especially Chinese workers; and connecting the South, Mexico, the Caribbean, and Latin America. Ex-Confederate general Jo Shelby pushed colonization to the Gulf of Mexico in the Tuxpan region; so did Texan John Henry Brown, whose Tumbadero colony lasted into the 1870s. Colonies with outlets to the Pacific Ocean also sprang up, while the promotional language of the *Mexican Times* and the *Two Republics* newspapers took a conciliatory tone to aid the longevity of these colonies. In the face of raids and banditry, southern colonization in central Mexico lost its hold, but other efforts sprang up and resuscitated southern transnational prospects.

After reviewing the legacy of Maury and Allen, we turn to see how the colonies in central Mexico began to collapse by 1867. One of the key factors of decline here and elsewhere in Mexico was the banditry and theft that undermined colonization. Next we examine continuing efforts after the fall of the Mexican Empire, when a new set of leaders emerged and cast the immigration movement into an arena of development that seemed more promising than doomed and more connected to trans-Pacific and trans-Atlantic routes of commercial exchange. By focusing on new immigration sites and by toning down or reversing the rhetorical support for the Imperialists, the new planners gave colonization new life. They also aligned themselves with larger economic forces spreading out from the United States into Latin America and thereby instilled longevity into the colonizers' dreams that persisted past the 1870s.

Southern Colonization in Mexico: An Enterprise Recast

At age sixty and in need of money, Maury turned to his scientific and technological expertise to earn a living. While in Europe, he decided to give lectures on electric torpedoes, or electrically detonated mines, a technology he had spent much time developing during the Civil War. Maury set out for Paris to give his first lecture in May 1866; he also gave a torpedo demonstration in the Seine River to the French emperor Napoleon III and other officials. He was subsequently asked to take a position at the meteorological observatory, but he declined.[6] Instead he received gifts of money from the many friends he had acquired over his lengthy career and a publishing contract from a New York firm. His March 1866 newspaper article had stressed the ruined state of the southern economy and the dire need to help the American South, and one way to provide aid was to support Maury's postwar economic plans, whatever the next step might be. Other offers to aid his efforts started to come in from the United States as well, including one for the vice chancellor position at the University of the South at Sewanee, Tennessee. In early July 1868 Maury and his family left England when the Virginia Military Institute offered him a more promising position as professor of physics.[7]

General Francis H. Smith, superintendent of the Virginia Military Institute, had initially offered Maury this professorship in mid-February 1868. Because Maury had not been included in President Andrew Johnson's amnesty proclamation of September 7, 1867, due to his rank of captain in the Confederate navy, he sought assurance of being permitted to return to the United States. He received such guarantees from friends back home in the coming months. In September 1868 Maury took up his position as professor and superintendent of the Physical Survey of Virginia. In December he published the first report from this survey, a thorough examination of his home state's geographic features and agricultural and commercial advantages.[8]

Even though Maury's plans for large-scale southern colonization in Mexico had failed, he did not abandon his quest to rebuild the South through commercial agricultural modernization. Instead, he returned to Virginia to aid his fellow southerners through a national and international development initiative. As Maury stated, the goals for his next postwar project were to develop "the physical resources of the State, to make known its geography, and to point out the great commercial advantages which naturally arise from its situation with regard to the seas and the interior." His plans also called for two transcontinental railroad routes and a steamship line running from Norfolk, Virginia, to Flushing, Holland. Collectively, he thought his plans would not only make great strides toward Virginia's economic recovery but also help resurrect the South by showing "the national importance" of his next venture. Thus Maury did not fade away with the failure of his southern colonization plans but reengaged the socioeconomic questions of his time back inside the borders of the United States.[9]

Along with numerous lectures and addresses, Maury completed the second installment of his survey report on Virginia in May 1871 (but it was not published until 1878). In the fall of the following year, Maury's health began failing, and he was forced to cancel a lecture at the Seaboard Agricultural Society in Norfolk, Virginia. Maury died from illness on February 1, 1873, at the Virginia Military Institute in Lexington. "Once more at home, on the soil of Virginia," the academic board wrote in his honor, Maury "bent his energies with the same vigor and enthusiasm which characterized those honor-reflecting labors of his former days." Although unsuccessful, his Mexico endeavors had been a key part of his active career. He likewise had constructed the framework for the ongoing development plans linked with southern colonization.[10]

Henry Watkins Allen had also given the colonization enterprise a foundation from which to continue, even under weakened circumstances. Although Allen had sorely missed his home state of Louisiana and expressed such longings in private correspondence, he had gained much confidence in Mexican colonization by the spring of 1866. As Allen had previously written, while he suffered from his "old wounds" and was sometimes "so lame" that he could "hardly walk" to his office, "I think of those dear ones I have left in Louisiana, of home, of all whom I love so much." During times when his injuries made him "feverish," he especially longed to somehow return eventually to his home state—it was difficult for even the staunchest supporters of immigration to be away from their native country. But he did not see how he could return, for on principle he would not ask for a pardon. Allen proclaimed privately that he would rather live out his days in honor than "ask pardon" for what he did not consider to be "a crime." These times of doubt seemed to pass at any rate, with Allen accepting his new role as editor of the *Mexican Times*, which provided such perks as "free admittance to all the theatres and operas."[11]

On another occasion, Allen had written back to a friend in Louisiana that he would never forget that brave state, but he seemed reconciled to his life in Mexico. "When it shall please God to consign this mutilated body to its last resting-place—be it among strangers in Mexico, or friends in Louisiana," he wrote, "I will want no better epigraph inscribed on my tomb than . . . 'Your friends are proud to know that Louisiana had a Governor who had an opportunity of securing a million of dollars in gold, and yet preferred being honest in a foreign land, without a cent.'" By New Year's Day 1866 Allen seemed even more reassured. Even though his newspaper afforded him only a modest income, he wrote, "I am making a living, a good, respectable living. I think I have obtained the respect and confidence of the people of this great city." By spring 1866 Allen appeared to be committed to his newspaper and the colonization initiative it supported.[12]

Rather than losing faith in the enterprise, Allen discussed the prospects of building railroads and importing low-wage Chinese labor to Mexico. These two subjects became major components of the ongoing colonization efforts in Mexico. In the *Mexican Times* in mid-April 1866 he argued in favor of issuing charters to private companies to speed development of railroad lines and to increase the amount of capital flowing into the country. "The opening of these railways," he thought, "will form new centres, around which workshops and villages will cluster." Allen also weighed in on the "labor question," which was "the great question just now in Mexico among farmers," and he came down decidedly in favor of the proposal by the Asiatic Colonization Company to bring in "Chinese, Asiatics—or as you all know better—Coolies." Rather than thinking about leaving Mexico, Allen wished "to impress upon the minds of our American colonists at Cordova, at Orizava," and other colonies that this company could provide "good, cheap, and reliable labor, without which your farming operations [were] useless and your efforts impotent." Allen thus pressed ahead with trans-Pacific plans to develop Mexico's economy.[13]

Both Maury and Allen shifted their sights to the next main source of labor in the Caribbean–Mexican–southern U.S. corridor. Although this turn to "coolie" labor signaled that their hopes of ex-slave labor rebuilding trans-southern dreams did not materialize, it also reflected a shared continuum of thought among ex-slaveholders across the South and beyond its borders. Southerners in Mexico and the South drew lessons from Cuba, in particular, about how to rebuild labor systems in the postemancipation world. John S. Thrasher, who resided in Louisiana and Cuba, for example, championed the "advantages of Coolie contract labor" because of its success in building Cuba's sugar economy. So did Jules H. Normand, a native Louisianan who had lived in Cuba and became involved in transporting Chinese workers from Cuba to Louisiana in 1867. He and other traders and planters surely agreed with the *New Orleans Bee's* assessment: "They [the laborers] are stout, hardy looking young men, and will doubtless prove better laborers than the negroes." Allen's search for another labor supply reflected a will to carry on with southern colonization in Mexico that drew on wider Caribbean influences rooted in exploitation and unfree labor.[14]

In March 1866 Allen expressed a triumphant tone in a private letter, writing that immigration was "setting in fast in to Mexico, *in earnest.*" While staying in Veracruz, he saw numerous ships carrying emigrants arrive from Tennessee, Georgia, Mississippi, Louisiana, South Carolina, and Missouri. "There is land enough for all the South," he proclaimed, even if survey efforts were taking longer than expected. He did caution migrants to "bring some money" but voiced no reason to turn away from colonization. He was thinking of going to Europe "to

consult a surgeon about [his] wounds," but this seemed like a temporary trip, as Maury's was supposed to be.[15] Allen made plans "to live
permanently abroad, without any hope of ever seeing my old and be-
loved friends again." In March 1866 he purchased land near Córdoba and expected to settle down there. He planned to go to Paris in
May for an operation because his health was deteriorating after his
return to Mexico City from the coast, but his permanent residence
was Mexico.[16]

He never made it to the operation. Allen died in Mexico City on
April 22, 1866, from health problems associated with his Civil War bat-
tlefield wounds. Even after his death, though, the colonization venture
moved onward because of his promotional efforts. On June 2, 1866, his
newspaper resumed operations under the guidance of another southern migrant, John N. Edwards, who continued to promote southern
immigration with a fervor similar to Allen's.[17] Not only did the new
editor champion colonization, but Edwards also supported the next
group of leaders, who breathed new life into the initiative. This next
phase owed a debt to Maury, Allen, and William M. Anderson, for it
carried on their economic development plans.

After Anderson's capture and escape in northern Mexico, he quit the
immigration enterprise and returned to Ohio. Before his departure,
however, he still believed in the potential of southern colonization
and was still allured by Mexico's agricultural promise. For example, he
mused about the lands around Querétaro in central Mexico, "These
lands are finely cultivated—astonishingly well cultivated" and observed that this high level of cultivation for "these hundreds and thousands of acres" could be replicated in "the millions on and around
the Sabinas, the Salado, the Monclova, and the Carmen [in northern
Mexico]," if and when "good farmers are brought to them." In his official report, he recommended establishing villages surrounded by
one-hundred-acre farms as well as constructing a railroad line, to create stability and prosperity in Coahuila. He thought it was "not only
possible, but practicable to reverse [the unsettled] state of affairs most
splendidly." So even though his role in colonization was coming to a
close, he was not giving up on its future.[18]

Anderson thought that U.S. interference in the affairs of Mexico was primarily to blame for pushing the Mexican nation in the wrong direction. He believed that most Mexican people "would prefer a settled monarchy to an ever changeable and changing Republic" and that the people of the United States had surrendered their will and power to "Politicians" set on determining Mexico's future by forcing the French out (in accordance with the Monroe Doctrine). "A fixed and firm government in Mexico," he thought, "would soon be followed by peace and prosperity." Anderson still believed in the imperial course and that southern colonization could contribute to the country's stability. He seemed to express a conflicted sense of his place in the world as he embarked for the United States, longing to leave Mexico but still championing "peace and prosperity" through "a fixed and firm government."[19]

To add to his misfortunes in Mexico, Anderson fell ill with yellow fever on his voyage to the United States and, on board the "French Steam-packet Panama" from Veracruz to Havana, lost a purse with some jewelry and money in it. Ex-Confederate general Jubal A. Early recovered Anderson's belongings while sailing from Havana to St. Thomas. Early wrote to Anderson that he found the purse and its contents, including "the gold ear-rings and breastpin, the silver ear-rings, a $2 1/2 gold piece, a Mexican dollar, 4 small coins, [and] a sun glass." Anderson had apparently reported that there had been "8 or 10 dollars in gold," but Early assumed he was "mistaken in [his] estimate" and that he had not "kept a strict account" due to his sickness. Early had given the ship's steward and a servant "the piece of gold and the Mexican dollar" for their efforts and sent the rest with John C. Breckenridge, former Confederate secretary of war, to return them to Anderson. The whole incident was reminiscent of Anderson's time in Mexico—his belongings scattered about foreign lands with no definite path for his development plans in northern Mexico, while he shrank back to Ohio a haggard-looking man (see photo).[20]

By mid- to late 1866 prospects for southern colonization itself fluctuated within this transnational-transoceanic world but still appeared quite promising. It would take a new direction in Mexico and follow different leadership, but hemispheric dreams of revitalization persisted. As a sign that perhaps all was not lost, Jacobo Küchler, the Mexican engineer and companion of Anderson, was discovered to have not been killed, as Anderson had feared. He was alive and well in Coahuila, and his survey report had been published in *El Coahuilense*, a Mexican liberal newspaper.[21] Perhaps this was a sign that southern immigration could continue under a restored Mexican Republican government if the Imperialists in fact faltered.

Carlota and Central Mexico

During the first half of 1866, southern colonization proceeded largely as planned in central Mexico. Prominent southerners such as Jo Shelby had established themselves on large haciendas, his about two miles from Córdoba. A verdant landscape surrounded Shelby, his wife, Betty, and their two sons (Joe and Orville), who had joined them in the fall of 1865. They took advantage of their new surroundings by cultivating a burgeoning coffee crop. Ex-Confederate general Sterling Price had also acquired 640 acres at the main colony, Carlota. Meanwhile, other southerners followed their lead and were making headway on smaller plots of land.[22]

By early 1866 the Carlota colony started to produce some successful crops and other worthwhile enterprises. One case was a coffee plantation owned by one Mr. Fink that earned $16,000. Sterling Price, who oversaw the colony, had likewise planted coffee and tobacco crops, along with beans, sweet potatoes, and fruits. As one southern colonist stated, "If I only had forty good negroes here from Virginia, I could make a fortune in two years."[23] An ex-slave labor force never did materialize in central Mexico, but the focus on agricultural development proceeded at a quick pace. Some southerners chose to work on the main railroad project running from Veracruz, while former Confederate general James Slaughter ran a steam mill, an undertaking that Price also pursued.[24]

Signs of successful colonization in central Mexico were so evident that even more reluctant white southerners from the state of Virginia ventured to Carlota in early 1866. As one U.S. newspaper reported,

"Some twenty young men, belonging to the first families of Virginia," were making their way to "the land of the Montezumas."[25] One of Maury's letters sent back to Virginia in early March 1866 helped entice migrants by describing the beautiful valley and plains of the central district, where crops, cattle, and orange trees flourished. Price corroborated these encouraging signs by writing at this time, "I never expect to return to the United States. I am entirely satisfied with my prospects here." Martha Price surely agreed with her husband; she had acquired "a beautiful grove of mangoes, two orange trees, a zapota and an [n]opal." "I hope to have in a few years," she wrote, "a great variety of fruits and flowers."[26]

Life was setting into a predictable routine in Carlota, which undoubtedly helped continue to draw emigrants. "We have Episcopal services in Carlotta every Sunday and Methodist preaching in Cordova," wrote Mrs. Price. Housing and living conditions were certainly rudimentary—even Price's home was described as "a straw roofed, low built, massive cottage." The only solid social retreat appeared to be the Confederate Hotel in Córdoba, itself only a two-story brick building, where male migrants congregated for card playing, gambling, smoking, drinking, and cotillions with the ladies.[27] Despite these rough conditions, the central colonies moved forward with a firm resilience, with social evenings alleviating the drudgery of building farms and towns.

By 1866 U.S. newspapers as well as personal correspondence indicated that "whole families" were "assembling to emigrate to Mexico." Among those departing were Judge W. G. Swan, "a member of the late Confederate Congress from Georgia," who left with twenty other families. General John S. Williams had preceded him with sixty migrants from Tennessee. Even in the old guard state of South Carolina, southern colonization stirred interest. "Mexico is the country now upon which all the eyes are turned," reported the *Charleston Courier*, "and we hear of a great many families preparing to leave."[28] John B. Magruder, in charge of the land office in Mexico, likewise received favorable news: "The letters of General Price, Imperial Commissioner Maury, and his son, Colonel [Richard] Maury, [had] been extensively published and universally read in this country [the U.S.]," making it clear that "the coming spring and summer will witness the exodus of the best and most desirable population of our country."[29]

Carlota continued to be the main area of colonization for these migrants. As reported in early March 1866, three ships had arrived at Veracruz in the last week, bringing "quite a number of emigrants," including "104 men, women and children, nearly all of whom are settling in the colony of Cordova [i.e., Carlota]." The state distribution for these arrivals ranged considerably: twenty-three were from Alabama, seventeen from Louisiana, sixteen from Texas, thirteen from Kentucky, eight from Virginia, and four from Mississippi. Families made up a large portion of the travelers by this point. For example, the list included Mrs. Grin and child; Mr. Mellard, wife, and seven children; and J. G. Stondermire, wife, and seven daughters.[30]

Even after the Office of Colonization closed down in April 1866, colonization and immigration continued largely unabated. The closure of the office was certainly "a serious set back" to southern colonization, but it by no means spelled its end. As the *Mexican Times* reported, "Notwithstanding the suppression of the bureau of colonization from motives of economy, the disposition of the Government [was] still favorable to emigration." By May 1866 there was even a proposal before the Mexican Ministry of Development "to establish a line of agricultural colonies from Cordova to Matamoros," to rekindle "the flame of emigration which was overspreading the South like a conflagration."[31] To be sure, southern colonization faced increasing difficulties, but it appeared that Maury and his coplanners had given enough impetus to the project for others to continue where they had left off.

The first sign of significant trouble for the central colonies came in mid-May 1866 when Mexican Liberal troops captured twenty-six southern colonists in the Córdoba area. In a manner quite similar to what was already occurring in northern Mexico, the Republican bandit Luis Pérez Figueroa robbed and then captured this migrant group from their small settlements at Omealca and Tolequilla, the sites of former haciendas, about twenty miles from Carlota. Pérez Figueroa was reportedly the same bandit responsible for robbing and killing

Confederate general Mosby M. Parsons on the road to Monterrey, Nuevo León. Now he roamed the countryside around central Mexico and struck another blow at the core area of colonization.[32]

Brigadier General Pérez Figueroa and his bandits reportedly destroyed the southern migrants' homes, killed or stole all of their animals, and ruined their crops. These colonists had accepted lands confiscated by the imperial government, angering agriculturalist Indians already living on them and prompting them to call for aid from local Mexican Republican forces. They also had disagreements with indigenous laborers over work terms. One of the captured colonists, Tom J. Russell, revealed that three southern families were living at the Omealca colony, along with "several single gentlemen." This group was "robbed of everything except their wearing apparel," he reported. At Tolequilla, where Russell and ten others lived (four with families), the colonists were merely taken prisoner by a detachment of soldiers.[33]

Pérez Figueroa and his army marched the captives southward, promising to release the colonists at a new settlement site. Along the way, Russell and the other colonists destroyed their immigration papers and the declaration of their intention to become citizens of the empire, shedding evidence implicating them with the colonization initiative. After a week they arrived in the state of Oaxaca and were released to the authorities at the town of Tuxtepec. The group soon made arrangements with Captain Thomas Soublet of Louisiana, whom Pérez Figueroa knew, for the return of their passports in exchange for leaving Mexico. They then made their way to Veracruz, but instead of departing, these southerners went to the city of Córdoba.[34]

Such disruptions were not enough to prompt an abandonment of the colonization plans. As Russell reported afterward, the "Carlota settlement ha[d] not been disturbed yet." The released colonists issued a statement in October 1866 testifying that the main colony was in fact quite prosperous, with the imperial government "giving to colonization all the encouragement that could be reasonably expected or desired." Besides, there was still much promise in Mexico, especially in the central areas. One correspondent in the Córdoba valley for the *Daily Picayune*, calling himself "Cordovan," wrote in the fall of 1866

that the raids on Omealca and Tolequilla had scared away some immigrants. Yet he remained quite optimistic, noting that the second
crop of corn was about ready for harvesting and the market was "full
of vegetables . . . of fruits," including "peaches, apples, pears," along
with "an abundance of fish." "Cordovan" actually knew of "no working man who ha[d] failed to do well here."[35]

Throughout 1866 the prospects for colonization through the con-
duit of commercial agriculture appeared more promising here than
in northern Mexico. As in the borderlands, though, one of the major
problems that would confront Carlota and other southern colonies
in central Mexico were the bandits, who were becoming more aggres-
sive as the year progressed. Especially after the withdrawal of French
troops in early 1867, Republican bandits such as Pérez Figueroa increased their control over central Mexico, a process that had already
been underway in the north. As Russell indicated, Pérez Figueroa was
"pronounced by all parties . . . to be nothing more than a cutthroat
and robber, fighting only for the purpose of stealing—not for the good
of the Liberal cause of his country."[36] More accurately, Pérez Figueroa
managed to tuck the Liberal cause into his quest for self-enrichment
through theft and trade, as other Republican bandits had done in
the borderlands. One of the key elements of the decline of southern
colonization in Mexico was the banditry and theft that undermined
the immigrants' nerve and confidence. But it was not so evident at
the time that banditry, theft, and raiding would bring the downfall
of colonization.

In early June 1866, as the French began to scale back some of their
forces in central Mexico, Republican bandits attacked Carlota.[37] Sterling Price, however, seemed quite determined to proceed onward.
He wrote afterward to his son about this raid "by a band of robbers
claiming to be liberal troops" and how he had arranged for an "Imperial Military Post" to prevent future incidents.[38] After the Omealca
raid, colonists also began to organize their own protection (beyond
the French military force).[39] The colonists at Carlota did indeed re-
double their efforts to form "an organization for self-defense" after
their "serious interruption." Concurrently, it was reported that there

was "as much activity in the acquisition and surveys of lands for Colonization as have ever been known on the part of the Government." The minister of development duly encouraged immigration while a number of surveys were underway in the summer of 1866.[40] Instead of caving in to pressure, southern colonization took a new direction, carrying on without Maury, Allen, and Anderson. They had given it the start it needed, and now the Mexican Ministry of Development and individual colony leaders aimed to bring the venture to completion.

The southern colonies in central Mexico did not survive, but their decline did not truly set in until the spring and summer of 1867, when the French forces completely withdrew and Emperor Maximilian met his fate before a firing squad.[41] Before then it was hard to tell which way southern colonization would go. No doubt the boldness of Mexican Republicans and their increasing control derailed much of the initiative's strength. But it remained to be seen whether the project could be carried forward under the Mexican Republican government if the imperial one indeed failed.

While some colonists returned to the United States by the end of 1866, others stayed on, waiting to see if colonization could still be achieved under one governmental guise or another. Among the returning Texas migrants was Judge C. H. Randolph (the former state treasurer); he left Orizaba and came back to Galveston in early November. Judges O. M. Roberts and W. S. Oldham also returned to Texas, the former from a colony in San Luis Potosí.[42] On the other hand, some migrants, such as Jo Shelby, instead of heading back across the border pushed onward with the colonization efforts at Tuxpan, north of Veracruz along the Gulf of Mexico. This area was to be an important site for the continued immigration efforts.

Tuxpan and the Colonization Plans:
"Southward to the Gulf and northward to the gates of Mexico"

By the summer of 1866 southern colonization in Mexico entered a new phase. The *Mexican Times* printed a letter from the town of Tuxpan in June that alluded to these changes. "Immigration is beginning to turn in our direction," the letter stated. "Several directors of

American companies" were presently "measuring lands" along the main river that flowed inland from Tuxpan on the Gulf of Mexico. "By the month of October," the newspaper reported, "these lands will be inhabited by two hundred families."[43] The colonization movement in central Mexico may have stumbled upon hard times, but other areas spurred the operation forward.

By late August 1866, Robert Jones Laurence had completed a survey of the lands in the Tuxpan region. Laurence was a farmer from Tennessee and was among the early Confederate migrants in Mexico, having arrived at the capital a year earlier with John N. Edwards (the one who recounted Shelby's expedition over the border and was now the editor of the *Mexican Times*). Laurence had recently returned from "an extensive survey of the lands of Metlaltoyuca, which extended from Tuxpam [the town of Tuxpan], on the Gulf of Mexico, nearly to Hunchinango, among the mountains." He wrote that the lands of Tuxpan contained soil with "a dark rich loam," making for "profitable productions" in "coffee, cotton, sugar, tobacco, corn, rice, cocoa," and other crops. "Two planting seasons occur[red] yearly" in this area, he said, "which give two crops per year." Moreover, fifty bushels of corn per acre was about the average yield, usually bringing one dollar per bushel. Sugar was planted only every seven years and cotton every four. But, as Laurence explained, "with improved machinery for manufacture and advanced implements of cultivation," a persistent theme of the overall colonization initiative, "this mode must certainly change." These surroundings along the gulf side of Mexico, a region that Maury had also sought to settle before he left for England, offered a whole new pathway to prosperity.[44]

Ripe for development, Tuxpan attracted the attention of southern migrants. As Laurence explained, "Capitalists could invest in lumber with every prospect of success and with golden promises of a heavy and valuable trade between Tuxpa[n] and the outside world." With only a few roads, and those in poor condition, Tuxpan presented challenges for potential colonists, but Laurence believed these difficulties were quite surmountable. There were already "some American colonists now on the Metlaltoyuca lands," and he anticipated that a "heavy

emigration [was] preparing to locate in this section of the country."
William T. Townsend led one of the "large companies" from Colorado County, Texas, and had recently "returned for a goodly number of his old friends and neighbors." Townsend also endorsed John Henry Brown's colonization efforts at a neighboring site called Tumbadero, along the Tuxpan River. Laurence was quite sure that Townsend and other emigrants would "bring with them stock, farming utensils, wagons, household furniture, and everything to commence life readily and earnestly in a new country."[45]

Ex-Confederate general Jo Shelby likewise saw the potential of Tuxpan and became the de facto leader of this initiative. Shelby relocated from Carlota to Tuxpan in the fall of 1866, acquired a sizeable land grant, and set to work attracting colonists to this location. He acquired his tract of land from Baron Enrique Sauvage, a European who had previously been granted it from Emperor Maximilian. The baron was "a distinguished financier and energetic business man" who transferred his claims to Shelby in order to more effectively and "speedily open up this splendid Metlaltoyuca country to emigration and capital." Shelby thereby organized a company with a president, three directors, and two hundred shares to be purchased at five hundred dollars per share (and to be offered "in the New York market"). He set the price of land at one dollar per acre, to be sold in tracts of 320 acres. In addition, "two schooners" were to be run from New Orleans and Tuxpan, with "every emigrant" transported "free of cost." With his wife, Betty, and two sons already with him, Shelby went straight ahead with setting his sights on this next stage of southern immigration.[46]

Maury's original plans sparked these ongoing colonization efforts. Shelby, like Maury, made specific provisions for land and transportation and intended to send agents to the United States, particularly to the cities of New Orleans, New York, Galveston, St. Louis, Chicago, and Baltimore. Shelby also sent out pamphlets to promote immigration, containing the names of the company's directors. William P. Hardeman of Texas was one of them, someone who reportedly could bring "two hundred families immediately to these lands." Another director was H. W. Keith, "one of the best business men that ever came from New York." Shelby was thus building upon the previous pattern of colonization but expanding its investment base to include northerners.[47]

Shelby's efforts coincided with John Henry Brown's to collectively give the colonization initiative a new direction within the broad framework laid out by Maury. While Shelby pressed his efforts at the Metlaltoyuca site, Brown continued to develop the neighboring colony at Tumbadero, also in the Tuxpan region but to the north between the Tuxpan and Panuco Rivers (closer to Tampico). By February 1868 Brown reported that his colony had forty families living there, along with "47 single men; 13 single ladies; 66 children, [and] *six native infants* [born]."[48] By September 1868 Brown reported, "This colony is proceeding in the right way to reflect honor and profit on the colonists, while they prove to be an advantage to the country of their adoption." That the focus of colonization had switched to this location did not surprise Brown. In 1866 he had discovered "this Tuxpan river country," and since then it had become his home, as well as "the home of over fifty American families" (by the fall of 1868). This colony was growing by the month, according to the agricultural plans for settlement. "All but two or three families [were] engaged in agriculture," and even those emigrants who had arrived "as late as January last [1868]" now had "good log cabins and luxuriant, though usually small[,] crops growing."[49] This colony represented one of the success stories in the unfolding colonization venture. (See map in chapter 3.)

On the opposite side of Mexico, in the state of Jalisco, Dr. Cornelius Boyle conducted another survey in the fall of 1866 that pushed the colonization plans ahead. Dr. Boyle examined lands that belonged to Mr. Eustace Barron and informed potential migrants that Barron intended to open lands "immediately for colonization" and had already "laid out a town sufficiently large to contain at first 200 families," appropriately named Barronville. "Within the town," the *Mexican Times* stated, "there will be a beautiful plaza, a large Court House in the centre and the lots upon this square are to be sold and the proceeds applied to the improvement and benefit of the town." Along the town's perimeter, colonists could obtain 160 acres of land for free and could acquire more at "a nominal price." As with Tuxpan, the lands here were "a dark chocolate color, soil several feet deep, and grow with unsurpassed vigor cotton, rice, sugar, tobacco, coffee, corn, wheat," and other vegetables and fruits. These plans were bringing agricultural production and a new market for them close together. The colonizers would also seek out international trade, since Barronville was "about 40 miles from San Blas, a Pacific port, where California steamers, whalers, and merchantmen continually stop, thus always creating a brisk and healthy market." Barronville and its surrounding farms opened interlocking avenues for production, consumption, and trade, with the Pacific Ocean as the gateway to prosperity.[50]

Coinciding with the plans for Barronville, southern colonization was also taking root at a nearby hacienda called San Lorenzo. This site also contained "all the advantages of soil, position, climate, and water communications" to make for a thriving colony. It also held "none of those broken and torn relations between master and slave, no sudden liberation of four millions of negroes," as the South was then experiencing. The call for immigration here and elsewhere returned to the idea that many white southerners wished to remove themselves from "the desolated and unprofitable cotton-fields of the South" and come to Mexico, where "the emigrant can build his home upon lands of unequalled fertility and well adapted to the growth of this valuable and needful staple." This was not a new vision for colonization; the emphasis had only shifted to lands along the coasts of Mexico.[51]

As editor and publisher of the *Mexican Times*, John N. Edwards supported this change in direction and the new leadership behind it. "Colonization, unfortunately mismanaged at first [by the imperial government]," he wrote, "comes back again to the vision upon the horizon of Mexico, and when Shelby, Laurence, Keith, Boyle and others of similar energy and intelligence put their shoulders to the wheels, success is easy, and colonization already commenced."[52] As Edwards indicated, new leadership (including himself) had emerged that was steering immigration toward new destinations. A web of new southern colonies appeared to be taking off by the fall of 1866. As Edwards reported, "The American settlers at Metlaltayuca [*sic*], in Durango,

[and] in Tuxpan are prosperously engaged in opening farms for themselves and their expected friends at home." Instead of shriveling away to nothing, these colonies had "gone on prosperously, unmolested and increasing." "The same can be said," claimed Edwards, "of Col. Mitchell's colony on the Rio Verde in San Luis Potosi Department." These sites of immigration away from central Mexico had come to fruition and taken on a life of their own. Edwards and other planners could not "account for the recent unfortunate occurrences near Cordova [the summertime raids]. It [was just] one of those exceptions that invariably occur to establish a general rule." From the new leadership's perspective, the raids on Omealca and Carlota were aberrations and not cause to consider abandoning colonization.[53]

As Edwards mentioned, the colony in San Luis Potosí had become a shining example of the possibilities outside of central Mexico. Colony leader F. T. Mitchell came forward at the end of September 1866 to fully endorse this site of immigration. "I have been carefully observing for the last fifteen months," Mitchell wrote, "the current events connected with emigration from the Confederate States to this country." Before this time, he had "sedulously withheld any advice until [his] own observations," combined with other reports he had obtained, enabled him "to make an intelligible statement" to potential migrants. Now the time seemed ripe to make a firm pronouncement in the colony's favor.[54]

Mitchell expressed outright confidence in his burgeoning colony, located between the cities of San Luis Potosí and Tampico. "The body of lands is immense," he wrote, "sufficient to accommodate a settlement of gigantic proportions." Labor was also "abundant and cheap" as well as "very tractable," a reference to the debt peonage that kept mostly Indian laborers tied to the land in northern areas. More importantly, he pointed out, southern migrants and local Mexicans had started to forge a relationship "of the most friendly character," with "all desiring the introduction of American skill and enterprize into the country." Mitchell continued to stress the promise of agriculture and labor but also the "easy transportation" that traversed "nearly all the way on a good road for wagons or carts to the interior, to which point we may look for the best market in the world for many years to come, for our great staples of sugar, coffee, tobacco, rice, &c., &c." Plans for a railroad running from Tampico to this interior market were underway, and, as with Tuxpan, emigrants could reach Mitchell's colony either by land from Texas or by sea from New Orleans or Galveston. He also planned to sell the land "at a cost not exceeding one dollar per acre" and to offer parcels through sharecropping arrangements.[55]

By the end of 1866 the colonies in San Luis Potosí, Tuxpan, and Jalisco were at the forefront of the colonization plans. While Mitchell's site lured migrants with five-year sharecropping offers, the equally rich lands owned by Shelby and Barron also reoriented the enterprise outward from the center. These latter two colonies, in particular, were set to be "the gates, one on the Gulf and the other on the Pacific, through which a hardy industrious immigration will enter," establish itself, and then spread to other locations. Some supporters of immigration even came to believe that had "the management of affairs at Cordova been entrusted to [Shelby's] keeping, to-day a great growing colony would have been stretching its browned hands southward to the Gulf and northward to the gates of Mexico, holding up the white beacon of cotton bales and beckoning from the world commerce, enterprize and capital."[56] The southern commercial agricultural enterprise still held claim to a larger modernizing dream.

As this last quote conveys, the enterprise had changed its direction and leadership, but not its goals of economic development. Those "browned hands" juxtaposed against "the white beacon of cotton" may also disclose the underlying racial tones of southern colonization, but the geographical and rhetorical emphasis had changed, while the economic premises came even more to the forefront. By January 1867 the *Mexican Times*, the main organ of promotion, had likewise changed hands again. The new editor, Bradford C. Barksdale, was a professional newspaperman who provided subscriptions from London, New York, and elsewhere to Mexico. Barksdale gave a more reserved tone to colonization and subtly shifted the paper's one-sided support for Emperor Maximilian. All the same, he firmly backed the colonies on the two coasts: "The two schemes we referred to in the

Times as safe and promising are those of Eustace Barron Esq., and the Tuxpan colony." Barksdale was not a promoter of southern immigration in the way Allen and Edwards had been, but he did favor the next phase of colonization. As he stated, "We know of no better place where, our friends can enrich themselves so speedily in agricultural pursuits as on these lands." Coming from the pen of a more objective editor, these comments seemed to grant the colonies even more legitimacy.[57]

Barksdale's control of the *Mexican Times* helped reshape the colonization venture around a few select plans and distance it from a strident anti-Juarista and pro-Maximilian position. As he stated in January 1867, the newspaper would not use its columns "to call Juarez a half blood Indian and the Liberals brigands and thieves." It would also not "invite Americans to 'come to Mexico,' merely to accomplish the ends of some enthusiastic speculator," a somewhat oblique criticism of previous efforts. Barksdale would endorse southern colonies only when "solid and advantageous terms [were] secured to immigrants by responsible and able parties."[58] These measures, combined with the movement away from central Mexico, gradually changed the course of colonization. By focusing on new immigration sites and reversing the rhetorical support for the Imperialists, the new group of leaders began to prepare for the possible downfall of Maximilian's empire and to plan for how to continue without it.

Southern Colonization after the End of the Empire

Like the *Mexican Times* under Barksdale, the *Two Republics* instilled a more inclusive and less abrasive tone into colonization. As the other major promoter of southern immigration in Mexico, this English-language newspaper began publication in 1867, following the collapse of Emperor Maximilian's government. Ex-Confederate major George W. Clarke (a former editor of the *Arkansas Intelligencer*) still wished to encourage immigration, but by taking an impartial political stance while emphasizing the development of Mexico's natural resources and industry.[59] This rhetorical shift was a wise move on the part of those promoting colonization, since it had become increasingly clear that the French army planned to leave and that the Mexican

Republican forces were gaining ground. Then again, in the haze of rumors that circulated about the French withdrawal and the war effort, it was quite difficult to determine the direction of Mexican politics and nationhood, and correspondingly, the outcome of southern colonization. Hence, the more reserved tone of the colonization initiative reflected a keen desire to persevere within unpredictable circumstances.

By late June 1866, John N. Edwards had recognized the improved position of the Mexican Republicans in the face of French withdrawal. As he wrote, "We regret to say that the dissidents stimulated by the prospect of the withdrawal of French support have gained lately some advantages." In one instance of imperial defeat, "a column of Mejias army [General Tomás Mejía], escorting a train of merchandize from Matamoros, ha[d] been cut off and defeated with severe loss." The towns of Matamoros and Tampico were "seriously threatened" by this Republican victory.[60] Edwards was correct to cite this incident as serious because the Imperial Army in the north had in fact suffered a devastating defeat at Santa Gertrudis (along the Matamoros–Camargo Road) on June 16, 1866, with around 400 men killed, 165 wounded, and hundreds taken prisoner. The *Brownsville (TX) Daily Ranchero* wrote that it signaled "a death blow to the reign of [the] Empire in Northern Mexico." Soon afterward, Imperialist general Mejía evacuated both Bagdad and Matamoros; in early August 1866, after 350 Mexicans deserted the Imperial Army, Tampico also surrendered.[61]

Edwards wrote more about the imperial reversal at Santa Gertrudis in early July 1866. He had received news that almost an entire company of the Imperial Army had been captured or killed. About one month later, he also reported on the rumors that the Mexican Republican forces had captured Tampico; then again, in the same issue the *Mexican Times* reported that the Imperialists had retaken the city soon thereafter.[62] Such rumors characterized the atmosphere of Mexico at the time—the Republican forces seemed to be advancing, but it was not certain to what extent, or whether it would be permanent.

By August 1866 French forces had apparently evacuated Saltillo, the capital of Coahuila, with Republican lieutenant colonel Ruperto

Martínez sending congratulations to this effect to the *ayuntamiento* (city council). In September it appeared that Liberal forces had taken control of the northern cities of Matamoros and Monterrey as well.[63] These actions in the northern areas of Mexico were matched by an important victory in the south central region in November. The Republican troops commanded by General Porfirio Díaz defeated the French at the city of Oaxaca (in Díaz's home state). The next month, reports came in that the Imperialist forces had surrendered at Jalapa, and rumors were in the air about Emperor Maximilian abdicating the throne of Mexico and leaving for Europe. By the end of 1866 the war effort seemed to be turning against the Imperialists.[64]

On the other hand, the empire still showed significant signs of life. In late September it continued to draw support from the most populated sections of the country. The Mexican states occupied mostly by Republican forces were outlying areas such as Chihuahua and Sinaloa, while the Imperialists held central states like Zacatecas and Jalisco, as well as Mexico. Both combatants meanwhile occupied and contended for such areas as Coahuila and Nuevo León.[65] Moreover, even with the impending French withdrawal, arrangements were to be made to build up the Mexican Imperial Army, including leaving French officers and members of the Foreign Legion behind to help direct it. With such continued, albeit diminished, military support, the colonization efforts stood a solid chance of carrying onward under the Imperialist banner.

There was also another idea for how colonization could continue even if the current imperial government did not remain in place. As the *Mexican Times* reported, "Hundreds of French soldiers, whose term of service ha[d] expired, instead of returning to France," had decided to stay in Mexico, "settle upon small tracts of land," and become citizens. The newspaper estimated that by the time the French army left Mexico in the fall of 1867 "no less than 5,000 of these voluntary French settlers" would be left behind, "many of them, no doubt, married to Mexican girls." These reports may have only been rumors too, but if true, these French soldier-colonists could aid the growth of the southern colonies and, if needed, reenlist in the Mexican army.[66]

William M. Anderson likewise thought the prospect of French colonization held promise. Even while he packed his bags and set sail himself, he thought that colonization might be secured through the support of foreign soldiers who remained after completing their term of service. "There are hundreds and thousands of French and Belgian and German soldiers," wrote Anderson, "who would doubtless be glad of a home in this country, where both soil and climate are unequalled." He specifically recommended that, after their discharge, "let them march north, with their arms in their hands, let them keep up a military organization while they cultivate their farms." In this way, stretches of northern Mexico, like those around the Sabinas River in Coahuila, would become "the most prosperous and peaceful in Mexico."[67] This protective panoply could provide the cover that southern colonization needed to continue without the empire.

By 1867, however, the tide seemed to be turning more definitively to Juárez's advantage. His forces were said to be fifty thousand strong, with a majority of them moving on the capital. The leader of the French forces, Marshal Achille Bazaine, had also recommended that Emperor Maximilian should take his leave.[68] Yet, again, it was hard to tell whether this spelled the definitive end of the imperial regime or of colonization. "Rumors from Queretaro and Puebla," as the *Mexican Times* reported in mid-March 1867, had been "multitudinous" and "as contradictory." The latest word was that Emperor Maximilian had personally led a contingent of troops out from Querétaro and gained a key victory. Shortly thereafter there were reports of a series of Imperialist victories that had dislodged the Liberal forces. By the end of the month, the tide appeared to be turning back toward the empire.[69]

Through the pages of the *Mexican Times*, we gain a sense of the state of mind of southern migrants. The mid- to late 1860s in Mexico were characterized by miscommunication, slow communication, and an unclear future. In this topsy-turvy situation where rumors flew rapidly and battles continued inconclusively, it was very difficult to predict the outcome. No one could deny that imperial Mexico was on more unstable ground than it had previously been, but it was not certain whether a truce might establish a coalition government or whether another political arrangement could be forged. As one witness observed at the time, "The thousand and one false rumours constantly flying from mouth to mouth, through town and city," worked their way "far and wide over the country."[70] This was the atmosphere that enveloped southern colonization, casting it with both uncertainty and hope.

The final siege of Querétaro that led to Imperialist defeat also came through a haze of rumors. In April 1867 it was reported that thirty thousand Liberal troops had been "baffled and defeated" by nine thousand Imperialist troops over the course of two months. The state capital had a larger defensive force, and it too was deemed certain to hold out. By May the news was more uncertain, with "no less than *three* different versions" of stories about the possible capture of Querétaro having been reported. Even in June it was not clear whether Emperor Maximilian had been captured, and the Imperial Army was rumored to be regrouping after abandoning Querétaro. In fact, Maximilian had been captured and his forces surrendered on May 15. He was executed by firing squad on June 19, 1867, along with two Mexican generals, and Mexican Republican forces entered Mexico City two days later. The war ended and so did publication of the *Mexican Times*.[71]

Leading up to this dramatic outcome were the events of the previous year, which turned out to be a crucial one for the Imperialist-Republican war and southern colonization. Just as 1866 was a pivotal year for gaining local support for the Mexican Republican cause in Coahuila, it was also a crucial period for determining whether colonization would continue as planned, take another course, or be extinguished altogether.[72] As it turned out, southern immigration did not proceed as planned, but it did not end either.

In 1868, for example, a year after the fall of the imperial government, southern migrants were still coming to Mexico. John H. Brown reported a steady arrival of new migrants at his colony in Tuxpan, especially from Texas. Corresponding with the change in Mexican governments, he stressed that this colony was filling up with "quiet, industrious, law-abiding farmers, friends to the Republic of Mexico," who were "determined to succeed by legitimate industry." This more humble, toned-down description of southern migration matched the reality of the situation. The restoration of the Mexican Republic did not necessarily mean the end of colonization, but it did prompt a change in where and how it would be carried out. The grand and boastful promotions of the Maury and Allen years were now replaced by the steady, quiet labor of yeoman farmers looking for a new start. This message of hard work had always been a part of the colonization plans, but it was now reflected much more in word and deed. Moreover, it was a time for more reconciliation and less confrontation with the Mexican people. As Brown said, "We have lived, and expect to live, in peace and harmony with the Mexican people around us." The goal, by necessity, was not to take expropriated land and install a new Old South on foreign ground. Instead, it was to ensure that "peace and goodwill" prevailed between colonists and the Mexican population.[73]

Shelby's colony at Metlaltoyuca had succumbed to the misfortunes of disputed land claims and hostilities around the time of Maximilian's fall. Many of those colonists then relocated to Brown's Tumbadero site and engaged with the other migrants in more mutually constructive activities. For instance, the Tumbadero colonists formed an agricultural society to make more of an effort to contribute to the advancement of the Mexican nation. "Among the later emigrants" contributing to this shift in focus was "Dr. Gideon Linseatur, an able writer on geology and mineralogy, botany, &c." The scientific and developmental emphasis, of course, had been at the forefront of the original colonization plans. Yet now both were placed at the behest of the rebounding Mexican Republic and not at the heels of a grand imperial design. Brown actually put himself in league with the *Two Republics* in its quest to aid Mexico through "its tone of progress, firmness, impartiality and generosity." "I trust your able and indefatigable efforts," wrote Brown to editor George W. Clarke, "to get this naturally great country on the high road of prosperity, unity and real national glory, may be fully appreciated by the statesmen and people of Mexico, and crowned with abundant success." Clarke and Brown continued the drive toward a better economic future in Mexico along a declared path of cooperation.[74]

The Tumbadero colony did not thrive, but it continued into the early 1870s. By March 1870 "the number of American residents in the [Tuxpan] Valley," was reported to have been "greatly reduced." Yet "those who have remained" were said to be "industrious and enterprising planters," even if on "a small scale." Among the problems that caused this colony to later falter were such financial matters as import duties that deprived the colony of funds and sparked debates in the halls of the Mexican Congress. This southern colony, for example, cited "the duty on flour" and other "articles of prime necessity" as "a great grievance."[75] More serious impediments to this colony and Mexican modernization included the delayed construction of railroad lines, the continuing problem of banditry, and perennial fiscal problems. Just as Mexico's development initiatives would continue to be hindered by political disagreements and funding issues during the Restored Republic, so would the ongoing colonization efforts never fully take shape in the ways that promoters described them.

All the same, southerners did not completely vanish from Mexico with the fall of the empire. In 1868 two Texans, Dr. D. McKnight and ex-Confederate general Hamilton P. Bee, for example, worked steadily on developing their vineyard and building a paper factory in cooperation with local Mexicans in Parras, Coahuila. The following year, Bee's young son was baptized as a Catholic, a sign of integration into the community. In 1870 Bee made a visit to Laredo, Texas, but returned to Mexico "to carry out his agricultural enterprises." His wife also came back "to her home in Mexico." Some southern immigrants found Mexico hospitable enough under a Republican government to continue with their colonization plans.[76]

Colonization did not reshape the Mexican landscape in the ways envisioned in 1865, but it was by no means a doomed enterprise from the start and it did leave a lasting legacy. The war brought on by the French Intervention made for turbulent times and presented no clear outcome. Under these circumstances, southern colonization persisted and still held great potential to connect the American South to Mexico through transborder and transoceanic commerce. The ongoing colonization efforts after the collapse of Maximilian's empire, as well as the plans and ideas that preceded them, subtly altered the course of U.S. and Mexican history.

Most directly, the continuing colonization plans sparked interest in and contributed to the forging of a hemispheric economy. Railroad building was one prominent manifestation of this movement by U.S. southerners and northerners to forge greater economic links with Latin America. Southern colonization intersected with the larger currents of economic development running southward from the United States, offering routes of cross-border trade and commerce. The southern plans played a key role in both forwarding these economic visions of the nineteenth century and distancing southerners from the expansionist tendencies of northern promoters.

Chapter Five

Southern Colonization, Railroads, and U.S. and Mexican Modernization

During the post–Civil War era, southern migrants were not the only foreigners with economic development plans for Mexico. Union general William S. Rosecrans was among the northern business promoters in Mexico who helped spearhead a new era of economic relations between the two nations, especially in terms of railroads. General Rosecrans became U.S. minister to Mexico in 1868. Upon his arrival, he made it clear that he favored U.S. economic expansion across the border through railroad development. In April 1869 he recommended to the U.S. secretary of state, Hamilton Fish, a comprehensive program for railroads in Mexico, with the possibility of buying the main artery that ran from Veracruz to the capital.[1]

Rosecrans likewise sent two petitions to the Mexican Congress for railroad construction projects during the Restored Republic period (1867–76). One proposed to go from Tampico or Tuxpan on the Gulf coast to Mexico City and the other from Antón Lizardo to Cuernavaca (south of Veracruz to south of the capital), with a possible extension to the Pacific Ocean. Soon afterward Rosecrans published a letter to President Juárez recommending American capital investment and enticements for immigrants to spur modernization. As with southern promoters, Rosecrans linked immigration and railroads as key initiatives to spur the Mexican economy. As he stated to Juárez, "a beneficent progress" depended on "*railroads* and *immigration*," and it was "the paramount duty of every friend of Mexico, every friend of humanity, to promote the adoption of these means for her salvation and regeneration." To this end, he continued to urge the approval of the two extensive railroad lines named above, with the intention of establishing a link across the continent.[2]

Rosecrans's railroads never materialized under his watch, but his efforts help reveal a mesh of business activity in Mexico that intersected with southern economic plans. A brief review of his involvement with Mexico establishes a basis for recognizing that the economic plans associated with southern colonization were not the only ones that failed in the era following the American Civil War and the French Intervention. More importantly, Rosecrans allow us to see that the modernization plans of southern colonization were part and parcel of U.S. efforts to strengthen economic ties with Mexico and establish a greater presence in the Latin America. The primary difference was that the southern plans tended to target joint southern-Mexican benefits instead of U.S. industrial advantages.

One level of southern influence on the course of U.S. and Mexican history is the role of southern colonization in the hemispheric economy. Southern promoters' search for an alternate destiny to Reconstruction contributed to the larger impulse toward bridging borders and crossing oceans that defined the second half of the nineteenth century. The postwar South's focus on railroad development and southern commerce reflected two prominent ways in which southern colonization intersected with and informed main currents of economic revival after the Civil War and the fall of Maximilian's empire.

Rosecrans in Mexico after the Civil War

The idea of a transcontinental railroad from the Gulf of Mexico to the Pacific was not a new one. In 1849 the Mexican Congress had authorized construction for such a line from Veracruz, and over the next twenty years it granted several concessions through central Mexico, as well as to the south across the Isthmus of Tehuantepec and to the north through Sonora. However, by the end of the French Intervention in 1867 only the railroad line between Veracruz and Mexico City had made significant progress. By 1867, desiring the completion of the Veracruz line, Mexican president Benito Juárez prompted the Mexican Congress to renew a British concession. His presidential successor, Sebastián Lerdo de Tejada (brother of Miguel Lerdo de Tejada), oversaw the completion of this project in January 1873, calling it the Mexican Railway.[3]

Rosecrans helped redirect attention from this railway focal point to a line from Mexico City to Tuxpan, where, as we have seen, at least one colony of southerners had settled and continued to grow. As the *Two Republics* reported in September 1868, the prospect of a railroad running from Tuxpan to the Pacific Ocean had already been "favorably received by [the Mexican] Congress," and work seemed ready to commence.[4] Other promoters became interested in similar lines, including the Englishman Edmund Stephenson, who submitted a plan during the summer of 1869 that would extend a railroad to both coasts and the Rio Grande (called the National Mexican Pacific and Rio Bravo Railroad). The *Two Republics* had reported on these plans back in June 1868, indicating that Stephenson was forming "a company to be composed of the Governors; the States and others to carry out this great project." Meanwhile, Rosecrans returned to the United States in July 1869 but left behind agents to represent him to the Mexican government; these men petitioned the Mexican Congress for over a year to build a railroad and telegraph line from Tampico or Tuxpan on the Gulf coast to the Pacific Ocean.[5]

Rosecrans's Tuxpan concession was finally passed in December 1870, but negotiations over the final proposal and arrangements for funding dragged on into 1872. By then rival promoters had created new obstacles, especially Edward Lee Plumb of the International Railroad Company of Texas, who proposed to build a railroad line from Laredo, Texas, to San Blas, Mexico, on the Pacific Ocean, along with branches going to Mexico City and Durango. Nonetheless, when Mexican president Juárez died of a heart attack in July 1872, it seemed fortuitous for Rosecrans, because the incoming president, Sebastián Lerdo de Tejada, had previously supported him. Yet Lerdo had also worked with

Plumb, setting up a competition between the two promoters, and by the spring of 1873 the continued impasse between Rosecrans and the Mexican Congress pushed the advantage to Plumb. After years of delays and debates over funding and construction that stalled his project, Rosecrans resigned and his business partner, William J. Palmer, took over the project, but he too failed to finalize the deal. Not until 1880 did Palmer successfully secure a concession for a shorter line from Laredo to Mexico City.[6]

In May 1873 President Lerdo granted a concession to Plumb for a railroad running to the Pacific coast and the border, but this project stalled with the financial panic of that year, which dried up American capital.[7] Plumb had experience in the railroad business and seemed assured of success in Mexico, but he too failed in his endeavors. In August 1871 he had become an agent of the International Railroad Company of Texas; in September he went to Mexico City and began plans to construct two main lines—one from Laredo to San Blas (or from the Rio Grande to the Pacific) and the other from Mexico City to Durango, with branches to Guanajuato and Morelia.[8] But like Rosecrans, Plumb ran into problems, including the turbulence caused by the unsuccessful revolt of Porfirio Díaz (the Rebellion of La Noria) and dwindling support from members of the Mexican Congress. Meanwhile, a group of fourteen Mexicans and Europeans formed a company, informally called Los Catorce (The Fourteen), to build a railroad to the Pacific under Mexican control and petitioned the Mexican Congress for authorization in September 1873. Plumb's concession was withdrawn in November, while the Mexican government signed a contract with the new group.[9]

In the spring and summer of 1874 Plumb's plans rebounded when Lerdo nullified Los Catorce's concession because of their inability to raise the necessary funds. In December the minister of interior development granted Plumb another concession, which was approved by Congress in the spring of 1875. After Lerdo was elected in 1875, though, he cancelled all concessions except the one for the Mexican National Railroad. Leading U.S. financiers and industrialists, in turn, decided to back Díaz and provided financial assistance that helped to overthrow

Lerdo. When revolution broke out in Mexico in 1876, Lerdo lost power, and out went Plumb's hopes that this would finally be his year.[10]

Coupled with Rosecrans's attempts to develop railroads in Mexico, Plumb's topsy-turvy tale illuminates the serious difficulties U.S. railroad promoters faced in Mexico. The political situation in Mexico was unstable in the 1860s and 1870s. Moreover, most Mexican politicians, even those actively promoting railroad projects, were rightfully suspicious of U.S. and foreign investment. The economic plans for southern colonization thus failed alongside other endeavors after the Civil War. On the one hand, we can see southern colonization and immigration plans as very much a main thread of U.S. economic expansionism into Latin America during the second half of the nineteenth century. On the other hand, the southern plans emphasized the bilateral benefits of trade and economic development to Mexico and the South. The later colonies described in the previous chapter and the economic plans outlined below contributed to a sense of bi-regional and hemispheric trade instead of a focus on U.S. business and expansion.

A Hemispheric New South?

By the late 1860s and early 1870s, U.S. and southern plans for a transcontinental railroad across the Southwest through Mexico to the Pacific Ocean had become a well-formed vision. One example, as the *Two Republics* reported in June 1868, was the plan for the National Mexican Pacific and Rio Bravo Railroad, which aimed to establish "a great railway from the Northern frontier to the Pacific." During the spring of 1869 the U.S. Senate likewise introduced two bills for railroad lines, one extending from "New Orleans to the Rio Grande in the direction of Mazatlan" and the other for "the International Pacific Railroad from Cairo, Illinois, to the Rio Grande, in the direction of San Blas or Mazatlan." Northern promoters such as Rosecrans and Plumb backed such postwar hemispheric commercialism, as did southern promoters. But only after a decade of work did Plumb partially succeed in his transportation plans.[11]

As the *Two Republics* and other southern promoters were aware, the reinstalled Mexican government sought the development of transcontinental railroad routes. The Mexican Congress and President Juárez spent considerable time and energy attempting to connect Veracruz and Mexico City with a railroad and telegraph line across the Isthmus of Tehuantepec to the Pacific Ocean.[12] Earlier proponents of such ideas included Confederate secretary of state Judah P. Benjamin, who had spent more than twenty years trying to establish an international link across this very isthmus before the Civil War. By 1857 Benjamin and other delegates to the Southern Commercial Convention in Knoxville, Tennessee, gained support for such plans based on state and federal funding and Central American and Mexican cooperation.[13] As with proposals from the late 1860s, however, the problems confronting such plans were not just financial or technical.

As Mexican congressman Ramón G. Guzmán pointed out in his opposition to a modification of General Rosecrans's railroad concessions, Mexico was tired of outside investors not living up to their commitments, as well as leery of foreign domination. Guzmán stated that he and others wanted the same outcome as those who supported Rosecrans's plans—Mexico "traversed by those wonderful trains which shed prosperity and which chant civilization's hymn of victory." However, Rosecrans's initiative, along with others going back over thirty years in relation to the isthmus, had failed to materialize because of delays in funding and construction and a distrust of U.S. intentions in Mexico. As Guzmán wrote, Mexico had "granted everything that has been demanded of her, in order to open to the commerce of the world this new interoceanic route." Yet these foreign companies had delivered "neither the railroad, nor the canal, nor any other work whatever." He also "feared" that the current proposal "would give rise to reclamations that would involve the Republic in difficulties of an international character" (i.e., the seizure of more territory or the loss of control over the national economy).[14]

Other Mexican statesmen joined Guzmán in opposing U.S.-backed railroad endeavors. One member of the Mexican Congress spoke against modifications to Rosecrans's concession for the Tuxpan and Pacific Railway. Again, this representative insisted, "The urgency of giving a powerful and decisive impulse to the construction of lines of railway in our country [was] not for a moment overlooked." But not everyone agreed on "*the means* to be adopted in order to realize this inestimable improvement." Many members of Congress were "fearful of the impulse" that was being granted to "the spirit of enterprise and speculation of the American people" through such concessions. The entry of railroads might serve as "the precursors of armies that over the same route would be sent by the neighboring people to undertake a second invasion of our territory." The fear of invasion or annexation was still present alongside the desire to expand Mexico's infrastructure.[15]

Guzmán and other Mexican congressmen were correct to be concerned. Railroads proved to be the fundamental element of U.S. power and influence in North America during the second half of the nineteenth century. They provided the material basis that allowed U.S. capitalists to expand operations into other sectors of the Mexican economy, such as banking, communications, urban land development, export agriculture, ranching, mining, and oil production. Mining companies, for example, built their smelters next to railroads and depended on rail lines for transporting ore and shipping silver and copper to the United States.[16] The eventual result was that Mexico's economy stagnated, while the United States' grew exponentially. By the early 1880s, when the Porfirian boom (under President Porfirio Díaz) was underway, the total product of Mexico was only about 2 percent of the total of the United States.[17]

While Mexican politicians sought out avenues of modernization, they struggled to find development plans that would truly aid the Mexican economy. In addition, expenses on such projects as the railroad line from Mexico City to Veracruz ballooned out of control. By 1873, when the line was completed, the Mexican Railway had cost more than twelve times the original $5 million estimated cost. More than half of the cost had been covered by federal government subsidies, depleting funds for other developmental projects. It was not until the 1880s that Mexico's railroad boom actually began and transborder commerce and binational trade became realities. Yet, apart from the growth of the export sector, railroads contributed little to the industrial growth

of Mexico during the Porfirian era (1876–1910), while they heavily en-
riched the American side of the border.[18]

The grander and more humble southern modernization plans represented a move away from such one-sided economic growth. Beyond
commercial agriculture colonies, southerners in Mexico advanced
multiple economic development plans to ignite a transborder partnership. In 1867, for instance, the *New York Tribune* reported that a contract for "draining the valley of Mexico, by cutting a channel through
the eastern range of mountains, according to the plan of Gen. G. W.
Smith of the Confederate States Army" was under consideration for
the purpose of transregional trade.[19] Southerners infused themselves
into the "March of Improvement" in Mexico in multiple ways, as the
New Orleans Daily True Delta reported, helping to form "steamship
companies" on "both sides of the continent, to form the nucleus of a
commerce for which few countries in the world offer a more substantial basis." Colonization had been attached to the larger contours of
"Steamships, Railroads, and Telegraphs" that would form "the great
system of internal improvement."[20]

The *Two Republics* especially carried forth a message of economic development through collaboration. In late 1868, for example, the newspaper voiced its approval of the completion of the railroad line running
from Veracruz to Mexico City. "With the completion of this road," it
stated, "this capital and several other cities will be brought into immediate and direct communication with the commercial world." The
railroad would also "open to enterprise a vast agricultural and mining
country, rich enough to support a dozen railroads." Likewise, it would
"bring in immigration, so much needed in this extensive and inviting region." The promotional publication did not stop there, though.
It insisted, "What we want next is a railroad in the North-Western
section—say from the upper Rio Grande through to the Gulf of California, to open that vast and valuable region of the Republic."[21] As
with Maury and Allen, as well as Rosecrans and Plumb, this voice of
southern colonization stood behind the economic promise of a railroad line running through northern Mexico. The connecting ideas
of commercial agriculture, immigration, and railroad development

were thus supported by a confluence of Anglo-American promoters in Mexico. Yet these plans aimed to provide the American South and Southwest with a cross-border economic partner, not co-opt Mexico's economy for U.S. benefits.

This goal can be seen in the way southern development initiatives intersected with liberal Mexican political programs. In the 1850s, for example, leading liberal politicians such as Manuel Payno y Flores and Sebastián Lerdo de Tejada championed select foreign investment, immigration, and infrastructure projects. Payno served as the treasury minister and worked toward settling Mexico's internal and foreign debt while encouraging French, British, and Spanish investment. Lerdo specifically championed a close economic partnership with the United States and courted the exploitation of Mexico's natural resources with a mind toward transnational benefits for each country. While Payno changed course after the French Intervention and pursued more nationalist aims, Lerdo, as the next president, supported railroad construction and the re-entrance of foreign capital on a large scale as long as it was not aimed at transborder domination.[22]

While the Juárez government of the Restored Republic pursued the development of the Mexican Railway, the *Two Republics*, as the main promotional organ of continued southern immigration, prompted it to go further. The newspaper enthusiastically supported such developmental measures but also spoke of how southern migrants would allow Mexico to flourish. "All [Mexico] wants to make it one of the great, powerful and wealthy nations of the world," it stated in 1868, "is a numerous and enlightened population bred to habits of industry, for they bring railroads, telegraphs, canals, machinery and all the concomitants of improved civilization and husbandry." The following year it harked on this theme, proclaiming, "One of the greatest needs of Mexico and of the times is *immigration*." These were themes that Mexican politicians and northern promoters echoed as well, but this message of innovation and improvement through increased immigration had already been carried out by southern migrants (not merely proposed), and by this time southern colonization came to mean adjusting to the political and social world of the Restored Republic.[23]

The postimperial colonization plans did not just blindly support Mexican government proposals either. They also critiqued evolving policy on immigration to edge it toward more comprehensive benefits. One example comes from a March 1869 article in the *Two Republics* that analyzed a proposal published in the Mexican newspaper *Siglo XIX* concerning plans before the government about colonization and immigration. The article pinpointed the main problem with the current proposal. "The 'project' referred to, and published in the *Siglo*," it stated, "contains in it nothing of an *immigration* policy. It simply proposes to encourage proprietors to collect laborers on their estates." The current strategy thus encouraged "the *landowner*, but not the *immigrant*." A more balanced immigration policy would benefit immigrants by specifying measures to include them as productive members of society and not mere workers to labor for landowners. For example, exemption from taxation in the proposed plan was directed only at proprietors and not immigrants.[24] By the time southern efforts shifted to the coasts, the initiative reflected more of a concern for community development alongside economic pathways across the border.

The Mexican government, in turn, supported southern colonization and development plans for their advantageous conduits of trade and less threatening intentions. In 1870, for instance, the Mexican Congress granted "a concession to Mr. J. D. O. Castro of New Orleans and his associates" to establish "a line of steam packets" between Veracruz and New Orleans. As with the overall southern immigration efforts, this was another attempt at connecting the U.S. southern and Mexican economies. Such a steamship line was of "the highest importance to the commerce" of Mexico, as it was for the American South. Through this line "a brisk commerce will spring up with New Orleans, and by that port, with all cities in the vallies of the Mississippi and Ohio." Here was one of the goals toward which southern colonization had aimed from the start. Through such commercial agricultural endeavors, the "tropical productions of Mexico" would find a "ready market in all those places," with southern colonists contributing to the agricultural output while Mexico likewise received products from the American South.[25]

In these biregional and hemispheric economic endeavors, southern colonization intersected with scientific politics and the Científicos in Mexico, bestowing it with further credibility for reshaping Mexican-southern commercial relations. The Científicos were a circle of intellectuals inspired by the positivism of Auguste Comte, who emphasized a scientific view of politics in which societies went through evolutionary stages of progress. The Científicos became prominent under the administrations of Porfirio Díaz and shaped public policy through their political positions and their writings in government-sponsored newspapers that advanced a conservative liberalism centered on order, material progress, and administrative government. During the 1870s and 1880s *La Libertad* newspaper, for example, voiced these goals, as did *El Mundo (Semanario Ilustrado)* in the 1890s and early 1900s. This latter publication was started by the Científico Rafael Reyes Spíndola and became the most widely distributed newspaper in Mexico City. These publications promoted the "civilizing process" that could be achieved especially through railroad development and envisioned how material progress would ensure national stability. Scientific expertise and technical management were among the ideas that made economic progress possible, according to the Científicos. Their intellectual leader, Justo Sierra, especially promoted agricultural commercial development alongside an evolving constitutionalism. Sierra was a modernizing theorist who reconciled liberal reform with social conservatism in ways that mirrored the perspective of the leaders of southern colonization.[26]

Although southern migration to Mexico contained elements of preserving southern culture and identity, the leaders of southern colonization were not the same as backward-looking Lost Cause spokesmen.[27] For such writers as Daniel Harvey Hill, who published the magazine *Land We Love* in 1866 in North Carolina, the Lost Cause meant not only defending the South and the Confederacy, even in defeat, but also attacking the pursuit of material success that seemed to be overtaking the region through the influence of the North. Edward A. Pollard, who had provided the name for the Lost Cause movement, also voiced concern about industry and materialism and their effect on the

South. In 1866 he had written of a "danger" from without and within based upon *"material* prosperity." He warned against bringing in "Northern capital and labour; to build mills and factories and hotels and gilded caravansaries" or making the South into "rivals in the clattering and garish enterprise of the North."[28] Instead, the white southern planners of colonization promoted such changes and had more affinity with the New South spokesmen who arose in the postwar period and, ironically, often blended into Lost Cause terrain.

New South promoters entangled themselves in the aura of the Lost Cause in ways that made the two frames of thought compatible and almost inseparable. In April 1870 Edwin DeLeon published an essay that might have given the New South movement its name. "The New South: What It Is Doing, and What It Wants" appeared in *Putnam's Magazine* of South Carolina and voiced approval of industrial and railroad expansion in the region as well as reconciliation with the North. DeLeon wrote that he welcomed "utterly overturning the old system," and in 1874 he published a series of articles about his tour of the South in magazines such as *Harper's* and *Southern Magazine*. These articles were read widely and the term "New South" became attached to a growing movement that embraced industrial and commercial pursuits but did not forget about the Old South.[29] As one study of the remaking of the South states about the New South–Lost Cause continuum, "The South would accept the industrial revolution, railroads, steam engines, and electricity, but southerners would adapt the modern world to its own purposes, ensuring the maintenance of white supremacy, patriarchy, and one-party rule."[30] These attitudes can be detected in both New South supporters and southern colonization leaders in Mexico, but the latter distanced themselves from the past more readily as the enterprise unfolded in Mexico.

In other words, colonization boosters struck out in new economic directions while paying less homage to the Lost Cause. New South advocates sought to elevate the region through appeals to industrialization and change but also had to elicit support by respecting the Old South (genuinely or not).[31] Henry W. Grady, editor of the *Atlanta Constitution*, promoted industry and scientific agriculture and became the leading New South spokesman, but he also knew that this social and economic message would need to be clothed in deferential terms to appeal to a broader audience.[32] J. D. B. DeBow's magazine in New Orleans, *DeBow's Review*, began to issue this corrective call back in 1866. In its "After the War" series, southerners were told about the necessity of industrialization, diversification, immigration, and reconciliation alongside remembrance of a sanctified past.[33]

The sentiments of economic revival thus transcended the border, but it was in Mexico that they took on larger dimensions of economic liberalism. Some business promoters in the South likewise recognized the wellspring of opportunities running westward and across the border. In May 1869 Charles Anderson, William M. Anderson's younger brother, presided over the first post–Civil War Southern Commercial Convention in Memphis, Tennessee. As a Republican who spoke against southern slaveholding before the war and a partial-term governor of Ohio during it, Charles struck different political chords than his brother William had. Yet they both shared an interest in reviving the South through expanding the commercial agriculture base of the region and forging larger connections with Latin America and beyond. The need for a southern railroad link to the Pacific Ocean was a top priority, along with steamship lines connecting the South to Europe and South America.[34] A few years before this convention, the revived idea of a southern transcontinental route was likewise circulated in such publications as *DeBow's Review*, which voiced support for a railroad line going through "the Southern part of Texas, thence to Monterey, with Guayamas," Mexico, as its terminal point on the Pacific.[35] This idea of connecting the South to Mexico and establishing reciprocal trade ran parallel to plans for southern colonization.

In July 1869 another business convention, this one held at the Greenlaw Opera House in Memphis, specifically connected with southern colonization in Mexico. Presiding as this convention's chairman was the ex-governor of Tennessee and returned southern migrant Isham G. Harris. Harris had migrated to Mexico in early July 1865 and became highly involved with the planning of the Carlota colony, where he acquired 640 acres of land for a coffee plantation on which he planned to "nestle down, constantly inhaling the odors of the rich tropical fruits, and gaudy, colored, and fragrant tropical flowers." By March 1867, however, Harris had left Mexico, first for England and then for Tennessee (in late November), bringing back with him ideas for "coolie" labor. Harris appointed a committee at the Memphis convention that endorsed the recruitment of contract Chinese laborers for the South. This unfree labor proposal mixed with ideas about building railroads and agricultural development in ways that aligned with Henry W. Allen's labor solutions in Mexico. The layered circuits of economic development were transported back to the South by returning southerners such as Harris, who had given up on Mexico but not on visions of how to resurrect their social and economic position in the postemancipation world. Harris was not transporting dreams of economic and social equality, but he did reflect the influence of economic modernizing priorities that came to more fully define southern plans in Mexico by the late 1860s and early 1870s.[36]

As the previous head of Mexican colonization, Matthew F. Maury had carried back his own sort of modernizing vision to Virginia. Before he died in 1871, Maury focused on the opportunities abounding from Norfolk as a seaport and railroad terminus for two potential transcontinental railroads. He also looked across the Atlantic Ocean and revived ideas about direct steamship lines to Europe. Maury especially favored steamers running from Norfolk to Holland. While veering away from his past inclinations for unfree labor, Maury maintained his belief in immigration. This time he foresaw European immigrants streaming into the South through Norfolk. Immigrants, steamships, and railroads would not only rebuild the South, he thought, but also produce conduits of exchange with South America. Maury's time in Mexico bolstered his vision of hemispheric trade, which he readily applied to a rebounded complex of southern economic inspirations.[37]

As one of the main leaders of colonization in Mexico after Maury's departure, Jo Shelby also became involved with railroads in the South after he returned to Missouri in the summer of 1867. Shelby carried back his experience in overseeing railroad construction and running a freighting line from Vera Cruz to Mexico City. In 1869 he became involved in two Missouri railway projects: in the first, he was elected director of a line that ran from Lexington to St. Louis; the second was a St. Louis and Santa Fe line that dissolved in a bond scandal, although Shelby was not implicated in it.[38] The first project had been planned before the war and was resurrected during the era of postwar railroad building in the United States. Shelby's developmental ideas were more insular to the South but still carried a modernizing impulse that placed the South looking outward to the West and beyond its shores. Another indication of his desire to push the South outward was how Shelby distanced himself from the Lost Cause and bygone plantations by supporting immigration into Missouri to advance its industrial economy. As one account indicates, Shelby "mocked as 'mossbacks' those who wanted to hold on to antebellum notions of Missouri as a transplanted medieval Scotland."[39] Shelby was among a cadre of southerners who searched for economic engines of progress and mobility for the South after the Civil War.

These planners of southern colonization in Mexico continued to plot a course of economic development even after their dreams of establishing Mexican agricultural colonies had evaporated. We can thus see the influence of their time in Mexico and how they transported back to the South ideas that continued to look toward biregional and hemispheric economic connections. They were part of postwar U.S. expansionist tendencies but inclined to bestow the economic blessings upon the South and Mexico. These promoters reached out to the hemispheric possibilities of economic development as they had during the colonization venture. They helped instill new pathways of prosperity and steer a course of transnational connections between the United States and Mexico during the second half of the nineteenth century.

Conclusion
Regions and Nations

The leaders of southern colonization in Mexico were not the only ones who instilled the American South with a sense of economic promise after the Civil War. The actions of more average white migrants also carved out, or attempted to carve out, new pathways of prosperity along the U.S.-Mexico border. Southwestward-moving white migrants moved against a dependent economic relationship that came to characterize the U.S. North and South after the Civil War. Paradoxically, they did so by drawing on their antebellum habits of migration—moving west to new lands with unfree labor—that had originally stunted the South's economic growth. The main difference after the war was that they moved without slaves—either taking former slaves or not taking laborers at all—and sought to create agricultural colonies in Mexico and take part in a brisk hemispheric trade. They set out on a new course toward upward mobility after the prospects of advancement through slave labor had vanished. In effect, they drove the agricultural profit game across the border once they determined that Mexico represented a better opportunity, and they sought to create agricultural sites of transnational exchange.

During the antebellum period, high rates of migration for large and small slaveholders spoke to the fact that they were not so much interested in investing in land as in investing in slaves and taking those slaves to more fertile agricultural surroundings. Small slave-holders who sought out new lands to be worked by their slave labor force may have been acquisitive and motivated by self-interest (some-what akin to their northern neighbors), but they carried with them a set of calculations different from those in a free-labor society. That is, aspiring small planters' first consideration was whether a new geo-graphic area would allow them to more fully capitalize on their slave labor investment as well as acquire more slaves.[1]

With the slave system abolished at the end of the Civil War, these "laborlords" mostly transitioned to "landlords," Gavin Wright has ar-gued, as the basis of wealth shifted to investment in land rather than slaves. This development helped reorient farming toward investment in particular localities (a "localization of economic life") rather than movement onward to greener pastures with a movable labor force.[2] However, the white southern migrants who went to Mexico did not follow this path but instead carried on with their antebellum tradi-tion of migration. They continued with a way of life that resisted the turn toward localized farm production, which tied landowners and workers to one location. Instead they sought out new lands in Mexi-co upon which to build a postwar life.

The example of John Henry Brown helps illustrate this point. Brown had moved southwestward from Missouri to Texas in 1845. During the Civil War he served as a private in the Texas Conscripts regiment. At the end of June 1865, he and his family left for Mexico. In his efforts to establish a colony in the Tuxpan region along the Gulf of Mexico, Brown captures the continued pursuit of upward mobility through migration. By 1868 this agricultural colony had attracted over fifty southern families to it. Among the crops they produced were coffee, cotton, sugar, rice, and tobacco. This colony, as we have seen, led the shift toward the coasts after the fall of Emperor Maximilian and con-tinued to grow into the 1870s.[3]

This movement of people across the border went against the eco-nomic dependency of the postwar South, even while it carried on with antebellum habits that were largely responsible for such dependency.[4] While the South did industrialize during the postwar period, it did so in a skewed and underdeveloped manner, as in North Carolina, with its focus on the cotton, textile, and tobacco industries, which resulted in a limited range of industries and industrial capabilities. The national bank system, government subsidies to railroads, and the concentration of capital in the North likewise moved the nation toward lopsided regional economic growth.[5] White southern migration to Mexico was an attempt to move beyond an isolated regional economy while, paradoxically, continuing with customs that had originally stunted the South's regional economic growth. White southerners such as the migrant group from Clinton, Texas, continued with the same antebellum impulses (except without slave labor), but instead of retarding economic growth, they were the forerunners of southern economic possibilities beyond the South.[6]

In some ways white southern migrants were correct about the South's future, although they were wrong about why it developed as it did. Many white southerners blamed the collapse of the slave system for the economic problems that ensued. They did not recognize that slavery had prevented the region from developing a balanced economy and placed it in a mostly dependent relationship with the North; they were also not prescient enough to see that sharecropping, a dependency on one crop, and a separate labor market would continue to trouble the postwar southern economy.[7] All the same, white southerners did move southwestward in hopes of improving their situation, with some five thousand pushing onward into Mexico, and by doing so they attempted to break beyond the boundaries of an increasingly hemmed-in southern economy and society. In this sense, white southern migration to Mexico helps recast the Reconstruction period in the South beyond the parameters of regional dependence.

Black southerners who went to Mexico likewise subtly influenced the postwar American South. Black southern migration to Mexico corresponded with other forms of African American agency in the Civil War and Reconstruction era. Whether through political mobilization, attempts to independently own land, efforts to obtain greater control over their own labor, or migration to Mexico, black southerners reflected a sense of what might be possible in the postemancipation

South. All of these efforts were geared at gaining a larger degree of economic and social control and autonomy. Moreover, black southern migration to Mexico set a precedent for renewed emigration to Liberia in the late 1860s and mid- to late 1870s.

As ex-slaves took to the roads in the early postwar period, in search of family members, food, or better work conditions, they made strides toward securing new freedoms. These mobile freed people sought out new lands or cities upon which to erect their postwar independence. At a base level, they pushed for greater control over their own labor. As the Union major general and Republican politician Carl Schurz reported from his tour of the South in the summer of 1865, there was tremendous opposition from white southerners against "the negro's controlling his own labor, carrying on business independently on his own account—in one word, working for his own benefit."[8] Some former slaves took this quest for greater control over their work lives all the way across the border.

Obtaining a degree of control over their own economic freedom was a top priority for African Americans in the postwar South. That meant getting out from under white southern control. Black southerners sought independent ownership of land during Reconstruction as a means to gain economic autonomy. The drive for land was a large motivating factor for African Americans who remained in the South as well as those who sought to leave the region behind. While some freed people who stayed in the South refused to sign labor contracts or to leave plantations, in an effort to claim a portion of plantation lands as their own with the justification that they had labored on it for years (especially in the Lowcountry of South Carolina and Georgia), former slaves who took to the road pursued another course of action to obtain a larger degree of control over their economic and social lives.[9] They either tried to use their ex-masters as a means of gaining landownership in a new country or state or left on their own with a bold determination to obtain work or land independently. We can think of Domingo in Córdoba and James Boyd in Matamoros as examples of black southern migrants who were able to work more independently in Mexico and perhaps inspired other African Americans.

Black southern migration to Mexico and elsewhere across the South corresponds with other forms of African American agency in the post-war period. For instance, many African Americans joined local Union League chapters and Republican clubs or participated in other forms of grassroots political mobilization in the South in order to exercise their newly won independence.[10] Most black southerners entered their postemancipation lives without any means to purchase land or any access to credit, so they had to rely on whatever tools were available in order to advance themselves. They confronted a situation in which whites owned the land and so black southerners increasingly had to accept work for wages or shares. This reality became more certain in early 1866, when the prospect of gaining land through redistribution or purchase dried up and most black southerners reluctantly signed labor contracts as sharecroppers in order to survive. This compromise between owning land and gang labor cemented the sharecropping system in to place in the cotton South.[11] Nonetheless, African Americans continued to push for landownership either by fighting for it in the South or by leaving their homes in hope of finding it elsewhere.

William D. Kelley, the Pennsylvania congressman who would become a strong proponent of the New South movement, offered advice to freed people. In 1867, while he toured the South, Kelley called for former slaves "to get independence for themselves by mechanical pursuits and by acquiring land." This message echoed the later sentiments of Booker T. Washington and his appeal to black southerners to pursue economic equality through agricultural and industrial education and work before grasping for social equality. As freed people already knew, one practical strategy for economic advancement was to move about, perhaps across the border, and push for better wages to enable them to buy land. Kelley likewise encouraged freed people to get farms through the Homestead Act of 1862, a federal government program that had opened up lands in the West.[12] Some black southerners did pursue this course of action, seeking out better opportunities in the American Southwest and northern Mexico.

Black and white southern migration to Mexico ultimately brings together nineteenth-century U.S. and Mexican history. This movement of southern leaders of colonization and more average southerners helps demonstrate that the histories of the American South and Southwest and Mexico are linked together. In the U.S.-Mexico borderlands we can see these connections most clearly, bringing together regions and nations.

Many of the white southerners moving southwest across the border believed they were charging across presumably empty space, or at least space inhabited by bands of "marauding Indians" who did not legitimately occupy the borderland region. Clearly Indians within this space thought otherwise and attempted to retain control of an area that they had lived in for centuries. Mexicans along the border also vied for power and autonomy from both the national Mexican government and U.S. encroachment.

The U.S.-Mexico borderlands reflected a process and place of contestation during an era of unclear national directions and outcomes. The political and economic outlook hung in the balance between nations and regions into the mid-1870s and beyond, while the United States and Mexico forged transregional, transnational, and hemispheric connections. By the late 1860s and early 1870s, southern migration to Mexico contributed to these multiple connections through its concerted efforts at bridging borders for mutual benefits. Alongside U.S. business ventures, southern economic plans sought out routes of hemispheric trade but pressed in directions that would not have left such lopsided growth. Always an imperfect process, and filled with more failure than achievement, the southern exodus to Mexico was both part of U.S. expansionism and a departure from it, helping frame the way we should interpret U.S. and Mexican history during the second half of the nineteenth century.

Notes

Abbreviations

AFP, HL   Anderson Family Papers, Manuscripts Department, Huntington Library, San Marino CA

AGEC   Archivo General del Estado de Coahuila, Ramos Arizpe, Mexico (C = caja, F = fólder, E = expediente; all cited materials were translated from Spanish to English by the author)

FHC   Los Angeles Regional Family History Center, Church of Latter-Day Saints, Los Angeles

IMN   Independent Mexico in Newspapers, Nineteenth Century, Reel 259, Nettie Lee Benson Latin American Collection, University of Texas at Austin

LSU   Middleton Library, Louisiana State University, Baton Rouge

MT   *Mexican Times*, Microfilm N51, Huntington Library, San Marino CA

VHS   Virginia Historical Society, Richmond

Introduction

1. [Isham G. Harris], "The Rebels in Mexico: Interesting Letter from Ex-governor Isham G. Harris, of Tennessee," *New York Herald*, December 18, 1865, Proquest Civil War Era, 1 (quotes); Elliott, *Isham G. Harris of Tennessee*, 182–86.

2. [Harris], "Rebels in Mexico," 1.

3. For two recent studies that reveal the impact of raiding on northern Mexico, see DeLay, *War of a Thousand Deserts*; and Hämäläinen, *Comanche Empire*.

4. For an account that underscores the ways in which white supremacy and reconciliation based on racial exclusion provided the common bond to reunite northern and southern whites after the Civil War, see Blight, *Race and Reunion*.

5. For an overview of the French Intervention in Mexico and the reasons behind it, see Cunningham, *Mexico and the Foreign Policy of Napoleon III*; Wasserman, *Everyday Life and Politics*, 112–16; Ridley, *Maximilian and Juárez*; Hanna and Hanna, *Napoleon III and Mexico*; Corti, *Maximilian and Charlotte of Mexico*.

6. Ridley, *Maximilian and Juárez*, 102–10, 121–31, 158–75; Hanna and Hanna, *Napoleon III and Mexico*, xiii–xv, 7, 85–89, 108–9, 133–35; Hanna and Hanna, "Immigration Movement of the Intervention."

7. Rolle, *Lost Cause*, 211. Similarly, William C. Davis concludes, "The Confederates failed due to their own inabilities, illusions, and poor adaptability to the wild country in which they settled." Davis, "Confederate Exiles," 43.

8. Robert C. Black III supports Rolle's conclusion when he writes that "the Confederate hegira to Mexico was no more than an intriguing episode in the disintegration of the southern effort at independence, of no lasting importance to the South, to Mexico, or to the emigrants themselves." Black, "Review of *The Lost Cause*," 702. A recent study of ex-Confederate Charles Swett's journey to British Honduras recounts the existing interpretation of Confederate migration to Latin America after the Civil War. The authors frame the movement to Mexico as an effort by "diehard 'Chivalrics,'" politicians, and other Confederate elites who were engaged in a doomed enterprise from the start. See Strom and Weaver, *Confederates in the Tropics*, 23–25, quote on 23.

9. For two recent works that analyze this Caribbean context, see Rugemer, *Problem of Emancipation*; Guterl, *American Mediterranean*. The initial strategy of ex-planters in the South sought to keep ex-slaves in near-bondage conditions by restricting property ownership, work contracts, and even the movement of African Americans. The Civil Rights Act of 1866 and the Fourteenth Amendment counteracted these state laws. See Foner, *Reconstruction*, 239–80.

10. M. F. Maury, "Mexico and the South," newspaper article written in London, March 26, 1866, in Minor Family Papers, Section 72, VHS.

11. Davis, "Confederate Exiles," 32–33. As one study has indicated, Confederate officers seemed most ready to emigrate during two periods of time: (1) from the spring of 1865 to the early part of 1866, and (2) from the spring of 1867 to the end of 1868. During the first period, high-ranking Confederates feared reprisals and left the country, but they started to feel more reassured when President Andrew Johnson vetoed the Freedmen's Bureau Bill and the Civil Rights Act in early 1866, indicating a more lenient course for Reconstruction. Johnson's actions helped assuage the fears of some Confederates, who remained in the South or started to return to the United States (especially to Virginia and South Carolina). During the second period, Congress eventually passed the vetoed bills and the president's coalition suffered a serious setback in the congressional elections of 1866. By March 1867, with the first of Reconstruction Acts passed, a renewed panic ensued in the South, sparking a new wave of southern resolution to escape Republican oppression. See Sutherland, *Confederate Carpetbaggers*, 25–27.

12. Sutherland, *Confederate Carpetbaggers*, 18; May, *Southern Dream of a Caribbean Empire*, 14 (quoting Wickliffe in the *Texas Republican*, January 28, 1859); Guterl, *American Mediterranean*, 16–28.

13. Griggs, *Elusive Eden*, 4–5, 10–11. McMullen's acquisitive spirit was reflected in his joining up with William Walker for his second failed attempt to seize Nicaragua in 1857.

14. Cyrus B. Dawsey and James M. Dawsey, "Leaving: The Context of the Southern Emigration to Brazil," in Dawsey and Dawsey, *Confederados*, 11–23. Brazil did not abolish slavery until 1888, and it accorded formal belligerent status to the Confederacy while harboring and supplying southern ships.

15. Dawsey and Dawsey, *Confederados*, 27–35, quote on 27. McMullan's hopes of a prosperous future ran into difficulties when he returned to the United States in June 1866. First he discovered that Brazilian officials had simultaneously made an agreement with the United States that only the Brazil Steamship Company running from New York would provide transportation for American emigrants. While he worked through this problem, McMullan struggled to find and secure a suitable ship to transport the growing number of interested Texans. Even when he found the brig *Derby* to sail from New Orleans to Galveston, Texas, where the migrants would be waiting, he had to fend off multiple attempts to detain the ship through fines and repairs. Shortly after setting sail in January 1867, the troubles continued when the ship (with over 150 passengers) encountered a storm and hit a reef off Cuba. The migrants were stranded and had to make arrangements to go back to New York before they could finally sail for Brazil.

16. "The American Colony in Mexico," *DeBow's Review* (New Orleans) 1, no. 6 (June 1866), ProQuest American Periodical Series, 623; "A Visit to a Confederate Settlement in Mexico," *New York Tribune*, February 3, 1866, ProQuest Historical Newspapers, 9. The correspondent visited the Córdova district and the Carlota colony and met, among others, former judge John Perkins of Louisiana, who was the land agent of the region.

17. Matthew Fontaine Maury, "Letter Regarding the Possibilities for Colonization," from the Office of Colonization, February 7, 1866, 1–2, Manuscripts Dept., VHS.

18. Maury's emphasis on Mexico as a land with Eden-like qualities particularly connects with the boosterism of the "New West" promotional literature. See Wrobel, *Promised Lands*, chap. 1., esp. 29–45. For examples of how Maury linked geography with economic development, see Maury, "Railroad from the Atlantic to the Pacific; and Maury, *Amazon, and the Atlantic Slopes*. For an analysis of his scientific career, see Hearn, *Tracks in the Sea*.

19. Robert E. Lee to M. F. Maury, September 8, 1865, near Cartersville VA, Mss2 L515 a 32, Manuscripts Dept., VHS; *Richmond Daily Dispatch*, January 11, 1866, VHS; and *Richmond Dispatch*, January 31, 1866, VHS.

20. M. F. Maury, "Mexico and the South," newspaper article, March 26, 1866, VHS. For a study on the young Virginia field officers who reflected this duty to their home state, see Carmichael, *Last Generation*.

21. Robert Lewis Dabney to Charles Dabney, January 27, 1866, and Dabney to unknown recipient, March 1866, Dabney Family Papers, Section I, VHS. As the *Mexican Times* reported, a former surgeon in the Confederate army named Dr. Massie had recently returned to his home state and indicated that "the very best classes of the people of Virginia" were contemplating emigration either to another state like Texas or outside the country. In fact, he said, "There is a furor in the State on that subject." See *MT*, November 4, 1865.

22. Davis, "Confederate Exiles," 35–37, 41.

23. Rolle, *Lost Cause*, xi (quote). Other studies include Nunn, *Escape from Reconstruction*; Rister, "Carlota"; and Knapp, "New Source on the Confederate Exodus."

24. Most notably, Rolle, *Lost Cause*; Davis, "Confederate Exiles"; and Rister, "Carlota."

25. Rolle, *Lost Cause*, 93, 104–5; Nunn, *Escape from Reconstruction*, 51, 57–59.

26. Harmon, "Confederate Migrations to Mexico," 477–82; Nunn, *Escape from Reconstruction*, 79–101; Davis, "Confederate Exiles," 38–43; Rolle, *Lost Cause*, 139–86.

27. Minor, *Light Gray People*, ix, 109–10. As Minor writes, captive taking was prevalent among the Lipan Apaches, but because of Apache matrilineal social organization it was not as central to their cultural practices as it was to the Comanches. The capture of children, particularly boys ages nine to thirteen, was "a secondary strategy," with Apache women having power over the decision about incorporating captives into the group as potential sons-in-law (118–19). For a brief review of Kickapoo history and motivations for raiding, see Gesick, "Historical Essay." For studies on the Comanches, see the notes to chapter 3.

28. Antebellum southern railroad promoters had previously touted the benefits that railroads would bring to the American South. In the late 1850s, for example, they envisioned the Charleston and Savannah Railroad as a connecting link between Asia and New Orleans. See Majewski, *Modernizing a Slave Economy*, 94, 203n39. Likewise, northern promoters sought out Mexico with modernizing dreams of their own after the Civil War. See Hart, *Empire and Revolution*; and Truett, *Fugitive Landscapes*.

29. This sentence alludes to an important work on the Lost Cause and New South movements by Gaines M. Foster, *Ghosts of the Confederacy: Defeat, the Lost Cause, and the Emergence of the New South*. Foster places memorial associations,

the Southern Historical Society, the United Confederate Veterans, and the United Daughters of the Confederacy at the center of molding "Southern perceptions of defeat" and the "Confederate tradition, the dominant complex of attitudes and emotions that constituted the white South's interpretation of the Civil War" (5). That is, the Lost Cause formed around a continued belief in the justness of slavery and secession and the honor in defending the region from Yankee influence. Other important works on the Lost Cause and New South movements and their intersections include Gallagher and Nolan, *Myth of the Lost Cause*; Wilson, *Baptized in Blood*; Osterweis, *Myth of the Lost Cause*; and Gaston, *New South Creed*.

30. For the Científicos, see Hale, *Transformation of Liberalism*, 27–29, 102–4, 123–28. Los Científicos was a name given by the opposition; the official name was the National Liberal Union.

1. Migration across the Borderlands

1. Terrell, *From Texas to Mexico*, vii–10.

2. Gould, *Alexander Watkins Terrell*, 37–47. The next day at Pleasant Hill, Terrell, along with one of his companies, was cut off from the main Confederate force, but they managed to elude capture by marching behind Union lines that night to rejoin his regiment the next morning. The Red River campaign, whereby the Union sought to commandeer the rest of Louisiana and capture Texas, marked a late Confederate victory in the western theater of the Civil War. Afterward, in the fall of 1864, Terrell gained command of three regiments (equivalent to a brigade), and by war's end he was promoted to brigadier general. Although a Virginian by birth, Terrell had moved as a child with his family to Missouri, following a westward-gazing path that many southerners took in the antebellum period. Since 1852 he had lived in Texas, where he subsequently became a district judge and came to support the Confederacy's strike for independence.

3. Terrell, *From Texas to Mexico*, 2, 11–21, quote on 11; J. Thompson, *Cortina*, 37–39; Rolle, *Lost Cause*, 50; Shalhope, *Sterling Price*, 102, 179–84. After Price captured Lexington, Missouri, in late September 1861, his name began to appear in such southern newspapers such as the *Natchez Daily Courier* and *Daily Richmond Whig*, the latter of which ranked the "Brilliant Success in Missouri" second only to Manassas as the greatest victory of the war.

4. Sheridan, *Personal Memoirs*, 208–10. Sheridan had received orders from Lieutenant General Ulysses S. Grant on May 17, 1865, assigning him "command west of the Mississippi" in order "to restore Texas, and that part of Louisiana held by the enemy, to the Union in the shortest practicable time" (208).

5. Sheridan, *Personal Memoirs*, 211–12; Sheridan, *Report of Operations*, 3, 6.

6. Davis, "Confederate Exiles"; MT, January 6, 1866; Rolle, *Lost Cause*, 123–24.

7. Gallagher, "Jubal A. Early," 37, quote from a letter to John Goode, June 8, 1866.

8. For Maury's scientific achievements, see Hearn, *Tracks in the Sea*. Examples of Maury's economic thinking include "Railroad from the Atlantic to the Pacific"; and "On Extending the Commerce of the South and West by Sea," *DeBow's Review* (New Orleans) 2 (April 1852): 381–99.

9. A recent study by Sarah E. Cornell argues that Confederate migration to Mexico was based on the "hope that a system of unfree, racialized labor could be developed on the continent outside the purview of the victorious North." Cornell, "Americans in the U.S. South and Mexico," 189–90, quote on 189. This is a valuable insight, but it continues to frame southern colonization and migration as a movement solely bent on re-creating the Old South on slightly new terms and thus aligns with previous studies cited in the introduction.

10. J. Miller, *South by Southwest*, 35–60, quote on 50.

11. During the 1820s and 1830s nearly 30,000 Anglo-Americans had arrived in Texas. The population rose to 160,000 by 1845 and to 600,000 by 1860. After Texan independence in 1836, the number of slaves who accompanied these white migrants rose dramatically too; by 1860 they represented almost one-third of the population. See Anderson, *Conquest of Texas*, 3–4. Put another way, from 1850 to 1860 the population of Texas tripled, with half of the increase from slaves, and the number of slaveholders climbed from about eight thousand to almost twenty thousand. See J. Miller, *South by Southwest*, 124; Oakes, *Ruling Race*, 72–81, statistics on 79. As Oakes states, "There was no period before the Civil War when this massive movement of slaveholders slowed down for long. Indeed, it reached its climax with the migration into Texas in the 1850's" (79).

12. Oakes, *Ruling Race*, 79, 73–77, quote on 74. The movement of white Southerners from the coastal region had continued right past neighboring states like Alabama. By 1850 about one-fourth of Alabama's native-born free population already lived beyond the state's borders. In the next ten years, Alabama, Louisiana, and Mississippi actually saw more departures than arrivals. See J. Miller, *South by Southwest*, 124.

13. J. Miller, *South by Southwest*, 89–93. Manifest destiny certainly influenced the course of southern migration before the Civil War. Westward-moving slaveholders saw no reason why slavery should not be an engine driving forward economic growth and social mobility. See Morrison, *Slavery and the American West*, 115–47.

14. Starr, *Americans and the California Dream*, 65.

15. Truett, *Fugitive Landscapes*, 36–37. For works that speak to the idea of multiple "Wests" and the different experiences of nineteenth-century westward migration, see Casper and Long, *Moving Stories*, especially the essay by Gioia Woods, "Multiple Places, Multiple Selves"; and Cronon, Miles, and Gitlin, *Under*

an Open Sky, especially Sarah Deutsch, "Landscape of Enclaves: Race Relations in the West, 1865–1900."

16. Truett, *Fugitive Landscapes*, 38–49, quote on 39.

17. Schoonover, "Dollars over Dominion," 43; Olliff, *Reforma Mexico and the United States*, 65–82.

18. Tyler, *Santiago Vidaurri and the Southern Confederacy*, 55–58; Schoonover, "Dollars over Dominion," 43–44. As Tyler explains, Vidaurri went a step further than Quintero and proposed the annexation of northern Mexico to the Confederacy. This move was primarily aimed at securing greater leverage and protection for this northern caudillo; Confederate president Jefferson Davis declined the offer.

19. *MT*, September 16, 1865.

20. Corbin, *Life of Matthew Fontaine Maury*, 235.

21. Emmons, *Beyond the American Pale*, 127, 220–21 (quotes). For a recent reassessment of the layers and meanings of Confederate nationalism, see Bonner, *Mastering America*, esp. chaps. 7–9.

22. Truett, *Fugitive Landscapes*, 120–28.

23. Emmons, *Beyond the American Pale*, 213–16, 224–27, quotes on 213, 226.

24. Painter, *Exodusters*, 137–38 (quote); Hahn, *Nation under Our Feet*, chap. 7.

25. May, *Manifest Destiny's Underworld*, 20–38.

26. May, *Manifest Destiny's Underworld*, 40–43, 47–52.

27. May, *Southern Dream of a Caribbean Empire*, 138–39, 149, 150 (quote from Bickley to E. H. Cushing, editor of the *Houston Telegraph*, November 15, 1860); May, *Manifest Destiny's Underworld*, 44–45.

28. Gwin, *Speech of Mr. Gwin*; H. McPherson, "Plan of William McKendree Gwin," 357–58, 364–69, 374; Perrin, "Exodus of Southerners," 578–89; Hanna and Hanna, *Napoleon III and Mexico*, 167–68.

29. H. McPherson, "Plan of William McKendree Gwin," 386.

30. Terrell, *From Texas to Mexico*, 42–43, quotes on 43.

31. Beginning at the end of 1861, Maury was usually addressed as "Commodore" after he was placed in charge of constructing a fleet of gunboats for the Confederate navy. Although it was not an official rank in the Confederate Navy, this title refers to a captain commanding more than one ship. See Williams, *Matthew Fontaine Maury*, 386, 615–16n126.

32. The "Register of the Names of Emigrants from the United States" in the first issue of the *Mexican Times* indicates that Maury arrived on June 1, 1865. *MT*, September 16, 1865; Corbin, *Life of Matthew Fontaine Maury*, 225–26, 229.

33. Corbin, *Life of Matthew Fontaine Maury*, 25–26, 40–45, 56; Williams, *Matthew Fontaine Maury*, 27–33; Maury, *Physical Geography of the Sea*.

34. Maury, *Amazon, and the Atlantic Slopes*, 6, 49. See also Matthew Fontaine Maury, "On Extending the Commerce of the South and West by Sea," *DeBow's Review* (New Orleans) 2 (April 1852): 381–99; Dozer, "Matthew Fontaine Maury's Letter of Introduction."

35. "Project," included in Matthew Fontaine Maury to Richard Maury, June 27, 1865, and Richard Maury to Robert E. Lee, July 22, 1865, Robert E. Lee Headquarters Papers, Series II, Folder 32, Manuscripts Dept., VHS. While he was in Cuba, Maury expressed some of his ideas on colonization and establishing a "New Virginia" in Mexico in a letter to Francis W. Tremlett on May 19, 1865. Hanna, "Role of Matthew Fontaine Maury," 109. As Maury's daughter later wrote, Maury had formulated "a grand scheme in his mind for the colonization of a New Virginia in Mexico." Corbin, *Life of Matthew Fontaine Maury*, 232. Previous historians have also noted this objective. For example, Hanna, "Role of Matthew Fontaine Maury"; Hanna and Hanna, *Napoleon III and Mexico*, chap. 20; and Rolle, *Lost Cause*, 137.

36. Matthew Fontaine Maury to Rev. Francis W. Tremlett, August 8, 1865, in Corbin, *Life of Matthew Fontaine Maury*, 230–31.

37. First two quotes from Maury to Tremlett, August 8, 1865, in Corbin, *Life of Matthew Fontaine Maury*, 230–31; third quote, M. F. Maury to Mrs. Mary Minor Blackford (his cousin), December 24, 1851, in Corbin, *Life of Matthew Fontaine Maury*, 130–32 (Maury's emphasis); Williams, *Matthew Fontaine Maury*, 10–15, 596n3. For Maury's gradual emancipation views, see also Maury, *Amazon, and the Atlantic Slopes*. Other advocates of the "draining off" of the slave population included Thomas Jefferson and Robert J. Walker, senator from Mississippi. Walter Johnson, in *River of Dark Dreams: Slavery and Empire in the Cotton Kingdom*, recognizes Maury's ideas about draining away the slave population from the South during the antebellum period but emphasizes Maury's efforts to develop "a pro-slavery commercial empire centered in the Mississippi Valley." W. Johnson, *River of Dark Dreams*, 280–81, 296–302, quote on 298.

38. Matthew Fontaine Maury, "Mexico and the South," newspaper article written in London, March 26, 1866, in Minor Family Papers, Section 72, VHS. Another example of Maury's publication efforts is his "Letter Regarding the Possibilities for Colonization" from February 7, 1866, which was printed in *DeBow's Review* (New Orleans) as "The American Colony in Mexico" in June 1866. A copy of the original letter can be found in the Manuscripts Department of the Virginia Historical Society and at the Huntington Library.

39. M. F. Maury to Richard Maury, June 27, 1865, Lee Headquarters Papers, Series II, Folder 32, Manuscripts Dept., VHS (Maury's emphasis). Maury submitted his proposal, entitled "Project of a Design to Encourage the Immigration

into Mexico of Planters from Virginia and the South with their Freed Slaves," to Emperor Maximilian on June 11, 1865. See Hanna, "Role of Matthew Fontaine Maury," 112.

40. M. F. Maury to Richard Maury, June 27, 1865, items 5 and 6 of the "Project," Lee Headquarters Papers, Series II, Folder 32, Manuscripts Dept., VHS. Maury specified that apprentices of twenty-one years of age and older would serve for not less than ten years; those under age twenty-one would serve twenty-one years.

41. Matthew Fontaine Maury to Robert E. Lee, August 8, 1865, and item 6 of the "Project," June 27, 1865, Lee Headquarters Papers, Series II, Folder 32, Manuscripts Dept., VHS.

42. Maximilian's Decree and Regulation, September 5, 1865, in U.S. Congress, *Message of the President*, 29–30, VHS. See also Corbin, *Life of Matthew Fontaine Maury*, 234; and Hanna, "Role of Matthew Fontaine Maury," 115–16. Maximilian actually adopted some of Maury's ideas outright, such as religious freedom and exemption from military service for five years. Given the Catholic heritage of Mexico, freedom of religion was a topic of particular concern for potential migrants and one that Maury addressed directly in a meeting with Emperor Maximilian after the publication of the official decree. Among other questions, Maury asked the emperor, "Will Protestant clergymen be tolerated and permitted to enjoy their religious opinions and worship in these colonies, without molestation?" To which Maximilian replied, "Yes, and encouraged." See Matthew Fontaine Maury, "Letter Regarding the Possibilities for Colonization," Office of Colonization Mexico, February 7, 1866, 4, Manuscripts Dept., VHS.

43. Guterl, *American Mediterranean*, chaps. 4–5; Holt, *Problem of Freedom*, 55–61; Foner, *Nothing but Freedom*, 43.

44. Rugemer, *Problem of Emancipation*, 3–4, 185–97, 261–62, quote on 191. Rugemer stresses how British abolitionists drove this fear of insurrection in Jamaica and in the United States. British abolitionist agitation, he argues, inspired slave rebellions in Barbados (1816), Demerara (1823), and Jamaica (1831), and it played a key role in Nat Turner's Rebellion (1831).Together, these abolitionist-inspired rebellions drove southern slaveholder fears. See chaps. 2–4.

45. Rugemer, *Problem of Emancipation*, 164–70; Holt, *Problem of Freedom*, 55–61; Foner, *Nothing but Freedom*, 43.

46. Foner, *Reconstruction*, 199, 209, 372, 376; Craven, *Reconstruction*, 119–20. After passage of the Civil Rights Act of 1866 and the Reconstruction Acts of 1867, the Black Codes were dismantled.

47. Manuel Orosco y Berra, "Appointment, 1865 Septiembre 27, of Matthew Fontaine Maury as Imperial Commissioner of Colonization for the Empire of Mexico," Mss2 M4485 a 5, Manuscripts Dept., VHS; Matthew Fontaine Maury

to F. W. Tremlett, August 8, 1865, in Corbin, *Life of Matthew Fontaine Maury*, 231 (first quote); Corbin, *Life of Matthew Fontaine Maury*, 234 (second quote).

48. Sheridan, *Personal Memoirs*, 217–18.

49. Corbin, *Life of Matthew Fontaine Maury*, 235, 236.

50. Corbin, *Life of Matthew Fontaine Maury*, 232.

51. Corbin, *Life of Matthew Fontaine Maury*, 232.

52. Hale, *Mexican Liberalism in the Age of Mora*, 179; Hale, *Transformation of Liberalism*, chap. 7; Ruiz, *Triumphs and Tragedy*, 177–78.

53. Jarnagin, *Confluence of Transatlantic Networks*, 131–41.

54. Jarnagin, *Confluence of Transatlantic Networks*, 140–41, 219–20, 1–8.

55. See, for example, Henry Watkins Allen, in MT, September 16, 1865, and "The Empire of Mexico and its Great Resources," MT, September 30, 1865.

56. Mexican Diaries, April 18, 1865, February 8, 1866, and January 30, 1866, AFP, HL, Box 5.

57. Shalhope, *Sterling Price*, 283.

58. Shalhope, *Sterling Price*, 283–87, quote on 286.

59. Matthew Fontaine Maury, "Letter Regarding the Possibilities for Colonization," Office of Colonization Mexico, February 7, 1866, 3, Manuscripts Dept., VHS.

2. White and Black Southerners Migrate

1. Mexican Diaries, April 3, 1865, AFP, HL, Box 7.

2. Most notably, Rolle, *Lost Cause*; Davis, "Confederate Exiles";; Nunn, *Escape from Reconstruction*; Knapp, "New Source on the Confederate Exodus"; Rister, "Carlota"; Harmon, "Confederate Migrations to Mexico."

3. By bringing the subject of black and white migration together, this study follows the lead of James Gregory's study *The Southern Diaspora: How the Great Migrations of Black and White Southerners Transformed America*, on the twentieth-century migration of black and white Southerners to the U.S. North, Midwest, and West. As with Gregory's work, it is best to think of migration in this book in terms of the "circulation" of migrants rather than "as a one-way relocation because, in many instances [or most in this case], migrants at some point circle back toward home" (p. xii). As in *The Southern Diaspora*, white southern out-migration also outnumbered black southern out-migration by a large margin (see charts on 14–15).

4. Robert Marshall Anderson, "Summary Report and Biographical Sketch of William Marshall Anderson," November 1936, AFP, HL, Box 5, AD 64; Ruiz, *American in Maximilian's Mexico*, xxvi–xxviii.

5. Mexican Diaries, April 16, 1865, AFP, HL, Box 7; "A Visit to a Confederate Settlement in Mexico," *New York Tribune*, February 3, 1866, Microfilm N66:68,

Huntington Library, about a correspondent's visit to Córdoba on January 15, 1866; "Rebel Colony in Mexico," *New York Observer and Chronicle*, November 30, 1865, American Periodical Series Online, 382.

6. Based on an analysis of the migrant lists printed in the following issues of the *Mexican Times*: 1865: September 16, 23, 30; October 14, 21; November 4; 1866: January 27; February 3, 10, 17; March 10, 17, 24. Some of the total derives from an estimated count of families and from news items reprinted in the *Mexican Times*. For example, in the February 10, 1866, issue the newspaper reprinted accounts of migration from the *New York Daily News* and the *Memphis Appeal*, among others, for a total of about three hundred families who reportedly left for Mexico. There are no migrant lists after the March 24 issue, only scattered references to individuals and families.

7. The most common estimate of the total number of emigrants who left the South during the postwar period (approximately 1865 to the early 1870s) is eight thousand to ten thousand, with most going to Latin American and the majority of those going to Mexico. This "ballpark" figure would thus equal about six thousand to seven thousand total migrants who went to Mexico. Based on my analysis, this estimate seems too high; the total number was more likely around five thousand. See Rolle, *Lost Cause*, 9, 211; Davis, "Confederate Exiles," 32; Hanna, "Role of Matthew Fontaine Maury," 113–14; Harmon, "Confederate Migrations to Mexico," 469; Roark, *Masters without Slaves*, 121; Wyatt-Brown, *Shaping of Southern Culture*, 243; Strom and Weaver, *Confederates in the Tropics*, 4; Sutherland, "Exiles, Emigrants, and Sojourners," 238n2. Rolle estimates that the number of southerners who went to Mexico was probably less than five thousand (which is close to my estimate); Sutherland estimates that around twenty-five hundred went to Mexico and five thousand to Brazil. Gerald Horne, in *Deepest South*, 200, offers a "highly speculative guess" that around ten thousand southerners went to Brazil, also reflecting some historians' belief that the number of southerners who migrated to Brazil was higher than the number who went to Mexico.

8. *MT*, March 17, 1866; U.S. Census Bureau, 1860 Federal Census, Macon, Noxubee County MO, Roll M653_588,p. 8, Image 333, Ancestry.com; U.S. Census Bureau, 1860 Population Schedules, Slave Schedules, Noxubee County MO, Roll 602, Microcopy M-653, FHC. In the 1860 census, Lyles's occupation is listed as "planter," but this designation does not seem to fit, considering the definitions for a planter (see note 9) and that five out of his seven slaves were females (who usually were not as productive in the fields) and two were infants (one male, one female).

9. Oakes, *Ruling Race*, 51, 39, 249 (table C). As Oakes points out, "The average slaveholding was eight or nine, but the typical master owned fewer than that" (51). In other words, "The median slaveholding rarely strayed far from four to six

bondsmen per master" (39). As Oakes further indicates, the definition of a planter is a tricky one to pin down, given the variation between how historians (and contemporaries) have defined the term. He considers an owner of twenty slaves in 1860 (about 5 percent of slaveholders) to be "among the wealthiest men in America," (52). His larger point is not only that large slaveholders were a small proportion of southern society but also that boundaries between "slaveholder" and "planter" were very fluid and not static conceptions, not designated solely by the number of slaves owned (in some counties all farmers were designated as planters in the census records). In comparison, Kenneth M. Stampp defines a planter as an owner of at least twenty slaves (estimated at 12 percent of slave owners). Stampp places slaveholders into three groups: (1) fewer than ten slaves, (2) small planters with ten to thirty slaves, and (3) wealthy planters with thirty slaves or more. See Stampp, *Peculiar Institution*, 30, 36–38. As generally recognized, in 1850 about half of all slaveholders owned five or fewer slaves. Oakes, *Ruling Race*, 39.

10. *MT*, March 17, 1866; U.S. Census Bureau, 1860 Federal Census, Noxubee County MO, Roll M653_588, p. 23, Image 456 Ancestry.com; U.S. Census Bureau, 1860 Slave Schedules, Noxubee County MO, Roll 602, Microcopy M-653, FHC.

11. W. Johnson, *Soul by Soul*, 6, 26, 58.

12. U.S. Census Bureau, 1860 Slave Schedules, Noxubee County MO, Roll 602, Microcopy M-653, FHC; Fogel, *Without Consent or Contract*, 64–71.

13. U.S. National Park Service, Soldiers and Sailors Database, M818, rolls 15 and 7; M232, rolls 40 and 27; *MT*, March 17, 1866; U.S. Census Bureau, 1860 Federal Census, Lawrence MO, Roll M653_584, Image 325, Ancestry.com. At age thirty-one in 1860, J. A. McDonald more than likely served in one of the eight Mississippi infantry regiments that his name matches in the U.S. National Park Service, Soldiers and Sailors Database.

14. Gallagher, *Confederate War*, 28. Somewhere between 750,000 and 850,000 men fought for the Confederacy, representing 75 to 85 percent of the white military-age population. See also Long, *Civil War Day by Day*, 704–5.

15. *MT*, March 17, 1866, second migrant list in same issue as the first group from Mississippi; U.S. Census Bureau, 1860 Federal Census, DeSoto County MO, Roll M653_581, Image 231, Ancestry.com. The name that matches his initials is Henry C. Gillespie, but he was a lieutenant colonel in the Second Regiment of the Tennessee Cavalry.

16. A better-known Confederate officer named John Thrailkill also migrated to Mexico and arrived in October 1865. This other Thrailkill was a captain with the First Missouri Cavalry, F Company. The migrant John Thrailkill discussed above most likely served as a private with either the Twentieth Georgia

Infantry Division or the Thirty-Eighth Mississippi Cavalry. See U.S. National
Park Service, Soldiers and Sailors Database, M380, roll 14; M226, roll 60; M232,
roll 40; MT, October 21, 1865.

17. MT, January 26 and March 24, 1866; U.S. Census Bureau, 1860 Federal Census, Callaway County MO, Roll M653_610, Image 412, Ancestry.com; U.S. Census
Bureau, 1860 Federal Census, Mobile Ward 2 AL, Roll M653_17, p. 267, Image 268,
Ancestry.com. Ferguson most likely served in Company A of the Nineteenth
Alabama Infantry. His name matches with an E. C. Ferguson for that company. See U.S. National Park Service, Soldiers and Sailors Database, M374, roll 14.

18. As Donald Sutherland has argued, "Land, offered at unbelievably low
prices, sometimes free, served as the principal attraction for Latin American
emigration." Such attractions did not necessarily indicate a desire for slave labor
either, since ex-Confederates migrated west and north too. This was especially
true for these common white southerners. See Sutherland, "Exiles, Emigrants,
and Sojourners," 241.

19. They signed a statement on February 23, 1866, that placed four members
of the group in charge of making arrangements and contracts with the Mexican
government and had the document authorized by the district county court. MT,
March 24, 1866, statement reprinted with the heading "A Texas Colony for Mexico."

20. MT, March 24, 1866; U.S. Census Bureau, 1860 Federal Census, Clinton,
DeWitt County TX, Roll M653_1291, p. 460, Image 397, Ancestry.com; U.S. Census Bureau, 1860 Slave Schedules, DeWitt County TX, Roll 1309, Microcopy M-653,
FHC. Over half of his slave force had been under the age of twelve, which helps
explain a lower average value (under $1,000), and he also had only two slave cabins (in comparison, both Thomas and Lyles, each with eleven slaves, had three
cabins). William S. Booth might have served in the First Louisiana Cavalry Regiment, entering as a private and leaving as a second lieutenant. U.S. National
Park Service, Soldiers and Sailors Database, M378, roll 3. Booth's four sons were
named Russell, William, Gar, and John (ages thirty-five, twenty-seven, twenty-four, and twenty-two). His wife, Lucy, and two daughters, M. Catherine and Leander (ages twenty-nine and fourteen), did not make the initial trip.

21. MT, March 24, 1866; U.S. Census Bureau, 1860 Federal Census, DeWitt
County TX, Roll M653_1292, pp. 457 and 482, Images 390 and 440, Ancestry.com;
U.S. Census Bureau, 1860 Slave Schedules, DeWitt County TX, Roll 1309, Microcopy M-653, FHC. Felix B. Greer is listed with the First Mississippi Cavalry, Company G, with the rank of sergeant. The name Greer also appears with Company
C of the Houston Battalion, Texas Infantry, rank unknown, but most likely a
private. U.S. National Park Service, Soldiers and Sailors Database, M232, roll 16;
and M227, roll 14.

22. Milligan was originally from South Carolina and had his parents to support along with his wife. Stapp, who came from Kentucky, had a wife, three sons, and two daughters in his household. *MT*, March 24, 1866; U.S. Census Bureau, 1860 Federal Census, DeWitt TX, Roll M653_1292, pp. 470 and 457, Images 417 and 390, Ancestry.com. A Benjamin Milligan is listed with the Twenty-Seventh Georgia Infantry, Company I. This might have been the same person. If so, he was actually demoted from a sergeant to a private by the end of the war. See U.S. National Park Service, Soldiers and Sailors Database, M226, roll 42.

23. *MT*, March 24, 1866; U.S. Census Bureau, 1860 Federal Census, DeWitt TX, Roll M653_1292, pp. 456, 482, 457, and 499, Images: 388, 440, 391, and 474, Ancestry.com. M. V. King, the blacksmith, had served in the Confederate army as a private and then later as artificer in the Fourteenth Field Battery, Texas Light Artillery. Twenty matches appear for John R. Wright, but he most likely served in either the Tenth Confederate Cavalry, Company B, as a private, then corporal, or in the Twenty-Second Texas Infantry, Company H, as third and then first lieutenant. See U.S. National Park Service, Soldiers and Sailors Database, M227, roll 20; M818, roll 26.

24. *MT*, March 24, 1866; U.S. Census Bureau, 1860 Federal Census, DeWitt County TX, Roll M653_1292, p. 482, Image 440, Ancestry.com; U.S. Census Bureau, 1860 Slave Schedules, DeWitt County TX, Roll 1309, Microcopy M-653, FHC. According to family documents on Ancestry.com, Emerald Brigham (Nancy's husband) was born in 1793 in Massachusetts (not Mississippi), worked as a farmer, and died in 1863 in DeWitt County, Texas (at age seventy-three). In 1830 they married in Florida, then lived in Georgia. Nancy was born in 1806, probably in Florida (instead of Georgia) and died in Texas in 1890. Children: one son, Benjamin, and three daughters. See 1830, 1840, 1860, 1870, and 1880 Federal Censuses and Family Record and Family Tree, Ancestry.com. Table 2 compiled from same sources as for the above Texan migrants.

25. "Emigration," *MT*, March 24, 1866; "Colonization," *MT*, November 18, 1865; Sheridan, *Report of Operations*, 2. A. J. Hanna puts the figure at one thousand migrants by the early summer of 1865, but this estimate also seems too high (it probably reached this level by the fall). See Hanna, "Role of Matthew Fontaine Maury," 113–14.

26. Cyrus B. Dawsey and James M. Dawsey, "Leaving: The Context of the Southern Emigration to Brazil," in Dawsey and Dawsey, *Confederados*, 18.

27. Griggs, *Elusive Eden*, 50.

28. Griggs, *Elusive Eden*, 20–26, 24 (first quote), 26 (second quote).

29. *New Orleans Daily True Delta*, February 21, 1866, Microfilm 2038, Reel 28 (January 23, 1866, to March 30, 1866), LSU.

30. *New Orleans Daily True Delta*, August 4, 1865, Microfilm 2038, Reel 27, LSU.

31. Letter of Sterling Price, January 30, 1866, *New Orleans Times*, March 4, 1866, Microfilm NB719 (March 1 to April 30, 1866), LSU.

32. For the migrant group that Sheridan stopped, see *New Orleans Times*, February 18, 1866, and notice about the steamship *Savannah*, *New Orleans Times*, April 8, 1866, Microfilm NB719, (March 1 to April 30, 1866), LSU.

33. *New Orleans Daily True Delta*, August 29, 1865, from the *Matamoros Ranchero*, August 18, 1965, Microfilm 2038, Reel 27, LSU.

34. MT, January 27 and February 3, 1866.

35. *New Orleans Daily True Delta*, August 4, 1865, Microfilm 2038, Reel 27, LSU.

36. Litwack, *Been in the Storm So Long*, 30–33, quote on 33.

37. Rawick, *American Slave*, vol. 4, pt. 1, , 156–59, 202–11, quotes on 159 and 209; Rawick, *American Slave*, vol. 4, pt. 2, 71–72, quote from Mattie Gilmore on 72. The former slave Josh Miles recalled how in 1862 his former master brought all of his slaves from Richmond, Virginia, to Franklin, Texas—a trip that took two years. See Rawick, *American Slave*, vol. 5, pt. 3, 79–80.

38. Rawick, *American Slave*, vol. 4, pt. 1, 124, 130.

39. Isham G. Harris to George W. Adair, November 12, 1865, in U.S. Congress, *Message of the President*, 37, VHS; Rolle, *Lost Cause*, 79–81, 116, 119; MT, September 30, 1865.

40. Worley, "Letter Written by General Thomas C. Hindman," 367, quoting letter to Dr. J. C. Lee of San Antonio, Texas; reference to "Albert" in Rolle, *Lost Cause*, 119.

41. Litwack, *Been in the Storm So Long*, 41.

42. Rawick, *American Slave*, vol. 4, pt. 2, 188–89.

43. Elliott, *Isham G. Harris of Tennessee*, 183–86, 194.

44. Terrell, *From Texas to Mexico*, 8, 10.

45. Since its independence period, Mexico had a history of guarding emancipation. The federal act of July 13, 1824, specifically prohibited traffic in slaves from other countries; once slaves stepped foot on Mexican soil, they were automatically free. Mexican president Vicente Guerrero, himself a Mexican of African descent called "El Negrito," validated this de facto freedom by officially abolishing slavery on September 15, 1829. See R. Schwartz, *Across the Rio to Freedom*, 7, 13–14, 16, 24–26.

46. McHatton-Ripley, *From Flag to Flag*, 77, 86–88, 112, quote on 86.

47. McHatton-Ripley, *From Flag to Flag*, 119, 123; Guterl, *American Mediterranean*, 89–90. Apparently only one former slave remained with the McHattons when they went to Cuba at the end of the war.

48. Mexican Diaries, between July 6 and August 16, 1865 (no specific date recorded), in Diary for July 6 to November 20, 1865, AFP, HL, Box 7.

49. Tyler, "Fugitive Slaves in Mexico," 5–6. Rosalie Schwartz puts the estimate of fugitive slaves at three thousand. *Across the Rio to Freedom*, 33. Both of these figures may be inflated, but they nevertheless show "the difficulty that Texas slaveholders faced in holding onto their laborers," Nichols, "Line of Liberty," 414.

50. R. Schwartz, *Across the Rio to Freedom*, 7, 13–14, 16, 24–26, 32–33, 51, quote on 26, from *El Diario del Gobierno*, June 7, 1842; Tyler, "Fugitive Slaves in Mexico," 2; Nichols, "Line of Liberty," 417–18; Rawick, *American Slave*, vol. 4, pt. 1, 141 (quote). See also Mulroy, *Freedom on the Border*.

51. For an analysis of freed people's struggles over land and work contracts and the role of the Freedmen's Bureau, see Hahn et al., *Freedom*, 26–35, first quote from Joseph D. Pope to Major General Q. A. Gillmore, June 29, 1865, doc. 13, p. 108; second quote from Circular No.1, Freedmen's Bureau Superintendent at Camden, Arkansas, July 25, 1865, doc. 21, p. 144; Foner, *Reconstruction*, 153–70. General Oliver Otis Howard, commissioner of the Freedmen's Bureau, issued General Order 129 on July 25, 1865, in an effort to stop such discriminatory practices as limiting the movement of freed people.

52. Hahn et al., *Freedom*, 51–53, 56–60; Foner, *Reconstruction*, 198–204, 165–66; Litwack, *Been in the Storm So Long*, 323.

53. Rawick, *American Slave*, vol. 4, pt. 1, 117–18.

54. Rawick, *American Slave*, vol. 4, pt. 1, 118.

55. Rawick, *American Slave*, vol. 4, pt. 2, 130–32, quotes on 132. Haywood's parents had been purchased in Mississippi.

56. Hahn et al., *Freedom*, 38–39; Litwack, *Been in the Storm So Long*, 308–14, 322. For an example of railroad work, see Contract between Wilmington & Manchester Railroad Company and North Carolina Freedmen, August 26, 1865, in Hahn et al., *Freedom*, doc. 89, pp. 383–84.

57. Painter, *Exodusters*, 137–38. See also Hahn, *Nation under Our Feet*, chap. 7, esp. 318–37, 554n11.

58. Painter, *Exodusters*, 146–47, 184–85, quotes on 184, 191.

59. Rawick, *American Slave*, vol. 4, pt. 1, 108, 19–20. In addition to working in Texas, Wash Anderson ventured as far as Louisiana, Arkansas, and Oklahoma for employment.

60. El licenciado Francisco Garza Sepúlveda, juez de letras del distrito de Río Grande comunica al Secretario del Gobierno del Estado, February 23, 1875, Zaragoza, AGEC, Fondo Siglo XIX, C2, F3, E6; B. de Hoyos del ayuntamiento de Monclova al Presidente de Hidalgo, April 3, 1878, AGEC, Fondo Siglo XIX, C3, F1, E11; Julián Ríos, presidente municipal de la villa de Múzquiz, May 10, 1888, AGEC, Fondo Siglo XIX, C5, F8, E1. The last item discusses a land contract from 1884.

61. Jacoby, "Between North and South," 212–16, 221–23, quotes on 212, 213.

62. Rawick, *American Slave*, vol. 4, pt. 2, 132.

3. The Texas-Coahuila Borderlands

1. Anacleto R. Falcón, de la jefatura política y comandancia military del distri-to de Río Grande, comunica al Alcalde primero de Guerrero, May 30, 1865, AGEC, Fondo Siglo XIX, C2, F3, E6. The estimate of one thousand Confederates entering Mexico together was more than likely an exaggeration. They also probably split up into smaller groups before crossing the border, with some turning back.

2. Brown, *Two Years in Mexico*, 27.

3. Brown, *Two Years in Mexico*, 17–18; Worley, "Letter Written by General Thomas C. Hindman," 367.

4. Cassidy and Simpson, *Henry Watkins Allen of Louisiana*, 136–37 (first quote by Henry Davis of Allen's emigrant group); "To Emigrants," MT, March 24, 1866.

5. Cassidy and Simpson, *Henry Watkins Allen of Louisiana*, 137.

6. Hanna and Hanna, "Immigration Movement of the Intervention," 228; Knapp, "New Source on the Confederate Exodus." Clark also started the *Two Republics* newspaper after the empire fell.

7. Brown, *Two Years in Mexico*, 24; "American Colony at Tuxpan," *Two Republics*, February 29, 1868, IMN.

8. "Liberal Offer of Land for Colonization," MT, October 7, 1865. These offers of land in exchange for defense against Indian raids is very reminiscent of the situation in Texas in the 1830s.

9. J. O. Forns, "Ho for Mexico!," Notice to Emigrants, February 9, 1866, Manuscripts, Huntington Library.

10. Maury's response, with J. O. Forns Notice, February 10, 1866, Manuscripts, Huntington Library.

11. Forns, "Ho for Mexico!," Notice to Emigrants, February 9, 1866, Manuscripts, Huntington Library.

12. Matthew Fontaine Maury, "Letter Regarding the Possibilities for Colonization," Office of Colonization Mexico, February 7, 1866, 1, Manuscripts Dept., VHS.

13. Maury, "Letter Regarding the Possibilities for Colonization," Office of Colonization Mexico, February 7, 1866, 3, VHS. There were also colonization efforts at Tampico and Matamoros along the Gulf of Mexico.

14. Maury, "Letter Regarding the Possibilities for Colonization," Office of Colonization Mexico, February 7, 1866, 3, Manuscripts Dept., VHS; Rolle, *Lost Cause*, 108, 93. In his Immigration Decree and Regulation, Emperor Maximilian reduced the amount of uncultivated land offered to immigrants from Maury's suggestion of 640 acres to 320 and exemption from property taxes for one

year instead of five. Maximilian's Decree and Regulation, September 5, 1865, in U.S. Congress, *Message of the President*, 29–30, VHS.

15. Maury, "Letter Regarding the Possibilities for Colonization," Office of Colonization Mexico, February 7, 1866, 3, VHS.

16. *MT*, October 21 and December 2, 1865.

17. Maury's address, "To Persons Wishing to Settle in Mexico," dated November 18, 1865, printed in *MT*, December 9, 1865.

18. *MT*, September 30, 1865.

19. *MT*, October 21, 1865; U.S. Census Bureau, 1860 Federal Census, Travis County TX, Roll M653_1306, p. 252, Image 29, Ancestry.com; U.S. Census Bureau, 1860 Slave Schedules, Travis County TX, Roll 1312, Microcopy M-653, FHC. Sneed owned twenty-one slaves in 1860.

20. *MT*, October 21 and September 21, 1865; U.S. Census Bureau, 1860 Federal Census, Van Buren, Newton County MO, Roll M653_636, Image 481, Ancestry.com; and San Antonio Ward 1, Bexar TX, Roll M653_1288, p. 367, Image 259, Ancestry.com. Daniels was in his midtwenties, married, and had no children. See *MT*, October 21, 1865; U.S. Census Bureau, 1860 Federal Census, Beaver Dam, Butler County MO, Roll M653_610, Image 26, Ancestry.com.

21. Quotes from "A Vine-Growing Enterprise," *Two Republics*, March 18, 1868, IMN; Knapp, "New Source on the Confederate Exodus," 371. A Mr. Monthden from Georgia also joined in these farming operations.

22. On May 20, 1865, a party of "americanos" was reported to be crossing over a ranch at San José; on August 6, 1865, another group of fifteen "americanos" was at the Hacienda de Guadalupe. In all likelihood, these groups were southern migrants. M. Rodríguez, May 20, 1865, Piedras Negras; Serapio Ramírez, August 6, 1865, Hacienda de Guadalupe, AGEC, Fondo Siglo XIX, C2, F2, E9, and C3, FI, E8.

23. Gregorio Galindo, de la Comandancia principal del distrito de Río Grande, April 6, 1864, Gigedo, AGEC, Fondo Siglo XIX, CI, F7, E7.

24. See, for instance, Montejano, *Anglos and Mexicans*, 41–47.

25. Diary of Lieutenant General Jubal A. Early, "After Leaving the state of Virginia subsequent to Gen. R.E. Lee's surrender," Manuscripts, Jones Memorial Library, Lynchburg VA. Quote from entry for August 24, 1865.

26. Rister, "Carlota," 36; Rolle, *Lost Cause*, 18–19, quote on 19.

27. Edwards, *Shelby's Expedition to Mexico*, 262–64. Edwards would later take over the *Mexican Times*. *Shelby's Expedition* was first published in 1872 by the *Kansas City Times* Steam Book and Job Printing House; it was republished in 1889. Shelby was at Piedras Negras in late June or early July 1865; the exact date that he and his party crossed the border is not known, although Edwards indicates that it was July 4 when they went across the Sabinas River in Mexico.

28. Edwards, *Shelby's Expedition to Mexico*, 262–64; Beasley, *Shelby's Expedition to Mexico*, xx–xxiii; 32–34; Rolle, *Lost Cause*, 58. Viesca actually went a step further and reportedly offered Shelby military control of Coahuila, Nuevo León, and Tamaulipas, with Viesca retaining civilian authority. But Shelby's men voted against joining the Mexican Republican war effort. Viesca's motivations for this offer appear to stem from his desire to bolster his own regional authority.

29. Beasley, *Shelby's Expedition to Mexico*, xxiii, 35–39.

30. Edwards, *Shelby's Expedition to Mexico*, 264.

31. Edwards, *Shelby's Expedition to Mexico*, 272, 273.

32. Edwards, *Shelby's Expedition to Mexico*, 274–77.

33. Edwards, *Shelby's Expedition to Mexico*, 277; Beasley, ed., *Shelby's Expedition to Mexico*, 42–49.

34. Rolle, *Lost Cause*, 60–61. For a recent depiction of Shelby's encounter with Viesca and the fight at the Sabinas River, see Arthur, *General Jo Shelby's March*, 74–96. This account also describes a subsequent Apache and Mexican bandit night attack on Shelby's group before reaching Monterrey.

35. Brown, *Two Years in Mexico*, 18; Rolle, *Lost Cause*, 67–68, 70; Rister, "Carlota," 37.

36. Mexican Diaries, January 18, 1866, AFP, HL, Box 7.

37. Mexican Diaries, January 18, 1866, AFP, HL, Box 7; Report from William M. Anderson to Francisco Somera (minister del fomento), May 21, 1866, p. 7, AFP, HL, Box 7 (second quote).

38. Mexican Diaries, January 30 and 31, 1866, AFP, HL, Box 7. One of the major factors leading to escalated Comanche raiding in northern Mexico was the severe drought from 1845 to the mid-1860s that caused the already strained bison herds (due to hunting and lack of grazing lands) to precipitously decline in the American Southwest, prompting the Comanches to seek out alternatives in northern Mexico. See Hämäläinen, *Comanche Empire*, 296–97.

39. Brooks, "Served Well By Plunder," 26, 28, 42, 44. In *Captives and Cousins: Slavery, Kinship, and Community in the Southwest Borderlands*, Brooks analyzes the dynamics of an exchange network based upon theft, violence, and slave trading with an emphasis on its gendered dimensions. For Native Americans and the Spanish, masculine honor and status depended upon the exchange and control of women and livestock.

40. Hämäläinen, *Comanche Empire*, chaps. 4 and 5; Brooks, *Captives and Cousins*, 208–57.

41. Hämäläinen, *Comanche Empire*, 8, 11, 181–201, 219–32, 292–320, quote on 219. Disease, malnutrition from overtaxing the land and food supplies, and Anglo-American encroachment had seriously reduced Comanche strength and numbers;

the tribe's population dropped from a peak of about forty thousand in the late eighteenth century to less than twenty thousand by the 1850s and perhaps only five thousand by the early 1870s. Yet Comanche power actually revived in the latter part of the 1860s, in the aftermath of the Civil War, and their precipitous collapse would not occur until the mid-1870s (297–303, 331–41, 347–48).

42. Comisión Pesquisadora de la Frontera del Norte, *Reports of the Committee*, 322–32. In 1853 alone, it was reported, "all four districts of Coahuila were overrun by great numbers of Comanches" (332). Brian DeLay argues that revenge played a large role in Comanche-Kiowa raids into Mexico during the 1830s and 1840s, creating a "raiding-revenge cycle." See DeLay, *War of a Thousand Deserts*, chap. 4, esp. 129–35. The Comanches had built the economic foundation of their empire on bison hunting, horse pastoralism, and the raiding and trading of horses, livestock, and humans. Horses, in particular, were the most prized commodity, serving the needs of hunting, raiding, and warfare; one of the goals of raids across the borderlands was to replenish and maintain this source of wealth and power. See Hämäläinen, *Comanche Empire*, 240–41; Kavanagh, *Comanche Political History*, 57–60.

43. George H. Pettis, "Kit Carson's Fight with the Commanche and Kioway Indians, Read before the Soldiers and Sailors Historical Society, Providence RI, February 14, 1877," 4–5, 10, 21–22, Manuscripts Regarding the U.S. Army in the American Southwest, Huntington Library; LaVere, *Texas Indians*, 206. Pettis later indicated a higher number of Comanches, writing, "There were at least three thousand Indians opposed to us, more than ten to one." This was probably an exaggeration, but the Comanches appear to have numbered in the thousands at this battle with the U.S. Army, and they were able to fend off this campaign (28). Colonel Christopher Carson (better known as "Kit Carson") led the campaign with the First New Mexico Cavalry, attempting to protect the Santa Fe Trail and Union supply route.

44. Hämäläinen, *Comanche Empire*, 64, 128–29; Ogle, *Federal Control of the Western Apaches*, 8; Kavanagh, *Comanche Political History*, 10–121, 140–43. During the early nineteenth century, a temporary truce between the Comanches and Lipan Apaches combined with waning Spanish control over the northern frontier to allow for a renewal of Apache power along the present-day Arizona-Texas-Mexico border area. For the collapse of the presidio system, see Weber, *Mexican Frontier*, chap. 6. See chapter 3 for the disintegration of the missions after Mexican independence.

45. Weber, *Mexican Frontier*, 53–56, 108–21. As one observer from the midcentury noted, "the Apaches and Camanches" were "scattered over the extensive country, from Chihuahua to the river Nueces," running from the territory of

New Mexico to Texas and northern Mexico, with the Apaches known to make "excursions for robbing, every year, into several states in Mexico." Clarke, *Travels in Mexico and California*, 54.

46. Carmony, *Civil War in Apacheland*, 1–12, 92, 99, 101, 107, 110, 123, 146–47, 174. Another source claimed that "over 80,000 head of sheep and hundreds of horses, mules and burros" had been stolen from the Fort Craig area by Apache and Navajo raiders during the spring and summer of 1863. See George H. Pettis, "A Thirty Days Scout after Navajo Indians," 1863, 1–2, Manuscripts, Huntington Library.

47. During the 1850s Mexican towns in the north did have some success in curbing raids by offering lands for settlement. A large group of Lipan Apaches, for instance, settled near Zaragoza in Coahuila at this time. Yet this development only prompted the Lipans to redirect their raids northward into Texas. See Chebahtah and Minor, *Chevato*, 19, 22.

48. Minor, *Light Gray People*, 109–30.

49. The Lipan Apaches were one of six southern Athapascan-speaking ethnic groups in North America, which also included the Mescalero and Chiricahua Apaches. Because of Comanche expansion during the eighteenth century, the Lipans were pushed southward along the Rio Grande and became divided into two main groups. The first group, the Lipans *de arriba* (the upper Lipans), were composed of about ten loosely aligned bands that were situated to the east on the Texas side of the river. The Lipans *de abajo* (the lower Lipans), on the other hand, included about four bands and lived mostly to the west of the river. These western Lipans had an alliance with the Mescalero Apaches in New Mexico during most of the nineteenth century. See Chebahtah and Minor, *Chevato*, 7, 241n4, 9, 11–12. The western Comanches in Texas and New Mexico included groups of Penatekas ("Honey Eaters"), Hois ("Comanches of the Woods"), and Kotsotekas ("Buffalo Eaters"). See Kavanagh, *Comanche Political History*, xvi, 4–5; Hämäläinen, *Comanche Empire*, 25, 105.

50. Chebahtah and Minor, *Chevato*, 77. Chevato would later be adopted by a group of Mescalero Apaches, and still later by a band of Comanches.

51. T. H. Stribling and P. Smythe (from San Antonio) to President of the United States, October 14, 1865, in Winfrey and Day, *Indian Papers*, 87.

52. J. W. Throckmorton to D. M. Cooley, November 5 and December 6, 1866, in Winfrey and Day, *Indian Papers*, 124–25, 127–28.

53. Comisión Pesquisadora de la Frontera del Norte, *Reports of the Committee*, 411–12; Gibson, *Kickapoos*, 199–203, 205–6; Latorre and Latorre, *Mexican Kickapoo Indians*, 17–19. This latter group of Kickapoos also fought a contingent of Texas Confederate soldiers before reaching Mexico and, in January 1866, was granted land at Nacimiento, a site formerly abandoned by the Seminoles and Mascogos.

54. Gesick, "Historical Essay."

55. J. B. Devenport to Hon. W. B. Knox, December 22, 1866, and "Report on Indian Depredations in Medina County, 1865–66," in Winfrey and Day, *Indian Papers*, 129–30, 134–35. A report from Medina County also provides a glimpse into property losses from these raids; it claimed a total of $12,340 in lost horses and mules from July 1865 to December 1866. By early 1867 this county recognized the Kickapoo and Lipan Apache Indians as its foremost raiders.

56. "List of Animals Stolen by Apache in San Eluario [San Elizario]," August 10, 1865, to March 15, 1866, states $3,475 in stolen property; a second report ("List of Animals Stolen by Apache") from El Paso County from August 1865 to March 1866 lists $5,330 worth of stolen livestock, of which $3,090 was attributed to one raid on March 14, 1866. Winfrey and Day, *Indian Papers*, 91–93.

57. Petition from Lampasas County to J. W. Throckmorton, July 15, 1866; Petition from Wise, Cooke, Montague, Clay, Jack, and Young Counties to J. W. Throckmorton, July 18, 1866; Report from Lazardo De La Garza to J. W. Throckmorton, January 21, 1867; J. W. Throckmorton to L. V. Bogy, January 29, 1867; and Report from H. I. Richarz to J. W. Throckmorton, February 25, 1867, in Winfrey and Day, *Indian Papers*, 95–96, 97–99, 140–41, 144–45, 167–68.

58. Comisión Pesquisadora de la Frontera del Norte, *Reports of the Committee*, 333. By the mid-1860s, Mexican villages and towns were gearing up for a new cycle of raids. For instance, the alcalde of San Buenaventura anxiously wrote about the Indians who were circling around his town. Closer to the border at Piedras Negras, Gregorio Galindo, the political chief of the Río Grande district, informed this town's alcalde that he was pursuing Indians who had been marauding in the area. See Alcalde primero de San Buenaventura, March 3, 1864, AGEC, Fondo Siglo XIX, C1, F5, E2; Gregorio Galindo al Alcalde primero de Piedras Negras, July 3, 1864, AGEC, Fondo Siglo XIX, C2, FI, E3; Jesús Galván, alcalde primero de Morelos, August 5, 1864, AGEC, Fondo Siglo XIX, C2, F5, E2. By 1860 the population of Coahuila had actually declined from the previous decade, from around seventy-five thousand to about seventy thousand residents. See Rodríguez, *La guerra entre bárbaros y civilados*, 62, 79.

59. *El Coahuilense*, November 15, 1867, No. 25, T2, p. 2, AGEC, Fondo Periódico Oficial. The last quote actually reads, "Hablando de los pueblos y Estados que forma la parte septentrional de México ¿quien puede ignorar y no comprender que nos referimos a la guerra de los salvajes?"

60. Correspondencia, Saltillo, April 7, 11, 13, and 25, May 2 and 7, 1868, AGEC, Fondo Siglo XIX, C5, F3, E3; C5, F3, E12; C5, F4, E9; C6, F2, E13; C6, F5, E6; and C6, F7, E7; Isidro Treviño, comunica al Gobernador del Estado, Saltillo, April 16, 1868, AGEC, Fondo Siglo XIX, C5, F6, EI; Mujica, del ministerio de Guerra y Marina,

comunica al Gobernador del estado de Coahuila, April 22, 1868, AGEC, Fondo Siglo XIX, C6, F2, E2. Coahuila could expect to receive 5,000 pesos "para su defensa contra la Guerra de los Indios bárbaros."

61. Correspondencia dirigida al Ministerio de Hacienda y Crédito Público, Saltillo, April 22, 1868, AGEC, Fondo Siglo XIX, C6, FI, E14. As with the call for presidios, Mexico resorted to recruiting Native Americans who had previously migrated into Coahuila into the antiraiding efforts. During the 1840s Mexican president José Herrera had renewed efforts to establish a buffer zone in northern Mexico against Indian raids by establishing protective colonies. One of the largest defensive efforts came with the migration of Seminoles, Mascogos, and Kickapoos to Coahuila in 1850. The combined group (over three hundred total) received a large land grant at La Navaja between Monclova Viejo and Guerrero in exchange for participating in joint expeditions with the Mexican military to defend the area against attacks from Comanches and other "indios bárbaros." See Mulroy, *Freedom on the Border*, 36–41, 47–54; S. Miller, *Coacoochee's Bones*, 131–32.

62. Florencio Valdez, Monclova, March 30, 1867, AGEC, Fondo Siglo XIX, C2, F5, E4.

63. Report from William M. Anderson to Francisco Somera, May 21, 1866, p. 2, AFP, HL, Box 7.

64. Vidaurri had recognized his chance to gain power in northern Mexico when the Revolution of Ayutla erupted in 1854. The Revolution of Ayutla challenged the dictatorship of restored president Antonio López de Santa Anna, calling for constitutional reform and the end of autocratic government (it was also a protest against the Gadsden Purchase). Ironically, Vidaurri seized on this liberal revolutionary outbreak to install his own dictatorship in the North. See Tyler, *Santiago Vidaurri and the Southern Confederacy*, 17–30; Hale, *Mexican Liberalism in the Age of Mora*, 1–9; Garner, *Porfirio Díaz*, 34–35.

65. Tyler, *Santiago Vidaurri and the Southern Confederacy*, 45–58. Vidaurri even went a step further and proposed to Confederate president Jefferson Davis the annexation of northern Mexico, a move most likely aimed at securing greater protection from President Juárez. Juárez did not want Vidaurri to create an alliance with the Confederacy. Going against Juárez's orders, Vidaurri continued his commercial trade with the Confederacy, since it would aid his state's financial position (82). Although the railroad failed to materialize, Governor Vidaurri collected substantial customs fees from the cotton and trade goods that passed through his dominion to the Confederacy or back from the Confederate states to the global economy. The cotton trade initially centered on the port of Matamoros, Tamaulipas, but Union victories in the Gulf region rerouted shipments

to central and western Texas, through Laredo or Eagle Pass, the same crossroads of southern migration (98–121).

66. Tyler, *Santiago Vidaurri and the Southern Confederacy*, 128; Wasserman, *Capitalists, Caciques, and Revolution*, chap. 3. Terrazas eventually diversified his economic dealings to include banking, meatpacking, and sugar beet refining, among other activities. As an indication of the varying use of terms, Wasserman uses "cacique" to refer to "a regional political boss" and reserves "caudillo" to mean only "a national leader" (172n3).

67. Tyler, *Santiago Vidaurri and the Southern Confederacy*, 134–54. When Maximilian and his government became trapped in Querétaro in 1867, Vidaurri was named minister of finance and war.

68. Jacobo Elizondo to Sr. Dr. Miguel S. Maynes, January 6, 1864; and unsigned letter to Sr. General D. Manuel Pabolado, March 3, 1864, Sanchez Navarro Collection, Benson Latin American Collection, University of Texas at Austin.

69. Nicolás Ansures, teniente coronel de infantería, al Gobernador del estado de Coahuila, January 2, 1866, AGEC, Fondo Siglo XIX, CI, FI, E2.

70. Andrés S. Viesca a León Villarreal, April 4, 1866, Monclova, AGEC, Fondo Siglo XIX, C2, F6, E9; La Secretaría de Gobierno a Juan Rábago, April 21, 1866, Monclova, AGEC, Fondo Siglo XIX, C2, F6, E3; Andrés S. Viesca a Eugenio Jiménez, April 21, 1866, Monclova, AGEC, Fondo Siglo XIX, C2, F6, E6,. The Soledad hacienda, for example, was to be seized by the Republican government, and all other properties in the district of Monclova were subject to having their horses taken for military use.

71. Leonardo Villareal al Secretario del Gobierno del Estado, July 14, 1866, Monclova, AGEC, Fondo Siglo XIX, C3, F4, EIO; La Secretaría de Gobierno al Comisionado de secuestros del Estado, September 8, 1866, Saltillo, AGEC, Fondo Siglo XIX, C4, F2, E3; Andrés S. Viesca, un reglamento, September 12, 1866, Saltillo, AGEC, Fondo Siglo XIX, C3, FII, E5.

72. Iglesias, ministro de hacienda y crédito público, al Gobernador del estado de Coahuila de Zaragoza, September 13, 1866, Chihuahua, AGEC, Fondo Siglo XIX, C4, F3, E2. For an account of Viesca's role in the Republican military campaigns in Coahuila, see Tapia, *Andrés S. Viesca*, 32–63.

73. Some of the confiscated Sánchez Navarro family lands went toward colonization plans—those of the Mascogos and Kickapoos. In January 1866, for example, Viesca granted land and livestock to the Mascogos, and in November he was informed that President Juárez had officially approved a land grant at El Nacimiento for a group of Kickapoos. Both groups were expected to contribute to the northern defenses against "los comanches, lipanes, mezcaleros" and other "barbarians" attacking the Mexican nation. See Andrés S. Viesca, Concesión

de cuatro sitios de ganada mayor en la hacienda del Nacimiento a la tribu de los mascogos, Monclova, January 11, 1866, in Martínez Sánchez, *Coahuila durante la Intervención Francesa*, 307–8; Iglesias, ministro de hacienda y crédito público, al Gobernador y Comandante militar, November 8, 1866, Chihuahua, AGEC, Fondo Siglo XIX, C5, F4, E2.

74. In the central highlands around Mexico City, for example, the region of Chalco experienced one of the first rebellions against the reestablished Liberal government in 1868. In this instance, a local leader rallied peasant farmers against estate owners. Tutino, "Agrarian Social Change and Peasant Rebellion," 129–38. As Tutino notes, "occupying the national government was not equivalent to ruling Mexico" (129).

75. The high point of banditry was actually in the 1850s and 1860s, during the War of the Reform and the French Intervention. The beleaguered Republican troops under Juárez primarily hired bandits, but the Imperialists also drew upon their support. In essence, bandits demanded that they be paid well, or they threatened to fight for the opposing side. The best-known bandits of the period were the Plateados of Morelos, whose "social cause was [primarily] their own enrichment." There was no effective police force to control these and other bandits at the time, and to denounce them invited revenge. See Vanderwood, *Disorder and Progress*, xxvi–xxviii, 6–8. See also Taylor, "Banditry and Insurrection."

76. "Murder of Gen. Parsons," MT, September 23, 1865; see also "Particulars of the Murder of General Parsons and Others," reprinted from Matamoros, "Monitor of the Frontier," MT, October 14, 1865. According to the Confederate officer John N. Edwards, Parsons and his party had been murdered by a well-known Republican-bandit named Luis Pérez "Figueroa, a robber chief." See Edwards, *Shelby's Expedition to Mexico*, 294–99.

77. The other English-language newspaper in Mexico that promoted southern immigration, the *Two Republics*, provides a glimpse into the sustained presence of banditry and its impact on colonization. George W. Clarke, a Confederate migrant from Arkansas, began the publication in July 1867, after the fall of Emperor Maximilian. In 1868 he reported that highway robberies had become widespread. One such mail robbery occurred in Guadalajara in June of that year. Another happened in September, causing the editor to proclaim that they occurred with such regularity as "to fix this branch as one of the institutions of the country." Moreover, it looked "very much like [the] complicity" of the military escorts played a large role; "at the best" it could be attributed to their "neglect or cowardice." Fighters for the Mexican Republic who still served in the military thus chose a path of theft even after military necessity was gone. "Mail Robbery," *Two Republics*, June 10, 1868, IMN; and "Highway Robberies," *Two Republics*, September

12, 1868, IMN. Ironically, many bandits were later recruited into the rural police force, the Rurales, started under Juárez when he launched a public security initiative in 1861 and expanded it in 1867. The roles of bandits and policeman in later nineteenth-century Mexico were thus fluid and interchangeable—there was a shifting line between bandits and Rurales, as there was a thin line between order and disorder. The Rurales actually became a central part of the process of consolidating a strong central government under Porfirio Díaz. See Vanderwood, *Disorder and Progress*, 5–11, 49–51, 63.

78. J. Thompson, *Cortina*, 152, 158–59, 169–70, 207.

79. "Robbery on the Rio Grande," *Two Republics*, May 1, 1869, IMN; "American Bandits Again," *Two Republics*, April 24, 1869, IMN; "Serious Matters! Trouble on the Border!!" *Two Republics*, September 25, 1869, IMN.

80. Mexican Diaries, December 12–25, 1865 (first quote, December 25) and January 8, 1866, AFP, HL, Box 7; Report from William M. Anderson to Francisco Somera, May 21, 1866, p. 1, AFP, HL, Box 7 (second quote); Ruiz, *American in Maximilian's Mexico*, 118n3.

81. Mexican Diaries, January 8 (first quote), 14 (second quote), and 12 (third quote), 1866, AFP, HL, Box 7.

82. Mexican Diaries, January 18, 1866, AFP, HL, Box 7; Report from William M. Anderson to Francisco Somera, May 21, 1866, p. 1, AFP, HL, Box 7, writing about the date January 24, 1866.

83. Mexican Diaries, January 18, 1866, AFP, HL, Box 7 (first quote); Report from William M. Anderson to Francisco Somera, May 21, 1866, p. 2, AFP, HL, Box 7 (second and third quotes), writing about the area he saw in late January 1866; Mexican Diaries, January 29, 1866, AFP, HL, Box 7.

84. Report from William M. Anderson to Francisco Somera, May 21, 1866, p. 3, AFP, HL, Box 7, writing of late January or early February 1866.

85. Mexican Diaries, March 3 and 4, 1866, AFP, HL, Box 7; Ruiz, *American in Maximilian's Mexico*, 102n90. "As soon as they saw us coming," Anderson recounted, "they counted our horses and immediately divided them out among themselves."

86. Mexican Diaries, March 4 and 5, 1866, AFP, HL, Box 7; William Marshall Anderson (from Las Hermanas Hacienda) to his wife, Ellen Columba (Ryan) Anderson, April 6, 1866, AFP, HL, Box 7. Anderson's Mexican guide, Fruto Guzman, also helped the group by meeting with Captain Winker the previous night to explain the expedition's purported scientific purpose.

87. Anderson to Ellen Columba (Ryan) Anderson, April 6, 1866, AFP, HL, Box 7; Mexican Diaries, entry under March 4, but actually March 6, 1866, AFP, HL, Box 7 (last quote).

88. Report from William M. Anderson to Francisco Somera, May 21, 1866, p. 7, AFP, HL, Box 7.

89. Mexican Diaries, April 13 and 19, 1866, AFP, HL, Box 7. Anderson recorded that Viesca signed his passport with the town of Monclova superimposed over Saltillo.

90. Mexican Diaries, April 20, 1866, AFP, HL, Box 7, written subsequently.

91. Mexican Diaries, April 20, 1866, AFP, HL, Box 7, (first two quotes); Account by Robert M. Anderson (son), June 10, 1898, in Mexican Diary, June 2 to 6, 1866, AFP, HL, Box 7.

92. Mexican Diaries, April 20, 1866, AFP, HL, Box 7; and Account by Robert M. Anderson, June 10, 1898, in Mexican Diary, June 2–6, 1866, AFP, HL, Box 7. Robert Anderson specifies that his father "was taken as a prisoner to a hacienda where he had stopped several times previously. During these visits he had made friends with the women and children and the dogs as they came for water to the well." This presumably aided the hound's recognition of Anderson and his escape.

93. Mexican Diaries, April 21 and 29, 1866, AFP, HL, Box 7. Robert Anderson claims that his father's shoes were "nearly worn through," while Anderson recorded that he was barefoot.

94. Report from William M. Anderson to Francisco Somera, May 21, 1866, p. 10, AFP, HL, Box 7.

4. Fall of the Mexican Empire, 1866–67

1. M. F. Maury to Ann and their children, March 1, 1866, in Williams, *Matthew Fontaine Maury*, 437.

2. Matthew Fontaine Maury, "Letter Regarding the Possibilities for Colonization," Office of Colonization, Mexico, February 7, 1866, 3–5, Manuscripts Dept., VHS; and "Mexico and the South," newspaper article written for the London *Morning Herald* and *Standard*, March 26, 1866, in Minor Family Papers, Section 72, VHS. A copy of the first item can also be found at the Huntington Library. In addition to its publication in London and U.S. newspapers, Maury's article from March was reprinted in the *Mexican Times* in its May 26 and June 2, 1866, issues (only partially in the former).

3. M. F. Maury to Emperor Maximilian, July 1, 1866, in Williams, *Matthew Fontaine Maury*, 440. Maximilian still wished for Maury to return and work as the director of the Mexican observatory.

4. *El Cronista*, March 31, 1866, in Hanna and Hanna, "Immigration Movement of the Intervention," 245.

5. Hanna and Hanna, in "Immigration Movement of the Intervention," likewise argue, "An amazing amount was planned and begun in a short space of time" (246).

6. Williams, *Matthew Fontaine Maury*, 442–43. Maury also gave torpedo instructions to officials from Sweden and Norway in London.

7. Wayland, *Pathfinder of the Seas*, 126–30. Before leaving England, Maury received an honorary doctor of laws degree from Cambridge University.

8. Williams, *Matthew Fontaine Maury*, 449–50; Wayland, *Pathfinder of the Seas*, 140–41. In addition to 13,500 special pardons and the amnesty act of September 1867, President Johnson issued third and fourth amnesty acts on July 4 and December 25, 1868, that cleared the way for Maury's return. See Stampp, *Era of Reconstruction*, 68.

9. Maury, *Physical Survey of Virginia*, 3–4 (quotes), 12–16, 79–81. For an assessment of how Maury's antebellum and postbellum geographic-economic thinking informed southern political economy, southern nationalism, and a reformist, modernizing tradition within nineteenth-century southern thought, see Majewski and Wahlstrom, "Geography as Power."

10. Wayland, *Pathfinder of the Seas*, 145–52; *In Memorium, Matthew Fontaine Maury LL.D., Proceedings of the Academic Board of the Virginia Military Institute, Lexington, Va., on the occasion of the Death of Commodore M.F. Maury . . .* , 1873, 20, Huntington Library (quote).

11. H. W. Allen to Sarah Dorsey, November 1, 1865, in Dorsey, *Recollections*, 333–35.

12. H. W. Allen to R. C. Cummings, Esq., Shreveport LA, December 25, 1865, in Dorsey, *Recollections*, 336–37 (first quote); Allen to Dorsey, January 1, 1866, in Dorsey, *Recollections*, 338–39 (second quote).

13. Henry W. Allen, "The Public Works of the Empire" (editorial), MT, April 14, 1866 (first quote); "Asiatic Colonization Company," MT, April 14, 1866 (second and third quotes).

14. Jung, *Coolies and Cane*, 76–98, 76 (first quote), 83 (second quote).

15. H. W. Allen to unknown, March 16, 1866 (first three quotes), and Allen to Dorsey, March 15, 1866, in Dorsey, *Recollections*, 340–41.

16. Quote from Allen to "Colonel," March 26, 1866, in Dorsey, *Recollections*, 351–52 (Allen's emphasis); Cassidy and Simpson, *Henry Watkins Allen of Louisiana*, 153.

17. MT, June 2, 1866, 2. For a eulogizing article on Allen, see "Death of Governor Allen," MT, June 16, 1866.

18. Mexican Diaries, May 15, 1866 (first quote); Report from William M. Anderson to Francisco Somera, May 21, 1866, pp. 9, 11, both items in AFP, HL, Box 7.

19. Mexican Diaries, May 18, 1866 (first quote), June 6, 1866, AFP, HL, Box 7.

20. Jubal A. Early to W. M. Anderson and Early to John Breckinridge, August 6, 1866, AFP, HL, Box 7.

21. *El Coahuilense*, December 3, 1866, AGEC, Fondo Periódico Oficial.

22. Rolle, *Lost Cause*, 96–97; Harmon, "Confederate Migrations to Mexico," 468; Arthur, *General Jo Shelby's March*, 135–50.

23. Harmon, "Confederate Migrations to Mexico," 469; Perrin, "Exodus of Southerners," 32 (quote).

24. "From Orizava" *MT*, January 26, 1866; "To Emigrants," *MT*, February 17, 1866; Davis, "Confederate Exiles," 35.

25. *New Orleans Daily True Delta*, February 21,1866, microfilm 2038, reel 28 (January 23, 1866, to March 30, 1866), LSU.

26. M. F. Maury letter, March 1, 1866, in Rister, "Carlota," 46; Sterling Price and Martha Price letters in Perrin, "Exodus of Southerners," 34, 35.

27. Perrin, "Exodus of Southerners," 35 (first quote); *New York Herald*, January 12, 1866, in Harmon, "Confederate Migrations to Mexico," 467 (second quote); Rolle, *Lost Cause*, 94; Davis, "Confederate Exiles," 35.

28. "Southern Emigration," *MT*, February 10, 1866, reprinting items from the *New York Daily News* and the *Charleston Courier*.

29. Letter to John B. Magruder (from a friend in the United States), February 14, 1866, *MT*, April 14, 1866.

30. "Emigration," *MT*, March 10, 1866.

31. "Local Items," *MT*, May 12, 1866.

32. Nunn, *Escape from Reconstruction*, 82.

33. Nunn, *Escape from Reconstruction*, 82–85, quotes from Tom J. Russell on 84.

34. Nunn, *Escape from Reconstruction*, 86–94, quote on 86. Russell would remain in the Córdoba area until early October 1866.

35. Nunn, *Escape from Reconstruction*, 95–100, first quote on 95 (by Russell), second on 98, third on 100, fourth on 97 (last two by "Cordovan").

36. Nunn, *Escape from Reconstruction*, 93 (quote by Russell).

37. Rolle, *Lost Cause*, 180–81; Mahoney and Mahoney, *Mexico and the Confederacy*, 161.

38. Sterling Price to Edward W. Price, July 2, 1866, in Rolle, *Lost Cause*, 105.

39. *MT*, May 26 and June 9, 1866; Rolle, *Lost Cause*, 97. Another option was to strike deals with Mexican Republican bandit leaders, as Jo Shelby had previously done to protect his hacienda.

40. "Cordova and Colonization," *MT*, June 16, 1866.

41. The French army was originally supposed to remain in Mexico for five years after Emperor Maximilian's arrival. By early 1866 news started to leak that the forces would be withdrawn sooner, in three stages—one at the end of October

1866, the second in the spring of 1867, and the last in the fall of that year. In actuality, the bulk of French troops left Mexico City in early February 1867, sailing off from Veracruz at the end of March. By this time Maximilian was personally leading the war effort, taking command of an army composed of Mexican Conservatives, Austrian and Belgian troops, and the French Foreign Legion. See Blasio, *Maximilian, Emperor of Mexico*, 79, 125–27.

42. Nunn, *Escape from Reconstruction*, 100–101.

43. "Colonization," *MT*, June 23, 1866.

44. "To Emigrants Wishing Good Lands," *MT*, August 27, 1866. R. J. Laurence arrived in Mexico City on August 29, 1865, and was the nineteenth person listed in the emigrant list printed in the September 23, 1865, issue of the *Mexican Times*. Robert Jones Laurence was born in North Carolina in 1820 and lived in Tennessee with his wife, Susan, in 1860; his occupation is listed as a farmer. He was back in Tennessee in 1870 and died in 1883. See U.S. Census Bureau, 1860, 1870, and 1880 Federal Censuses, Ancestry.com.

45. "To Emigrants Wishing Good Lands," *MT*, August 27, 1866 (quotes); Brown, *Two Years in Mexico*, vii.

46. "Metlaltoyuca," *MT*, October 8, 1866 (quotes); Nunn, *Escape from Reconstruction*, 73; Rolle, *Lost Cause*, 97, 110–11.

47. "Metlaltoyuca," *MT*, October 8, 1866; "The Tuxpan Colony," *MT*, October 29, 1866 (quotes).

48. "Letter from Tuxpan River" *Two Republics*, February 2, 1868, IMN; "American Colony at Tuxpan," *Two Republics*, February 29, 1868, IMN (quote; Brown's emphasis).

49. John Henry Brown, "The Tuxpan Colony," letter to the editor, *Two Republics*, September 5, 1868, IMN.

50. John N. Edwards, "To Emigrants Desiring Splendid Lands," *MT*, September 3, 1866.

51. John N. Edwards, "The Hacienda of San Lorenzo," *MT*, September 10, 1866.

52. "Metlaltoyuca," *MT*, October 8, 1866.

53. *MT*, September 24, 1866.

54. F. T. Mitchell, letter to the editor, *MT*, September 27, 1866.

55. Mitchell, letter to the editor, *MT*, September 27, 1866. See *MT*, November 12, 1866, for an additional letter from Mitchell on the colony in San Luis Potosí. This more northern region of Mexico maintained large haciendas in the middle decades of the nineteenth century that tended to bind laborers to them through debt peonage. See Katz, "Labor Conditions on Haciendas," 31.

56. "Immigration," *MT*, December 11, 1866 (first quote); Edwards in "Shelby's Tuxpan Colony," *MT*, November 19, 1866 (second quote and section quote). The

Mexican Times under Edwards was briefly suspended with the November 19 issue; Bradford C. Barksdale, the owner of the American and Mexican News Company, bought the publication in early December and wrote the December 11 editorial.

57. Bradford C. Barksdale, "Colonization," MT, January 1, 1867. While in Mexico, William Marshall Anderson had received one of Barksdale's business cards, an indication of the interweaving circuits of colonization.

58. Bradford C. Barksdale, "Policy," MT, January 22, 1867. As an indication of this change in editorial tone, when Barksdale took over the *Mexican Times* with the December 4, 1866, issue, he added a new line to the masthead: "Mineralogy, Agriculture, Literature, Commerce and Politics."

59. Knapp, "New Source on the Confederate Exodus," 365–66. Clarke started the newspaper in Mexico City on July 27, 1867.

60. John N. Edwards, "Mexico," MT, June 30, 1866.

61. J. Thompson, *Cortina*, 178–81, quote on 180.

62. John N. Edwards, "Destruction of Olvera's Co.," MT, July 7, 1866; MT, August 13, 1866.

63. Felicitación, El teniente coronel Ruperto Martínez, Saltillo, August 4, 1866, Fondo Presidencia Municipal, Caja 109, Fólder 2, Expediente 3, Archivo Municipal de Saltillo; MT, September 3, 1866.

64. Boletín, "¡Viva la Republica!" Saltillo, November 22, 1866, Fondo Presidencia Municipal, Caja 109, Fólder 1, Expediente 6, Archivo Municipal de Saltillo; "Capitulación de Jalapa," *El Coahuilense*, December 14, 1866, 1, and December 3, 1866, 1, AGEC, Fondo Periódico Oficial. In October and November 1866, Maximilian seriously contemplated abandoning the throne of Mexico once it was confirmed that Napoleon III intended to withdraw the French army. But Mexican Conservatives helped to convince him to not to abdicate, particularly Generals Leonardo Márquez and Miguel Miramón (the latter was later executed with Maximilian). See Basch, *Recollections of Mexico*, 27–36, 43–51.

65. For tables showing population counts of various areas and the political party that occupied each of them, see MT, September 24, 1866.

66. "The Bright Side of Mexico," MT, August 27, 1866.

67. Report from William M. Anderson to Francisco Somera, May 21, 1866, p. 9, AFP, HL, Box 7.

68. MT, January 29, 1867.

69. "The Situation," MT, March 13, 1867 (first quote); MT, March 24, 1867; "The Situation," MT, March 31, 1867. By mid-March, the Republican forces encircled the Imperialists at Querétaro, but the latter continued to win military battles while the Liberals suffered heavy casualties. See Blasio, *Maximilian, Emperor of Mexico*, 145–49. As Samuel Basch, Maximilian's personal physician, recounted,

on March 14 and 24, 1867, the Imperialist forces repulsed Liberal attacks, and they waged one of their own offensives on April 1. *Recollections of Mexico*, 162.

70. Elton, *With the French in Mexico*, 174. The situation at this time in Mexico is reminiscent of the unpredictability of the outcome of the U.S. Civil War in the late summer of 1864, when Lincoln despaired about his chances for reelection before the capture of Atlanta, Georgia, made it more certain.

71. "The Situation," *MT*, April 18, 1867; "Rumors," *MT*, May 23, 1867 (quote, emphasis in original); *MT*, June 3 and 17, 1867; Blasio, *Maximilian, Emperor of Mexico*, 159–66, 174–81. The last issue of the *Mexican Times* was vol. 4, no. 15, June 17, 1867. With food supplies dwindling and the hope of reinforcements gone, an attempt to break through the Mexican Liberal lines was planned for May 15, 1867, but Colonel Miguel López of the Imperialist forces instead turned traitor and allowed the Republicans to enter the city. As Basch explained, "It seemed as if the enemy, themselves, were surprised and bewildered by a success that had exceeded their wildest hopes. They never would have dared to dream that they would successfully come into position of the Emperor, his Generals, and the entire garrison after all those actions which they had always lost." *Recollections of Mexico*, 205.

72. For an analysis of Coahuila's contribution to the Republican war effort, see Martínez Sánchez, *Coahuila durante la Intervención Francesa*, chap. 4.

73. John Henry Brown, "The Tuxpan Colony," letter to the editor, *Two Republics*, September 5, 1868, IMN.

74. John Henry Brown, "The Tuxpan Colony," letter to the editor, *Two Republics*, September 5, 1868, IMN.

75. *Two Republics*, April 2, 1870, IMN, from a report on the Tuxpan Colony dated March 11, 1870.

76. "Cultivo de la Viña," *El Coahuilense*, April 13, 1868, 2, and *El Coahuilense*, September 7, 1869, 3, AGEC, Fondo Periódico Oficial; "Gen. Bee at his Old Home," *Two Republics*, March 26, 1870, IMN.

5. Railroads and U.S. and Mexican Modernization

1. Hart, *Empire and Revolution*, 31–33; Pletcher, *Rails, Mines, and Progress*, 35–37. Rosecrans was previously known both for capturing Chattanooga, Tennessee, in August 1863 and for being defeated at the Battle of Chickamauga in September of the same year. For biographical information, see Lamers, *Edge of Glory*.

2. Pletcher, *Rails, Mines, and Progress*, 37–40. "Letter of General Rosecrans to President Juárez, Mexico, May 28, 1869," 1, included with the pamphlet "'Manifest Destiny,' 'The Monroe Doctrine,' and Our Relations with Mexico; a Letter from Gen. Rosecrans to the People of the United States, 1870," William S. Rosecrans Papers, Collection 663, Box 89, Folder 15, Department of Special Collections,

Charles E. Young Research Library, University of California, Los Angeles (emphasis by Rosecrans).

3. Pletcher, *Rails, Mines, and Progress*, 40, 23. By the mid-nineteenth century, investment in railroad construction in Mexico had been concentrated on this line (mainly British and Mexican funding).

4. "The Tuxpan Rail Road," *Two Republics*, September 12, 1868, IMN.

5. Pletcher, *Rails, Mines, and Progress*, 40–41; "The National Mexican Pacific and Rio Bravo Railroad," *Two Republics*, June 13, 1868, IMN. Richard White places Rosecrans among those railroad promoters who aspired, and often failed, to build transcontinental lines to the Pacific Ocean. Rosecrans's combined routes would have effectively linked El Paso, Tuxpan (on the Gulf of Mexico), and Acapulco on the Pacific. See White, *Railroaded*, 47–55.

6. Pletcher, *Rails, Mines, and Progress*, 45, 49, 51, 61, 66–69. Juárez and the Mexican Congress did approve two railroad projects by Pennsylvania developers in 1870 (granting the Tuxpan and Tehuantepec concessions, the first a nationwide rail system and the second a reestablished route across the isthmus connecting the Atlantic and Pacific; the latter project was sold to a British syndicate). Americans emphasized the construction of a north–south line from El Paso to Mexico City, but Juarez was concerned with U.S. intentions and died in 1872 without granting this railroad concession. See Hart, *Empire and Revolution*, 46–48, 52–55. For Rosecrans's struggle to obtain revisions to his concession and his partnership with Palmer, see also Pletcher, "General William S. Rosecrans."

7. "Anti-Americanism and the Panic of 1873 prevented much further railroad construction in Mexico before 1880." Pletcher, *Rails, Mines, and Progress*, 24. This is when President Porfirio Díaz approved two key railroad concessions—the Mexican Central (from Mexico City to El Paso, Texas) and the Mexican National (Mexico City to Laredo, Texas). These two lines were not completed until 1884 and 1888, respectively. White, *Railroaded*, 52–54, 84.

8. Pletcher, *Rails, Mines, and Progress*, 74–77, 80–81. In 1872 the International Railroad Company of Texas merged with the Houston and Great Northern Railroad to become the International and Great Northern Railroad. Some of Plumb's previous experience included launching the Mexican Pacific Coal and Iron Mining and Land Company in 1855 in New York (with the help of East Coast capital). He became the chargé d'affaires to Mexico in 1866 and befriended Lerdo. After Rosecrans was chosen for the ministry position, Plumb left Mexico at the end of 1868 and received the position of consul general to Cuba in 1869. He served for just over six months before returning to railroads in Mexico.

9. Pletcher, *Rails, Mines, and Progress*, 84, 89–91.

10. Hart, *Empire and Revolution*, 59–63; Pletcher, *Rails, Mines, and Progress*, 92–96.

11. "The National Mexican Pacific and Rio Bravo Railroad," *Two Republics*, June 13, 1868, IMN; "From New Orleans to the Rio Grande" and "From Cairo to the Rio Grande," *Two Republics*, April 17, 1869, IMN; Hart, *Empire and Revolution*, 43–45. By 1880 Díaz had become very interested in American capital and granted two concessions to the Mexican Central and Mexican National Railroad companies to build lines from Mexico City to El Paso and Laredo, respectively. By then the International and Great Northern Railroad, which Plumb represented, had already lost its leading position to two great railroad magnates, Collis P. Huntington and Jay Gould. By 1881 Plumb had sold his stake in the International concession in Mexico to Gould; that summer a Huntington subsidiary (the International Construction Company) secured a concession from the Mexican government from Piedras Negras to Mazatlán on the Pacific. Subsequently this Huntington company organized the Mexican International Railroad Company to unify competing grants, began building in 1883, and reached Monclova, Coahuila, in January 1884. Ironically, from 1881 to 1889 Plumb was vice president of this company and finally saw some of his work come to fruition, albeit not as he had imagined. In the end, this line was of secondary importance to the Mexican Central and Mexican National Railroads. See Pletcher, *Rails, Mines, and Progress*, 100–102.

12. See "Transcontinental Railroad of Mexico," *Two Republics*, January 7, 1871, IMN; "Vera Cruz, Anton Lizardo and Tehuantepec Railroad, Ministry of Fomento," *Two Republics*, January 21, 1871, IMN.

13. V. Johnson, *Men and Vision of Southern Commercial Conventions*, 106.

14. "The Railway Question; Speech by the Hon. Ramón G. Guzmán, Delivered in the Mexican Congress on the 12th and 15th of November 1872," *Two Republics*, December 14, 1872, IMN.

15. "The Railway Question; Speech by the Hon. Estanislao Cañedo, Delivered in the Mexican Congress on the 22d and 26th of November, 1872," *Two Republics*, December 21, 1872, IMN (emphasis by Cañedo).

16. Hart, *Empire and Revolution*, 122–23; St. John, *Line in the Sand*, 66–73.

17. Coatsworth, *Growth against Development*, 3–4. Between 1893 and 1907, Mexico's economy grew more rapidly than that of the United States (total product grew at a rate of 5.1 percent per year), with twenty thousand kilometers of railway built and the revival of the mining industry. Yet the transnational economic connections between the two countries brought forth issues of social inequality and foreign domination. "Both concentration of landownership and the foreign presence in Mexico's economy increased substantially during the

Porfirian period" (5). In contrast to the pure power and transformative nature of U.S. railroads, Richard White reveals in *Railroaded* that U.S. transcontinental railroad builders and operators were corrupt, and their poorly managed, indebted enterprises were made monumental through the owners' business and political connections.

18. Coatsworth, *Growth against Development*, 35; St. John, *Line in the Sand*, 63–89. When Porfirio Díaz came to power in 1877, Mexico only had 640 kilometers of railroad track, with 424 of it belonging to the Mexican Railway. For its first three years, the Porfirian regime was as unsuccessful as the Juárez government in developing railroads because of the lack of sufficient foreign capital. The period of most rapid expansion of railroad freight services began in 1884 with the completion of the Mexican Central's line from Mexico City to the U.S. border. For studies that disagree with the framing of the Porfirian era around the premise of one-sided and U.S.-controlled economic growth, see Ficker and Riguzzi, *Ferrocarriles y vida económica en México*; Schell, *Integral Outsiders*; and Van Hoy, *Social History of Mexico's Railroads*.

19. "Mexico, Our Special Correspondent," *New York Tribune*, September 2, 1867, ProQuest Historical Newspapers, 2.

20. *New Orleans Daily True Delta*, August 4, 1865, Microfilm 2038, Reel 27, LSU.

21. "The Vera Cruz Railroad," *Two Republics*, November 21, 1868, IMN. The November 7 and 14, 1868, issues also contain articles about the Veracruz–Mexico City Railroad.

22. Tenenbaum, "Manuel Payno, Financial Reform, and Foreign Intervention in Mexico," 213–17, 222–23, 228; Olliff, *Reforma Mexico and the United States*, chap. 1.

23. Editor, "Advantages of Emigration," *Two Republics*, October 3, 1868, IMN; and "The Destiny of Mexico," *Two Republics*, April 28, 1869, IMN.

24. "Colonization, vs. Immigration," *Two Republics*, March 10, 1869, IMN.

25. "Between Vera Cruz and New Orleans," *Two Republics*, January 22, 1870, IMN.

26. Hale, *Transformation of Liberalism*, esp. 21–27, 34–37, 102–4, 123–28; Matthews, *Civilizing Machine*, 11–13, 55–58, 126.

27. In the postwar South, the myths of the Lost Cause developed out of a white southern need to restore regional identity, "temporarily lost in military defeat and Reconstruction humiliation." The power of its ideology derived from its ability to reconsolidate a defeated and colonized region while masking over aspects of the past that disturbed this process. Hence, the Lost Cause rested upon a mythic history concerning a chivalrous, refined, and romantic plantation civilization that simultaneously placed the revered and vanquished Confederate nation, populated with countrified southern white gentlemen, at its center. More bluntly, however, this myth was directed at supporting white supremacy, the

distillation of memories of the war, and the purification of slavery. See Osterweis, *Myth of the Lost Cause*, x, 5, 7. Other important works include Foster, *Ghosts of the Confederacy*; and Wilson, *Baptized in Blood*. Wilson sees the Lost Cause forming from a confluence of Christianity and a sacred regional history, an interdenominational foundation to the cultural movement that put forward the "crusading Christian Confederate" as the virtuous symbol of the South.

28. Gaston, *New South Creed*, 31, 155–57. Hill specifically targeted the New South movement and its "new industrial oligarchy."

29. Gaston, *New South Creed*, 32–34.

30. Goldfield, *Still Fighting the Civil War*, 22. Another expression of conservatism in the South during Reconstruction, with which the original planners of southern colonization in Mexico would have agreed, was the argument that imperialism in the form of a stronger central government would thwart democratic reform and promote "an alternative route to stabilization in which the property of the South's self-styled best men would enjoy the protection of an authoritarian, centralized state." See Heath, "Let the Empire Come," 157.

31. Osterweis, *Myth of the Lost Cause*, 130.

32. Wilson, *Baptized in Blood*, 159; Gaston, *New South Creed*, 186, 7, 17. Grady spoke about removing the tensions between the regions as well as providing an "authentic Southern heritage." He paid homage to the "exquisite culture" of the Old South and even said, "The civilization of the old slave *regime* in the South has not been surpassed, and perhaps will not be equaled, among men." See Gaston, *New South Creed*, 84–86, 91–100, 173–74.

33. "Manufactures, the South's True Remedy," *DeBow's Review* (New Orleans) 3, no. 2 (February 1867): ProQuest American Periodical Series, 172. As DeBow stated, *"We have got to go to manufacturing to save ourselves,"* a reference to the necessity, not the value in itself, of turning to a more modernized region.

34. V. Johnson, *Men and Vision of Southern Commercial Conventions*, 76, 185, 196.

35. "Department of Internal Improvement, 2: Southern Railroad Route to the Pacific," *DeBow's Review* (New Orleans), 2, no. 5 (November 1866), ProQuest American Periodical Series, 532.

36. Jung, *Coolies and Cane*, 99–104; Nunn, *Escape from Reconstruction*, 38–47, 110; Elliott, *Isham G. Harris of Tennessee*, 194–200; [Isham G. Harris], "The Rebels in Mexico: Interesting Letter from Ex-governor Isham G. Harris, of Tennessee," *New York Herald*, December 18, 1865, Proquest Civil War Era, 1 (quote).

37. Majewski and Wahlstrom, "Geography as Power."

38. O'Flaherty, *General Jo Shelby*, 327–38. Shelby worked as a contractor to lay the track for the St. Louis and Santa Fe line, but that project ended with

bloodshed over attempted fraud in 1872. In the Gunn City, Missouri, massacre, citizens shot the court officials involved in the scandal.

39. Arthur, *General Jo Shelby's March*, 197–98, quote on 198.

Conclusion

1. Wright, *Slavery and American Economic Development*, 60–61, 67–68; Wright, *Old South, New South*, 17–20. The priority given to slave accumulation over land was not isolated among larger planters. An owner of just three slaves usually had a larger investment in human property than the average nonslaveholder had in all other forms of wealth. See also Huston, *Calculating the Value of the Union*, 32, 37, 40.

2. Wright, *Old South, New South*, 25–26, 34; Wright, *Slavery and American Economic Development*, 67.

3. Brown, *Two Years in Mexico*, 15–17; John Henry Brown, "The Tuxpan Colony," letter to the editor, *Two Republics*, September 5, 1868, IMN.

4. For the classic account of the colonial economy of the South and regional dependency, see Woodward, *Origins of the New South*. Even while emphasizing the regional economic problems of the South, Wright concludes *Slavery and American Economic Development* by acknowledging that the postwar South did experience "a significant economic invigoration on many fronts, including railroad investment, town-building, minerals-based industrial development, and a vigorous cotton textile industry" (125).

5. Bensel, *Yankee Leviathan*, 366–67, 417–19; Foner, *Reconstruction*, 161–63, 375–76, 603; Carlton and Coclanis, *The South, the Nation, and the World*, chap. 6. As Carlton argues in chapter 6 of *The South, the Nation, and the World*, it was not so much "economic colonialism" that characterized the postwar South but an "unbalanced industrial structure" that hindered the region. While industrialization materialized, the limited range of industrial capacities did not translate into regional economic growth.

6. During his trip to British Honduras, Charles Swett also commented on the economic drive, or more likely the necessity, behind migration to Latin America. "We find in our little vessel many gentlemen from Louisiana, Arkansas, Mississippi and from other Southern states, who before the war were in affluent circumstances," Swett wrote, "and consequently removed from the necessity of performing any kind of manual labor, now express their willingness to do as far as they are able, whatever may be necessary to enable them to make a support for themselves and families." See Strom and Weaver, *Confederates in the Tropics*, 62 (quote from January 2, 1868).

7. For a thorough analysis of the sharecropping system, see Ransom and Sutch, *One Kind of Freedom*.

8. Richardson, *Death of Reconstruction*, 17–19, quote on 19.

9. Foner, *Reconstruction* 103–6; Foner, *Nothing but Freedom*, 82–83.

10. Hahn, *Nation under Our Feet*, chap. 4.

11. Hahn et al., *Freedom*, 42–43, 587 (quote, from doc. 150, Tennessee Planter to the Freedmen's Bureau Superintendent of the Subdistrict of Memphis TN); Foner, *Reconstruction*, 106; Hahn, *Nation under Our Feet*, 154. Recent studies have directed attention to the variation in work arrangements, especially in the sugar and rice regions, where wage labor played a larger role. See Rodrigue, *Reconstruction in the Cane Fields*; and Saville, *Work of Reconstruction*. In Rodrigue's study, freed people adopted wage labor while continuing with gang-work routines.

12. Richardson, *Death of Reconstruction*, 36–37, 1–3, quote on 36. Congress also passed the Southern Homestead Act in February 1866, which opened public lands in the South and gave blacks and loyal whites preferential access. This bill proved to be unsuccessful, however, since these public lands were decidedly inferior to those held by existing plantations, and freed people lacked capital to invest in and improve them. By 1869 only four thousand black families had tried to gain land through this act, with three-fourths of them in Florida. See Foner, *Reconstruction*, 246.

Bibliography

Archives

Archivo General del Estado de Coahuila
Archivo Municipal de Saltillo, Coahuila
Benson Latin American Collection, University of Texas at Austin
Charles E. Young Research Library, University of California, Los Angeles
The Huntington Library, San Marino CA
Jones Memorial Library, Lynchburg VA
Southern Historical Collection, University of North Carolina at Chapel Hill
Virginia Historical Society, Richmond

Published Sources

Adelman, Jeremy, and Stephen Aron. "From Borderlands to Borders: Empires, Nation-States, and the Peoples in between in North American History." *American Historical Review* 104 (June 1999): 814–41.

Altman, Ida. "The Marqueses de Aguayo: A Family and Estate History." MA thesis, University of Texas at Austin, 1972.

Anderson, Gary Clayton. *The Conquest of Texas: Ethnic Cleansing in the Promised Land, 1820–1875*. Norman: University of Oklahoma Press, 2005.

Arthur, Anthony. *General Jo Shelby's March*. New York: Random House, 2010.

Ayers, Edward. *The Promise of the New South: Life after Reconstruction*. New York: Oxford University Press, 1993.

Basch, Samuel, M.D. *Recollections of Mexico: The Last Ten Months of Maximilian's Empire*. Translated and edited by Fred D. Ullman. Wilmington DE: Scholarly Resources, 2001. Originally published as *Erinnerungen aus Mexico*. Leipzig: Duncker and Humboldt, 1868.

Beasley, Conger, Jr., ed. *Shelby's Expedition to Mexico: An Unwritten Leaf of the War*. By John N. Edwards. Fayetteville: University of Arkansas Press, 2002.

Bensel, Richard Franklin. *Yankee Leviathan: The Origins of Central State Authority in America, 1859–1877*. New York: Cambridge University Press, 1990.

Black, Robert C., III. Review of *The Lost Cause*, by Andrew Rolle. *American Historical Review* 71 (January 1966): 702.

Blasio, José Luis. *Maximilian, Emperor of Mexico: Memoirs of His Private Secretary*. Translated and edited by Robert Hammond Murray. New Haven CT: Yale University Press, 1934.

Blight, David W. *Race and Reunion: The Civil War in American Memory*. Cambridge MA: Belknap Press of Harvard University Press, 2001.

Bonner, Robert E. *Mastering America: Southern Slaveholders and the Crises of American Nationhood*. New York: Cambridge University Press, 2009.

Bowman, Shearer Davis. "Industrialization and Economic Development in the Nineteenth-Century U.S. South: Some Interregional and Intercontinental Comparative Perspectives." In *Global Perspectives on Industrial Transformation in the American South*, edited by Susanna Delfino and Michele Gillespie, 76–104. Columbia: University of Missouri Press, 2005.

Brooks, James. *Captives and Cousins: Slavery, Kinship, and Community in the Southwest Borderlands*. Chapel Hill: University of North Carolina Press, 2002.

———. "Served Well by Plunder: *La Gran Ladronería* and Producers of History astride the Río Grande." *American Quarterly* 52, no. 1 (March 2000): 23–49.

Brown, John Henry. *Two Years in Mexico; or, the Emigrant's Friend*. Galveston TX: "News" Book and Job Office, 1867.

Burden, David K. "*La Idea Salvadora*: Immigration and Colonization Politics in Mexico, 1821–1857." PhD diss., University of California, Santa Barbara, 2005.

Carlton, David L., and Peter A. Coclanis. *The South, the Nation, and the World: Perspectives on Southern Economic Development*. Charlottesville: University of Virginia Press, 2003.

———. "Southern Textiles in Global Context." In *Global Perspectives on Industrial Transformation in the American South*, edited by Susanna Delfino and Michele Gillespie, 151–74. Columbia: University of Missouri Press, 2005.

Carmichael, Peter S. *The Last Generation: Young Virginians in Peace, War, and Reunion*. Chapel Hill: University of North Carolina Press, 2005.

Carmony, Neil B., ed. *The Civil War in Apacheland: Sergeant George Hand's Diary; California, Arizona, West Texas, New Mexico, 1861–1864*. Silver City NM: High-Lonesome Books, 1996.

Caskie, Jacquelin Ambler. *Life and Letters of Matthew Fontaine Maury*. Richmond VA: Richmond Press, 1928.

Casper, Scott E., and Lucinda M. Long, eds. *Moving Stories: Migration and the American West, 1850–2000*. Reno: Nevada Humanities Committee, 2001.

Cassidy, Vincent H., and Amos E. Simpson. *Henry Watkins Allen of Louisiana*. Baton Rouge: Louisiana State University Press, 1964.

Catton, Bruce. *The Civil War*. New York: American Heritage, 1960. Reprint, Boston: Houghton Mifflin, 1987.

Cayton, Andrew R. L., and Fredrika J. Teute. "Introduction: On the Connection of Frontiers." In *Contact Points: American Frontiers from the Mohawk Valley to the Mississippi, 1750–1830*, edited by Andrew R. L. Cayton and Fredrika J. Teute, 1–15. Chapel Hill: University of North Carolina Press, 1998.

Chebahtah, William, and Nancy McGown Minor. *Chevato: The Story of the Apache Warrior Who Captured Herman Lehmann*. Lincoln: University of Nebraska Press, 2007.

Clarke, A. B. *Travels in Mexico and California, Comprising a Journal of a Tour from Brazos Santiago, through Central Mexico, by way of Monterey, Chihuahua, the country of the Apaches, and the River Gila, to the Mining District of California.* Boston: Wright & Hasty's Steam Press, 1852.

Coatsworth, John. *Growth against Development: The Economic Impact of Railroads in Porfirian Mexico*. DeKalb: Northern Illinois University Press, 1981.

Comisión Pesquisadora de la Frontera del Norte. *Reports of the Committee of Investigation Sent in 1873 by the Mexican Government to the Frontier of Texas.* Translated from the official edition made in Mexico. New York: Baker & Godwin, 1875.

Corbin, Diana Fontaine Maury. *A Life of Matthew Fontaine Maury, U.S.N. and C.S.N., Author of "Physical Geography of the Sea and its Meteorology."* London: Sampson Low, Marston, Searle, & Rivington, 1888.

Cornell, Sarah E. "Americans in the U.S. South and Mexico: A Transnational History of Race, Slavery, and Freedom, 1810–1910." PhD diss., New York University, 2008.

Corti, Egon Caesar, Count. *Maximilian and Charlotte of Mexico*. Translated by Catherine Alison Philips. New York: Alfred A. Knopf, 1928.

Craven, Avery. *Reconstruction: The Ending of the Civil War*. New York: Holt, Rinehart and Winston, 1969.

Cronon, William, George Miles, and Jay Gitlin, eds. *Under an Open Sky: Rethinking America's Western Past*. New York: W.W. Norton, 1992.

Cunningham, Michele. *Mexico and the Foreign Policy of Napoleon III*. New York: Palgrave, 2001.

Davis, William C. "Confederate Exiles." *American History Illustrated* 5, no. 3 (June 1970): 30–43.

Dawsey, Cyrus B., and James M. Dawsey, eds. *The Confederados: Old South Immigrants in Brazil*. Tuscaloosa: University of Alabama Press, 1995.

DeLay, Brian. *War of a Thousand Deserts: Indian Raids and the U.S.-Mexican War.* New Haven CT: Yale University Press, 2008.

Delfino, Susanna. "The Idea of Southern Economic Backwardness: A Comparative View of the United States and Italy." In *Global Perspectives on Industrial Transformation in the American South*, edited by Susanna Delfino and Michele Gillespie, 105–30. Columbia: University of Missouri Press, 2005.

Del Paso, Fernando. *News from the Empire*. Translated by Alfonso González and Stella T. Clark. Champaign IL: Dalkey Archive Press, 2009. Originally published in Spanish as *Noticias del Imperio*, by Diana Literaria, in 1987.

Dorsey, Sarah A. *Recollections of Henry Watkins Allen, Brigadier-General, Confederate States Army, Ex-governor of Louisiana*. New York: M. Doolady, 1866.

Dozer, Donald Marquand. "Matthew Fontaine Maury's Letter of Introduction to William Lewis Herndon." *Hispanic American Historical Review* 28, no. 2 (May 1948): 212–28.

Edwards, John N. *Shelby's Expedition to Mexico: An Unwritten Leaf of the War*. In *Biography, Memoirs, Reminiscences and Recollections*, by John N. Edwards. *Kansas City Times* Steam Book and Job Printing House, 1872. Reprint, Kansas City MO: Jennie Edwards, 1889.

Elliott, Sam Davis. *Isham G. Harris of Tennessee: Confederate Governor and United States Senator*. Baton Rouge: Louisiana State University Press, 2010.

Elton, J. F. *With the French in Mexico*. Philadelphia: J.B. Lippincott, 1867.

Emmons, David M. *Beyond the American Pale: The Irish in the West, 1845–1910*. Norman: University of Oklahoma Press, 2010.

Ficker, Sandra Kuntz, and Paolo Riguzzi, eds. *Ferrocarriles y vida económica en México (1850–1950): Del surgimiento tardía al decaimiento precoz*. México DF: El Colegio Mexiquense and Universidad Metropolitana Xochimilco, 1996.

Fogel, Robert William. *Without Consent or Contract: The Rise and Fall of American Slavery*. 1989. Reprint, New York: W.W. Norton, 1994.

Foner, Eric. *Free Soil, Free Labor, Free Men: The Ideology of the Republican Party before the Civil War*. New York: Oxford University Press, 1970.

———. *Nothing but Freedom: Emancipation and Its Legacy*. Baton Rouge: Louisiana State University Press, 1983.

———. *Reconstruction: America's Unfinished Revolution, 1863–1877*. New York: Harper & Row, 1988.

Foster, Gaines M. *Ghosts of the Confederacy: Defeat, the Lost Cause, and the Emergence of the New South*. New York: Oxford University Press, 1987.

Freehling, William W. *The Road to Disunion*. Vol. 1, *Secessionists at Bay, 1776–1854*. New York: Oxford University Press, 1990.

———. *The Road to Disunion*. Vol. 2, *Secessionists Triumphant, 1854–1861*. New York: Oxford University Press, 2007.

———. *The South vs. the South: How Anti-Confederate Southerners Shaped the Course of the Civil War*. New York: Oxford University Press, 2002.

Gallagher, Gary W. *The Confederate War: How Popular Will, Nationalism, and Military Strategy Could Not Stave Off Defeat*. Cambridge: Harvard University Press, 1997.

———. "Jubal A. Early, the Lost Cause, and Civil War History: A Persistent Legacy." In *The Myth of the Lost Cause and Civil War History*, edited by Gary W. Gallagher and Alan T. Nolan, 35–59. Bloomington: Indiana University Press, 2000.

Gallagher, Gary W., and Alan T. Nolan. *The Myth of the Lost Cause and Civil War History*. Bloomington: Indiana University Press, 2000.

Garner, Paul. *Porfirio Díaz: Profiles in Power*. London: Pearson Education, 2001.

Gaston, Paul M. *The New South Creed: A Study in Southern Mythmaking*. New York: Alfred A. Knopf, 1970.

Gesick, E. John, Jr. "Historical Essay." In *The Texas Kickapoo: Keepers of Tradition*, 1–26. Photography by Bill Wright. El Paso: Texas Western Press, 1996.

Gibson, A. M. *The Kickapoos: Lords of the Middle Border*. Norman: University of Oklahoma Press, 1963.

Goldfield, David. *Still Fighting the Civil War: The American South and Southern History*. Baton Rouge: Louisiana State University Press, 2004.

Gould, Lewis L. *Alexander Watkins Terrell: Civil War Soldier, Texas Lawmaker, American Diplomat*. Austin: University of Texas Press, 2004.

Gregory, James. *The Southern Diaspora: How the Great Migrations of Black and White Southerners Transformed America*. Chapel Hill: University of North Carolina Press, 2005.

Griggs, William Clark. *The Elusive Eden: Frank McMullen's Confederate Colony in Brazil*. Austin: University of Texas Press, 1987.

Guterl, Matthew Pratt. *American Mediterranean: Southern Slaveholders in the Age of Emancipation*. Cambridge MA: Harvard University Press, 2008.

Gwin, William M. *Arguments of the Hon. William M. Gwin on the Subject of a Pacific Railroad, before the Senate of the United States*. Washington DC: Congressional Globe Office, 1860.

———. *Speech of Mr. Gwin, of California, on the Bill to Establish a Railway to the Pacific, Delivered in the Senate of the United States, January 13, 1853*. Washington DC: Lemuel Towers, 1853.

Hahn, Steven. "Class and State in Postemancipation Societies: Southern Planters in Comparative Perspective." *American Historical Review* 95 (February 1990): 75–98.

———. *A Nation under Our Feet: Black Political Struggles in the Rural South from Slavery to the Great Migration*. Cambridge MA: Harvard University Press, 2003.

Hahn, Steven, Steven F. Miller, Susan E. O'Donovan, John C. Rodrigue, and Leslie S. Rowland, eds. *Freedom: A Documentary History of Emancipation, 1861–1867*. Ser. 3, vol. 1, *Land and Labor, 1865*. Chapel Hill: University of North Carolina Press, 2008.

Hale, Charles. *Mexican Liberalism in the Age of Mora, 1821–1853*. New Haven CT: Yale University Press, 1968.

———. *The Transformation of Liberalism in Late Nineteenth-Century Mexico*. Princeton NJ: Princeton University Press, 1989.

Hämäläinen, Pekka. *The Comanche Empire*. New Haven CT: Yale University Press, 2008.

Hanna, A. J. "The Role of Matthew Fontaine Maury in the Mexican Empire." *Virginia Magazine of History and Biography* 55 (April 1947): 105–25.

Hanna, Alfred Jackson, and Kathryn Abbey Hanna. "The Immigration Movement of the Intervention and Empire as Seen through the Mexican Press." *Hispanic American Historical Review* 27 (May 1947): 220–46.

———. *Napoleon III and Mexico: American Triumph over Monarchy*. Chapel Hill: University of North Carolina Press, 1971.

Harmon, George D. "Confederate Migrations to Mexico." *Hispanic American Historical Review* 17 (November 1937): 458–86.

Harris, Charles, III. *A Mexican Family Empire: The Latifundio of the Sánchez Navarros, 1765–1867*. Austin: University of Texas Press, 1975.

Hart, John Mason. *Empire and Revolution: The Americans in Mexico since the Civil War*. Berkeley: University of California Press, 2002.

Hearn, Chester G. *Tracks in the Sea: Matthew Fontaine Maury and the Mapping of the Oceans*. New York: McGraw-Hill, 2002.

Heath, Andrew. "'Let the Empire Come': Imperialism and Its Critics in the Reconstruction South." *Civil War History* 60, no. 2 (June 2014): 152–89.

Holt, Thomas C. *The Problem of Freedom: Race, Labor, and Politics in Jamaica and Britain, 1832–1938*. Baltimore: Johns Hopkins University Press, 1992.

Horne, Gerald. *The Deepest South: The United States, Brazil, and the African Slave Trade*. New York: New York University Press, 2007.

Huston, James L. *Calculating the Value of the Union: Slavery, Property Rights, and the Economic Origins of the Civil War*. Chapel Hill: University of North Carolina Press, 2003.

Jacoby, Karl. "Between North and South: The Alternative Borderlands of William H. Ellis and the African American Colony of 1895." In *Continental*

Crossroads: Remapping U.S.-Mexico Borderlands History, edited by Samuel Truett and Elliott Young, 209–39. Durham NC: Duke University Press, 2004.

Jarnagin, Laura. *A Confluence of Transatlantic Networks: Elites, Capitalism, and Confederate Migration to Brazil*. Tuscaloosa: University of Alabama Press, 2008.

Johnson, Vicki Vaughn. *The Men and the Vision of the Southern Commercial Conventions, 1845–1871*. Columbia: University of Missouri Press, 1992.

Johnson, Walter. *River of Dark Dreams: Slavery and Empire in the Cotton Kingdom*. Cambridge MA: Belknap Press of Harvard University Press, 2013.

———. *Soul by Soul: Life Inside the Antebellum Slave Market*. Cambridge MA: Harvard University Press, 2000.

Jung, Moon-Ho. *Coolies and Cane: Race, Labor, and Sugar in the Age of Emancipation*. Baltimore: Johns Hopkins University Press, 2006.

Katz, Friedrich. "Labor Conditions on Haciendas in Porfirian Mexico: Some Trends and Tendencies." *Hispanic American Historical Review* 54 (February 1974): 1–47.

———. "Rural Rebellions after 1810." In *Riot, Rebellion, and Revolution: Rural Social Conflict in Mexico*, edited by Friedrich Katz, 521–60. Princeton NJ: Princeton University Press, 1988.

Kavanagh, Thomas W. *Comanche Political History: An Ethnological Perspective, 1706–1875*. Lincoln: University of Nebraska Press, 1996.

Knapp, Frank A., Jr. "A New Source on the Confederate Exodus to Mexico: *The Two Republics*." *Journal of Southern History* 19 (August 1953): 364–73.

Kolchin, Peter. *American Slavery, 1619–1877*. New York: Hill and Wang, 1993.

Lamers, William M. *The Edge of Glory: A Biography of General William S. Rosecrans*. New York: Harcourt, Brace, 1961. Reprint, Baton Rouge: Louisiana State University Press, 1999.

Latorre, Felipe A., and Dolores L. Latorre, *The Mexican Kickapoo Indians*. Austin: University of Texas Press, 1976.

LaVere, David. *The Texas Indians*. College Station: Texas A&M University Press, 2004.

Litwack, Leon F. *Been in the Storm So Long: The Aftermath of Slavery*. Reprint, New York: Vintage Books, 1980.

Long, E. B. *The Civil War Day by Day: An Almanac, 1861–1865*. Garden City NY: Doubleday, 1971. Reprint, New York: Da Capo Press, 1985.

Mahoney, Harry T., and Marjorie Locke Mahoney. *Mexico and the Confederacy, 1860–1867*. San Francisco: Austin & Winfield, 1998.

Majewski, John. *Modernizing a Slave Economy: The Economic Vision of the Confederate Nation*. Chapel Hill: University of North Carolina Press, 2009.

Majewski, John, and Todd W. Wahlstrom, "Geography as Power: The Political Economy of Matthew Fontaine Maury." *Virginia Magazine of History and Biography* 120, no. 4 (Winter 2012): 340–71.

Martínez Sánchez, Lucas. *Coahuila durante la Intervención Francesa, 1862–1867.* Saltillo, Coahuila: Consejo Editorial del Estado, 2008.

Matthews, Michael. *The Civilizing Machine: A Cultural History of Mexican Railroads, 1876–1910.* Lincoln: University of Nebraska Press, 2013.

Maury, Matthew Fontaine. *The Amazon, and the Atlantic Slopes of South America: A Series of Letters Published in the National Intelligencer and Union Newspapers, under the Signature of "Inca."* Washington DC: Franck Taylor, 1853.

———. *The Physical Geography of the Sea.* 6th ed. New York: Harper & Brothers, 1859.

———. *Physical Survey of Virginia, Geographical Position Of; Its Commercial Advantages, and National Importance.* Preliminary Report. No. 1, Virginia Military Institute, Lexington. Richmond VA: W.A.R. Nye, Book and Job Printer, 1868.

———. "A Railroad from the Atlantic to the Pacific: Where Shall the Railroad Begin on the Atlantic, and Where Shall It End on the Pacific?" *Merchants' Magazine and Commercial Review* 18 (June 1848): 592–601.

May, Robert E. *Manifest Destiny's Underworld: Filibustering in Antebellum America.* Chapel Hill: University of North Carolina Press, 2002.

———. *The Southern Dream of a Caribbean Empire, 1854–1861.* Baton Rouge: Louisiana State University Press, 1973.

McDaniel, Antonio. *Swing Low, Sweet Chariot, The Mortality Cost of Colonizing Liberia in the Nineteenth Century.* Chicago: University of Chicago Press, 1995.

McHatton-Ripley, Eliza. *From Flag to Flag: A Woman's Adventures and Experiences in the South during the War, in Mexico, and in Cuba.* New York: D. Appleton, 1889.

McPherson, Hallie M. "The Plan of William McKendree Gwin for a Colony in North Mexico, 1863–1865." *Pacific Historical Review* 2 (December 1933): 357–86.

McPherson, James M. *Battle Cry of Freedom: The Civil War Era.* New York: Oxford University Press, 1988.

Miller, James David. *South by Southwest: Planter Emigration and Identity in the Slave South.* Charlottesville: University of Virginia Press, 2002.

Miller, Susan A. *Coacoochee's Bones: A Seminole Saga.* Lawrence: University Press of Kansas, 2003.

Minor, Nancy McGown. *The Light Gray People: An Ethno-History of the Lipan Apaches of Texas and Northern Mexico.* Lanham MD: University Press of America, 2009.

Montejano, David. *Anglos and Mexicans in the Making of Texas, 1836–1986.* 1987. Reprint, Austin: University of Texas Press, 2001.

Mora-Torres, Juan. *The Making of the Mexican Border: The State, Capitalism, and Society in Nuevo León, 1848–1910*. Austin: University of Texas Press, 2001.

Morrison, Michael A. *Slavery and the American West: The Eclipse of Manifest Destiny and the Coming of the Civil War*. Chapel Hill: University of North Carolina Press, 1997.

Mulroy, Kevin. *Freedom on the Border: The Seminole Maroons in Florida, the Indian Territory, Coahuila, and Texas*. Lubbock: Texas Tech University Press, 1993.

Nichols, James David. "The Line of Liberty: Runaway Slaves and Fugitive Peons in the Texas-Mexico Borderlands." *Western Historical Quarterly* 44, no. 4 (Winter 2013): 413–33.

Nunn, W.C. *Escape from Reconstruction*. Fort Worth: Texas Christian University, 1956.

Oakes, James. *The Ruling Race: A History of American Slaveholders*. New York: Alfred A. Knopf, 1982, Reprint, W.W. Norton, 1998.

O'Flaherty, Daniel. *General Jo Shelby: Undefeated Rebel*. Chapel Hill: University of North Carolina Press, 1954.

Ogle, Ralph Hedrick. *Federal Control of the Western Apaches, 1848–1886*. Albuquerque: University of New Mexico Press, 1940.

Olliff, Donathon C. *Reforma Mexico and the United States: A Search for Alternatives to Annexation, 1854–1861*. Tuscaloosa: University of Alabama Press, 1981.

Osterweis, Rollin G. *The Myth of the Lost Cause, 1865–1900*. Hamden CT: Archon Books, 1973.

Painter, Nell Irvin. *Exodusters: Black Migration to Kansas after Reconstruction*. New York: Alfred A. Knopf, 1977.

Perrin, Mary Amanda. "Exodus of Southerners after 1865 to Mexico, Brazil, Venezuela, and Central America." MA thesis, Tulane University, 1941.

Pletcher, David M. "General William S. Rosecrans and the Mexican Transcontinental Railroad Project." *Mississippi Valley Historical Review* 38, no. 4 (March 1952): 657–78.

————. *Rails, Mines, and Progress: Seven American Promoters in Mexico, 1867–1911*. Ithaca NY: Cornell University Press, 1958.

Ransom, Roger L., and Richard Sutch. *One Kind of Freedom: The Economic Consequences of Emancipation*. 2nd ed. New York: Cambridge University Press, 2001.

Rawick, George P., ed. *The American Slave: A Composite Autobiography*. Vols. 4–5, *Texas Narratives*. 1941. Reprint, Westport CT: Greenwood, 1973.

Rhodes, James Ford. *History of the Civil War, 1861–1865*. New York: Frederick Ungar, 1961. Reprint, Mineola NY: Dover, 1999.

Richardson, Heather Cox. *The Death of Reconstruction: Race, Labor, and Politics in the Post–Civil War North, 1865–1901*. Cambridge MA: Harvard University Press, 2001.

Ridley, Jasper. *Maximilian and Juárez*. New York: Ticknor & Fields, 1992.

Rister, Carl Coke. "Carlota, A Confederate Colony in Mexico." *Journal of Southern History* 11 (February 1945): 33–50.

Roark, James L. *Masters without Slaves: Southern Planters in the Civil War and Reconstruction*. New York: W.W. Norton, 1977.

Rodrigue, John C. *Reconstruction in the Cane Fields: From Slavery to Free Labor in Louisiana's Sugar Parishes, 1862–1880*. Baton Rouge: Louisiana State University Press, 2001.

Rodríguez, Martha. *La guerra entre bárbaros y civilados: El extermindo del nómado en Coahuila, 1840–1880*. Saltillo, Coahuila: Centro de Estudios Sociales y Humanísticos, 1998.

Rolle, Andrew. *The Lost Cause: The Confederate Exodus to Mexico*. 1965. Reprint, Norman: University of Oklahoma Press, 1992.

Rugemer, Edward Bartlett. *The Problem of Emancipation: The Caribbean Roots of the American Civil War*. Baton Rouge: Louisiana State University Press, 2008.

Ruiz, Ramón Eduardo, ed. *An American in Maximilian's Mexico, 1865–1866: The Diaries of William Marshall Anderson*. San Marino CA: Huntington Library, 1959.

———. *Triumphs and Tragedy: A History of the Mexican People*. New York: W.W. Norton, 1992.

Saville, Julie. *The Work of Reconstruction: From Slave to Wage Laborer in South Carolina, 1860–1870*. New York: Cambridge University Press, 1994.

Schell, William, Jr. *Integral Outsiders: The American Colony in Mexico City, 1876–1911*. Wilmington DE: Scholarly Resources, 2001.

Schmidt-Nowara, Christopher. *Empire and Antislavery: Spain, Cuba, and Puerto Rico, 1833–1874*. Pittsburgh: University of Pittsburgh Press, 1999.

Schoonover, Thomas. "Dollars over Dominion: United States Economic Interests in Mexico, 1861–1867." *Pacific Historical Review* 45 (February 1976): 23–45.

Schwarz, Philip J. *Migrants against Slavery: Virginians and the Nation*. Charlottesville: University Press of Virginia, 2001.

Schwartz, Rosalie. *Across the Rio to Freedom: U.S. Negroes in Mexico*. Southwestern Studies, monograph no. 44. El Paso: Texas Western Press, 1975.

Shalhope, Robert E. *Sterling Price: Portrait of a Southerner*. Columbia: University of Missouri Press, 1971.

Sheridan, Philip Henry. *Personal Memoirs of Philip Henry Sheridan, General, United States Army, New and Enlarged Edition with an Account of His Life from 1871 to His Death, in 1888*. Vol. 2. New York: D. Appleton, 1904.

———. *Report of Operations of the United States Forces, and General Information of the Condition of Affairs in the Military Division of the South-West and Gulf and Department of the Gulf, from May 29, 1865, to November 4, 1866.* New Orleans, 1866.

Smith, Henry Nash. *Virgin Land: The American West as Symbol and Myth.* 1950. Reprint, Cambridge MA: Harvard University Press, 2000.

Stampp, Kenneth M. *The Era of Reconstruction, 1867–1877.* New York: Alfred A. Knopf, 1966.

———. *The Peculiar Institution: Slavery in the Antebellum South.* 1956. Reprint, New York: Vintage Books, 1989.

Starr, Kevin. *Americans and the California Dream, 1850–1915.* 1973. Reprint, New York: Oxford University Press, 1986.

St. John, Rachel. *Line in the Sand: A History of the Western U.S.-Mexico Border.* Princeton NJ: Princeton University Press, 2011.

Strickland, John Scott. "Traditional Culture and Moral Economy: Social and Economic Change in the South Carolina Low Country, 1865–1910." In *The Countryside in the Age of Capitalist Transformation: Essays in the Social History of Rural America,* edited by Steven Hahn and Jonathan Prude, 141–78. Chapel Hill: University of North Carolina Press, 1985.

Strom, Sharon Hartman, and Frederick Stirton Weaver. *Confederates in the Tropics: Charles Swett's Travelogue of 1868.* Jackson: University Press of Mississippi, 2011.

Sutherland, Daniel E. *The Confederate Carpetbaggers.* Baton Rouge: Louisiana State University Press, 1988.

———. "Exiles, Emigrants, and Sojourners: The Post–Civil War Confederate Exodus in Perspective." *Civil War History* 31, no. 3 (September 1985): 237–56.

Tapia, Oscar Flores. *Andrés S. Viesca: Soldado y maestro.* México DF: Secretaría de Educación Pública, 1966.

Taylor, William B. "Banditry and Insurrection: Rural Unrest in Central Jalisco, 1790–1816." In *Riot, Rebellion, and Revolution: Rural Social Conflict in Mexico,* edited by Friedrich Katz, 206–15. Princeton NJ: Princeton University Press, 1988.

Tenenbaum, Barbara A. "Manuel Payno, Financial Reform, and Foreign Intervention in Mexico, 1855–1880." In *Liberals, Politics and Power: State Formation in Nineteenth-Century Latin America,* edited by Vincent C. Peloso and Barbara A. Tenenbaum, 212–34. Athens: University of Georgia Press, 1996.

Terrell, Alexander Watkins. *From Texas to Mexico and the Court of Maximilian in 1865.* Dallas: Book Club of Texas, 1933.

Thompson, Guy P. C., with David G. LaFrance. *Patriotism, Politics, and Popular Liberalism in Nineteenth-Century Mexico: Juan Francisco Lucas and the Puebla Sierra.* Wilmington DE: Scholarly Resources 2002.

Thompson, Jerry. *Cortina: Defending the Mexican Name in Texas*. College Station: Texas A&M University Press, 2007.

Truett, Samuel. *Fugitive Landscapes: The Forgotten History of the U.S.–Mexico Borderlands*. New Haven CT: Yale University Press, 2006.

Tutino, John. "Agrarian Social Change and Peasant Rebellion in Nineteenth-Century Mexico: The Example of Chalco." In *Riot, Rebellion, and Revolution: Rural Social Conflict in Mexico*, edited by Friedrich Katz, 95–140. Princeton NJ: Princeton University Press, 1988.

Tyler, Ronnie C. "Fugitive Slaves in Mexico." *Journal of Negro History* 57 (January 1972): 1–12.

———. *Santiago Vidaurri and the Southern Confederacy*. Austin: Texas State Historical Association, 1973.

U.S. Census Bureau. 1860, 1870, and 1880 Federal Censuses (online database). Ancestry.com.

———. 1860 Population Schedules and Slave Schedules. Los Angeles Regional Family History Center, Church of Latter-Day Saints, Los Angeles.

U.S. Congress. *Message of the President of the United States, communicating, in compliance with a resolution of the Senate of December 19, 1865 . . . .* 39th Cong., 1st sess., 1866.

U.S. National Park Service. Soldiers and Sailors Database. The Civil War. www.itd.nps.gov/cwss.

Valerio-Jiménez, Omar Santiago. "'*Indios Bárbaros*,' Divorcees, and Flocks of Vampires: Identity and Nation on the Rio Grande, 1749–1894." PhD diss., University of California, Los Angeles, 2001.

Vanderwood, Paul. *Disorder and Progress: Bandits, Police, and Mexican Development*. 1981. Reprint, Wilmington DE: Scholarly Resources, 1992.

———. *The Power of God against the Guns of Government: Religious Upheaval in Mexico at the Turn of the Nineteenth Century*. Stanford: Stanford University Press, 1998.

Van Hoy, Teresa. *A Social History of Mexico's Railroads: Peons, Prisoners, and Priests*. Lanham MD: Rowman & Littlefield, 2008.

Wahlstrom, Todd W. "Defeated and Colonized: The Psychology of the Ex-Confederate Planter Class in the Postwar South." MA thesis, Michigan State University, 2003.

Wakelyn, Jon L. *Biographical Dictionary of the Confederacy*. Westport CT: Greenwood Press, 1977.

Wasserman, Mark. *Capitalists, Caciques, and Revolution: The Native Elite and Foreign Enterprise in Chihuahua, Mexico, 1854–1911*. Chapel Hill: University of North Carolina Press, 1984.

———. *Everyday Life and Politics in Nineteenth-Century Mexico*. Albuquerque: University of New Mexico Press, 2000.

Wayland, John W. *The Pathfinder of the Seas: The Life of Matthew Fontaine Maury*. Richmond VA: Garrett & Massie, 1930.

Weber, David J. *The Mexican Frontier, 1821–1846: The American Southwest under Mexico*. Albuquerque: University of New Mexico Press, 1982.

White, Richard. *The Middle Ground: Indians, Empires, and Republics in the Great Lakes Region, 1650–1815*. Cambridge University Press, 1991.

———. *Railroaded: The Transcontinentals and the Making of Modern America*. New York: W.W. Norton, 2011.

Williams, Frances Leigh. *Matthew Fontaine Maury, Scientist of the Sea*. New Brunswick NJ: Rutgers University Press, 1963.

Wilson, Charles Reagan. *Baptized in Blood: The Religion of the Lost Cause, 1865–1920*. Athens: University of Georgia Press, 1980.

Winfrey, Dorman H., and James M. Day, eds. *The Indian Papers of Texas and the Southwest, 1825–1916*. Vol. 4. Austin: Texas State Historical Association, 1995.

Woodward, C. Vann. *Origins of the New South, 1877–1913*. 1951. Reprint, Baton Rouge: Louisiana State University Press, 1999.

Worley, Ted R., ed. "A Letter Written by General Thomas C. Hindman in Mexico." *Arkansas Historical Quarterly* 15, no. 4 (Winter 1956): 365–68.

Wright, Gavin. *Old South, New South: Revolutions in the Southern Economy since the Civil War*. New York: Basic Books, 1986.

———. *Slavery and American Economic Development*. Baton Rouge: Louisiana State University Press, 2006.

Wrobel, David M. *Promised Lands: Promotion, Memory, and the Creation of the American West*. Lawrence: University Press of Kansas, 2002.

Wyatt-Brown, Bertram. *The Shaping of Southern Culture: Honor, Grace, and War, 1760s–1880s*. Chapel Hill: University of North Carolina Press, 2001.

Index

*The Limits of Liberty: Mobility and the Making of the
Eastern U.S.-Mexico Border*
by James David Nichols

*Native Diasporas: Indigenous Identities and Settler
Colonialism in the Americas*
edited by Gregory D. Smithers and Brooke N. Newman

Shape Shifters: Journeys across Terrains of Race and Identity
edited by Lily Anne Y. Welty Tamai, Ingrid Dineen-Wimberly,
and Paul Spickard

*The Southern Exodus to Mexico: Migration across the
Borderlands after the American Civil War*
by Todd W. Wahlstrom

To order or obtain more information on these or other University of Nebraska
Press titles, visit nebraskapress.unl.edu.

CPSIA information can be obtained
at www.ICGtesting.com
Printed in the USA
LVHW042218081220
673655LV00006B/395